D0847811

# WRITING IN
# THE COMMUNITY

# WRITTEN COMMUNICATION ANNUAL
## An International Survey of Research and Theory

### Series Editors
**Charles R. Cooper,** *University of California, San Diego*
**Sidney Greenbaum,** *University College, London*

### Editorial Advisory Board

Robert de Beaugrande,
*University of Florida*
Wallace Chafe, *University of California,
Berkeley*
Wolfgang Dressler,
*Institut für Sprachwissenschaft
der Universität Wien*
N. E. Enkvist, *Engelska Institusionen,
Abo Akademi*
Richard L. Enos,
*Carnegie Mellon University*
R. G. Fowler, *University of East Anglia*
Sarah W. Freedman,
*University of California, Berkeley*
M. A. K. Halliday, *University of Sydney*
Jerome C. Harste, *Indiana University*
Shirley Brice Heath, *Stanford University*
George Hillocks, Jr., *University of Chicago*
Barry M. Kroll, *Indiana University*

G. N. Leech, *University of Lancaster*
James J. Murphy,
*University of California, Davis*
Walter Nash, *University of Nottingham*
János S. Petoefi, *University of Bielefeld*
Louise Wetherbee Phelps,
*University of Southern California*
Alan C. Purves, *State University of
New York, Albany*
Harold Rosen, *University of London,
Institute of Education*
Marlene Scardamalia, *York University*
Robert J. Tierney, *University of Illinois,
Urbana-Champaign*
Hayden White, *University of California,
Santa Cruz*
H. G. Widdowson, *University of London,
Institute of Education*
A. M. Wilkinson, *University of East Anglia*

### Volumes in This Series

Volume 1   STUDYING WRITING: Linguistic Approaches
Charles R. Cooper and Sidney Greenbaum, editors

Volume 2   WRITING ACROSS LANGUAGES
AND CULTURES: Issues in Contrastive Rhetoric
Alan C. Purves, editor

Volume 3   THE WRITING SCHOLAR:
Studies in Academic Discourse
Walter Nash, editor

Volume 4   ORAL AND WRITTEN COMMUNICATION:
Historical Approaches
Richard Leo Enos, editor

Volume 5   A SENSE OF AUDIENCE IN WRITTEN COMMUNICATION
Gesa Kirsch and Duane H. Roen, editors

Volume 6   WRITING IN THE COMMUNITY
David Barton and Roz Ivanič, editors

# WRITING IN
# THE COMMUNITY

edited by

**DAVID BARTON**
*Lancaster University*

**ROZ IVANIČ**
*Lancaster University*

WRITTEN COMMUNICATION ANNUAL
An International Survey of
Research and Theory

Volume 6

LIBRARY
LINCOLN MEMORIAL UNIVERSITY
Harrogate, Tennessee

**SAGE** PUBLICATIONS
*The International Professional Publishers*
Newbury Park   London   New Delhi

223799

Copyright © 1991 by Sage Publications, Inc.

All rights reserved. No part of this book may be reproduced or utilized in any form or by any means, electronic or mechanical, including photocopying, recording, or by any information storage and retrieval system, without permission in writing from the publisher.

*For information address:*

SAGE Publications, Inc.
2455 Teller Road
Newbury Park, California 91320

SAGE Publications Ltd.f
6 Bonhill Street
London EC2A 4PU
United Kingdom

SAGE Publications India Pvt. Ltd.
M-32 Market
Greater Kailash I
New Delhi 110 048 India

P 211
.W 725
1991

Printed in the United States of America

International Standard Book Number 0-8039-3632-X (c)

International Standard Book Number 0-8039-3633-8 (p)

International Standard Series Number 0883-9296

Library of Congress Catalog Card No. 86-655578

**FIRST PRINTING, 1991**

Sage Production Editor: Judith L. Hunter

# Contents

Preface
CHARLES R. COOPER and
SIDNEY GREENBAUM                                              vii

Introduction
DAVID BARTON and ROZ IVANIČ                                   viii

1. The Social Nature of Writing
   DAVID BARTON                                                1

2. Because This Is Who We Are:
   Writing in the Amish Community
   ANDREA R. FISHMAN                                           14

3. Bilingual Written Language Use by
   Low-Education Latin American Newcomers
   CECIL KLASSEN                                               38

4. Roles, Networks, and Values in
   Everyday Writing
   DAVID BARTON and SARAH PADMORE                              58

5. Self, Education, and Writing in Nineteenth-
   Century English Communities
   URSULA HOWARD                                               78

6. Community Publishing as Self-Education
   GERRY GREGORY                                               109

7. The Schooling of Literacy
   JOANNA C. STREET and BRIAN V. STREET                        143

8. Learning to Write as an Adult
   SUE GARDENER                                                167

9. Bringing Community Writing Practices into Education
   ROZ IVANIČ and WENDY MOSS                                   193

About the Authors                                              224

# Preface

**Writing is required** in the education system and is often necessary at work. Less conspicuous are the varieties of writing needed in social life: personal letters, letters to officials, notes to oneself or others, personal records, completed forms, minutes of meetings.

This volume focuses on the social functions of writing and relates the writing practices in the community with those in the domains of education and employment. Drawing on empirical studies, it discusses and illustrates current theories and methodologies on community writing.

This is the sixth volume of the *Written Communication Annual: An International Survey of Research and Theory.* It is part of Sage Publications' publishing program in composition studies, which includes the quarterly journal *Written Communication.* This volume will be of particular interest to teachers of writing and researchers in composition. It will also appeal to community workers and to students and researchers who are interested in a variety of approaches to literacy—sociocultural, historical, linguistic, and ethnographic.

—*Charles R. Cooper and*
*Sidney Greenbaum*
Series Editors

# Introduction

## DAVID BARTON
## ROZ IVANIČ

**The unifying theme of** the chapters in this book is examining writing practices outside of educational institutions. They bring together two contemporary concerns: new views of literacy and a renewed focus on writing in schools and colleges.

The chapters are all original works written specially for this volume. We wanted a set of chapters that would reflect the range of work in this field in Britain and North America. Three of the chapters we commissioned for the volume are detailed case studies of everyday uses of writing. Two make links between writing and self-education in two historical periods. Two other chapters examine the relationship between community views of writing and education in very different communities. As editors, we have written an initial chapter that provides a context for discussing everyday uses of writing and a final chapter that brings out the implications of the volume for the teaching of writing.

In the first chapter, "The Social Nature of Writing," David Barton draws attention to phenomena in everyday literacy that are not normally mentioned when discussing theories of literacy. There are three aspects to this. First, to describe people's everyday literacy, we need to talk in terms of literacy practices and literacy events. Second, it is useful to see everyday literacy as being one of several domains of reading and writing. And, third, we need to see literacy practices as social practices involving the roles people take, the networks they are part of, and the values and attitudes they hold.

The next three chapters provide case studies of the uses of writing in three distinct communities. In Chapter 2, "Because This Is Who We Are: Writing in the Amish Community," Andrea Fishman describes an ethnographic study of literacy practices among the Amish in Lancaster, Pennsylvania, in the United States. She shows how values underlying writing practices in the Amish community are reinforced by writing practices in Amish schools. In the third chapter, "Bilingual Written Language Use by Low-Education Latin

American Newcomers," Cecil Klassen describes the multilingual uses of reading and writing among Spanish-speaking bilingual adult immigrants in Toronto, concentrating on their uses and strategies along with the ideological values underlying their practices. In the fourth chapter, "Role, Networks, and Values in Everyday Writing," David Barton and Sarah Padmore report on part of a study of everyday uses of literacy in Lancaster, England, giving concrete examples of some of the categories outlined in Barton's introductory chapter. Coincidentally, Barton and Padmore and Fishman all have carried out studies of literacy in places called Lancaster, one in England and the other in the United States. This fortunate coincidence helps us to realize why ethnographic studies of writing are so important. We can see in two communities that share the same name writing practices that are remarkably different: People in the two communities have different values and aspirations; their everyday lives are made up of different activities; and, as a result, how and what they write is different. Education needs to be sensitive to these differences; the way writing is taught should differ accordingly.

Chapters 5 and 6 contain accounts of adults teaching themselves to write, largely outside of educational institutions. One particularly interesting theme in these chapters is people's motivations to write outside of school and college. Another is the interaction between individuals and collective endeavor. "Self, Education, and Writing in Nineteenth-Century English Communities," by Ursula Howard, is an account of popular writing in a rural setting in Britain in the nineteenth century prior to the introduction of compulsory education. It is based on a detailed examination of autobiographical accounts and historical records. In Chapter 6, "Community Publishing as Self-Education," Gerry Gregory examines what goes on in community publishing. This includes giving, conducting, taping, transcribing, and editing interviews; writing with a variety of purposes for a range of readers and with length and time constraints; multiple drafting; editing; researching; bringing nonstandard language into print; involving people in public readings and group discussions; and designing, making, marketing, and distributing printed materials. Taken together, these activities act as a form of collective community self-education.

The next two chapters examine different types of interplay between community and education in learning to write. In Chapter 7, "The Schooling of Literacy," Joanna Street and Brian Street examine similarities between home literacy and school literacy in mainstream families in the United States. The emphasis in their chapter is on the way school literacy practices percolate into homes, perhaps even replacing the writing practices that might naturally arise in everyday life. In Chapter 8, "Learning to Write as an Adult," Sue

Gardener draws on accounts of learning given by adult students and by members of community writing groups. The accounts are used to criticize the dominant construction of how adults learn to write: that of a largely predictable child to adult developmental path. This standard approach makes it difficult even to ask the questions we need to ask about learning by adults. She examines three other possible ways of looking at how adults learn to write: activities drawn from the practice of competent writers, cultural and ideological contexting, and issues related to dialect and language variety.

In the final chapter, "Bringing Community Writing Practices into Education," Roz Ivanič and Wendy Moss are concerned with the implications of community literacy for the teaching of writing. They propose a critical view of writing in the community that recognizes the difference between "imposed" and "self-generated" writing. They synthesize the view of writing expressed in the earlier chapters and discuss how this can enrich the teaching of writing in educational contexts.

# 1

# The Social Nature of Writing

## DAVID BARTON

**How can we make sense** of the writing people do in their everyday lives? How does it fit into general theories of literacy, and how does it relate to other reading and writing, such as that done at school and at work? As a whole, this book is concerned with these questions about the role of writing in people's everyday lives. In different ways, the separate authors of the chapters put forward social views of writing, which draws our attention to phenomena not normally brought up when discussing theories of literacy. In this chapter, I want to outline some of these phenomena and to spell out ways they can contribute to our understanding of literacy. There are three aspects to this. First, to describe people's everyday literacy, we need to talk in terms of *literacy practices* and *literacy events*. Second, it is useful to see everyday literacy as being one of several *domains* of reading and writing. And, third, we need to see literacy practices as *social practices* involving the roles people take, the networks they are part of, and the values and attitudes they hold.

Everyday literacy is a very rich area to explore. We can see this clearly using an example. In going about their ordinary daily lives, people today are constantly encountering literacy. For someone waking up in Lancaster, England, tomorrow, the first voice he or she will hear in the morning might well be someone reading a written text—a news reader on the radio. Going downstairs, he or she finds a newspaper on the doormat along with some mail, at least glancing at these. Even before this English person's first cup of tea, there have been two literacy events quite different from each other. We could continue through the day with shopping, consulting a calendar, following the instructions for using a new watch, writing a check, on through to leaving a note for the milkman as a final task at night. The activities involving literacy in some way are many and varied.

AUTHOR'S NOTE: Writing of this chapter has been supported in part by a grant from the Economic and Social Research Council R000-23-1419 and has benefited greatly from numerous discussions with Mary Hamilton, Roz Ivanič , and Sarah Padmore.

1

We can use this example to see what a comprehensive view of literacy needs to include. The first point to be made is that literacy is embedded in the activities of ordinary life. It is not something that is done just at school or at work. In fact, several of the activities seem quite unlike those that are focused on in our educational system. For example, making notes or consulting a calendar may not sound like something typically taught in school, while listening to the news may not be thought of as having anything to do with literacy.

We can also see that there are many different ways of using the written word. Listening to the news being read, scanning through junk mail, or leaving a note for the milkman are all very different activities; in each, literacy has a distinct use. These uses are very different, and it may not be very useful to think of writing as one activity that is the same across all situations. Approaches using broader terms such as *literacy events* or *literacy practices* are important here. We also find we need to talk in terms of *literacies,* not just one literacy. Even if we focus just on writing, there are many ways of writing, not just one way.

These examples are also particular to a particular community at a particular point in history. It is only in some cultures that newspaper, milk, and mail are delivered to the door early in the morning. It is only in some cultures that it is thought normal to start the day sitting at a table and simultaneously listening to a radio, reading a newspaper, and drinking a cup of tea.

The social settings in which literacy occurs are particular to individual societies and have developed over time. Like other cultural activities, ways of being literate are passed on from generation to generation. They are reorganized and reinvented by each succeeding generation. We, therefore, also need to take a relativistic view where a historical perspective is included.

The scene we have described could include people of all ages, from young children to elderly people. People learn about literacy throughout life, not during just one age range, and all activities are forms of learning. To take account of this, we need a view of literacy that allows change, a dynamic view of people's constantly developing literacy rather than a static model. The literacy demands on a person go up and down during their lifetimes.

People have purposes. They have their own purposes and, at the same time, they are situated in a society that makes demands upon them. People see the point of literacy because it serves some of their everyday needs: it has a value to them. These purposes and values then act as guides to and constraints on action. Most of the examples above have kept to people's direct participation in literacy in their everyday lives. The examples have been very varied; nevertheless, they still cover only a narrow part of the full range of uses of literacy: The example of listening to a news reader on the radio indicates how literacy is a part of much broader activities of understanding what is going on about us—how we make sense of the world. Although we will not pursue the topic here, we could examine how, as a communication medium, literacy structures certain social relations.

We have already made several observations about literacy that are not covered by the most common views of literacy. Most theories of literacy start out from the educational settings in which literacy is typically taught. The dominant definitions then are school-based definitions of literacy and, to a lesser extent, work-based definitions of literacy. These views of what literacy is are often at odds with what people experience in their everyday lives. This can be in a very straightforward way, where the reading and writing people do in their everyday lives is different from that done in school. It can be in people's more general conceptions of literacy; an example of this is that society's view of what it is to be illiterate may be very different from the perceptions of a person with reading and writing difficulties. The position we take here is that school, work, and community are different domains of literacy and that we need to develop ways of talking about literacy in these different domains.

By looking outside the educational domain, different issues arise, and phenomena not highlighted in a school-based view of literacy suddenly have prominence. For example, we see that people learn from each other, and, as adults, people continue learning more about how to use their language. We see that people can have different roles in a literacy event. A much wider range of activities count as writing and reading and we get a far richer view of what literacy is. I will now examine these points in more detail, starting with events and practices, discussing the idea of separate domains, and bringing out some of the implications of viewing writing as a social practice.

## EVENTS AND PRACTICES

Reading and writing are carried out in everyday life. Our starting point is everyday life, and we need ways of talking about everyday activities. As we have said, it may not be very useful to think of writing as one activity that is the same across all situations. It is probably not very useful to try to abstract some general skill from all situations, and it is important to get away from something residing in the individual or in the product. We need to talk in broader terms, and it is here that the concepts of "events" and "practices" are useful. Several people have been using these terms. (Others have made the activity the central part.) We can start by drawing on other people's characterizations of literacy *events* and *practices*. These terms are part of newer conceptions of literacy that are being articulated in different ways by linguists, sociologists, anthropologists, psychologists, and others converging on the same issue.

The first general term that has become a basic unit of analysis is that of *event*. The notion of literacy event has its roots in the sociolinguistic idea of speech events. Heath (1983, p. 386) uses the term extensively, referring to it generally as being "when talk revolves around a piece of writing." Elsewhere, Heath (1984, p. 71) defines literacy events as communicative situations "where literacy has an integral role." This is important in demonstrating that literacy has a role in so many communicative activities. It is important to identify and describe these events to understand children's (and adults') learning of literacy.

Second, what do people mean by practices? The term is used in several disciplines, and several researchers have applied it directly to literacy. Street, an anthropologist, speaks of an "ideological" model of literacy that assumes that "the meaning of literacy depends on the social institutions in which it is embedded" and that "the particular practices of reading and writing that are taught in any context depend upon such aspects of social structure as stratification . . . and the role of educational institutions" (Street, 1984, p. 8). Coming from a psychological perspective, Scribner and Cole (1981) move away from a skills explanation of reading and writing. They are edging toward their alternative notion of a "practice account" of literacy, arguing that literacy can only be understood in the context of the social practices in which it is acquired and used. They conclude their study of Vai literacy in this way:

> Instead of focusing exclusively on the technology of a writing system and its reputed consequences . . . we approach literacy as a set of socially organized practices which make use of a symbol system and a technology for producing and disseminating it. Literacy is not simply knowing how to read and write a particular script but applying this knowledge for specific purposes in specific contexts of use. The nature of these practices, including, of course, their technological aspects, will determine the kinds of skills ("consequences") associated with literacy. (Scribner & Cole, 1981, p. 236)

Their discussion expands on this, and they suggest how practices can be seen as ways of using literacy that are carried across situations (see Scribner &

Cole, 1981, pp. 234-238). For links with broader sociological formulations of practiced theory, including the work of Bourdieu, see the discussion in Lave (1988). In another direction, Fairclough (1989) links the notion of discourse with social practices to reveal how social institutions and power relations structure our uses of language, both spoken and written.

We need to make use of both terms here. Literacy *events* are the particular activities in which literacy has a role; they may be regular repeated activities. Literacy *practices* are the general cultural ways of utilizing literacy that people draw upon in a literacy event. For example, leaving a note for the milkman is a *literacy event*. In deciding to do it, finding a pen and paper, and deciding what to write and where to leave it, we make use of our *literacy practices*. In this volume, Fishman contrasts Amish literacy practices and mainstream U.S. ones; Klassen shows how bilingual's literacy practices are distributed according to the language being used.

## DOMAINS OF WRITING

There may be different literacy practices in different *domains* of social life. The term *domain* has been used in the study of language for some time; for instance, it is a standard term in sociolinguistics going back at least to 1965 (see Fishman, 1965) and has been used more recently in studies of children's emergent literacy (e.g., Goelman, Oberg, & Smith, 1984, p. 28; Teale & Sulzby, 1986, p. 184). There are various uses of the term that are not necessarily identical.

The term is useful for us in this volume in that it enables us to contrast home, school, and work situations. School and work are two obvious domains that have been studied and where there might be distinct literacy practices. To these we add the domain of everyday literacy. For the moment, home and community are being treated as being one homogeneous domain. However, different breakdowns are possible. How we decide that something constitutes a separate domain is going to be defined partly sociologically—that it constitutes a distinct social situation—but more by the fact that it involves identifiably different types and uses of literacy.

Behind home, school, and work can be seen particular institutions that support these distinct domains. Particular definitions of literacy and associated literacy practices are nurtured by these institutions. They are definition-sustaining institutions. It is possibly true that different institutions define and influence different aspects of literacy or different literacies. Religion may influence ritual aspects of literacy; the family has an effect on habits of personal communication; work and school influence public and formal aspects of communication. It follows from this that domains are not equal, and, to some extent, the different institutions may be supporting conflicting literacy practices. However, the picture is not clear-cut: The domains overlap and there is movement between them. The various chapters in this volume cover slightly different domains. In addition, Street and Street argue that there are larger concerns such as national identity whose influence cuts across different domains.

Documenting and understanding everyday literacy is an essential part of understanding the learning of literacy. One reason for identifying the everyday as a distinct domain is the belief that the key to learning is in everyday activities and how people make sense of them. Beginning from everyday contexts and later moving out to study school and work situations should contribute to our understanding of learning and may give us different insights from studies that start from school or work.

## The Home Domain

In mainstream culture, the household is an ecological niche in which literacy survives, is sustained, and flourishes. Literacy is part of the web of home life. In addition to the example already given, many everyday activities invoke the use of literacy in some way. Sometimes it is central and its role obvious; at other times it is not so. There is a great deal of print in the house: It is on packaging, notice boards, instructions, junk mail as well as in magazines and books. Cooking, eating, shopping, keeping records, celebrating all make use of literacy in some way. Literacy is not the aim of these activities, their aim is something else—to survive, to consume, to act in the world—and literacy is an integral part of achieving these other aims.

In many households, literacy is an essential part of these everyday activities, and, although the aim is not literacy, in many ways the household is structured around literacy: Literacy mediates family activities. There are many ways of putting this. Heath locates literacy in the ways families use space and time and describes how literacy traditions

> are interwoven in different ways with oral uses of language, ways of negotiating meaning, deciding on action, and achieving status. Patterns of using reading and writing in each community are interdependent with ways of using space (having bookshelves, decorating walls, displaying telephone numbers), and using time (bedtime, meal hours, and homework sessions). (Heath, 1983, p. 234)

Another vision of home life is one where literacy flows through the household: The literate world pours in through the letterbox and goes out through the waste bin. In between, people act on it, use it, change it (see Leichter, 1984).

These examples are of very literate households. Even in less literate households, literacy has a significant role. Where researchers have taken very simple measures, such as the number of books in the home, it is very easy to find wide disparities—and to be shaken in one's literate world by the high number of homes in Britain containing almost no books. However, all homes in Britain are touched by literacy. There is still consumer packaging to get through, bills to pay, junk mail to sort, and various official forms and notices with which to deal. Junk mail cannot be avoided; you have to do something with it, and people develop individual solutions to cope with the continuous tide (see Taylor 1983, p. 27).

It is not a question of households being literate or not. It is not adequate to characterize this as a simple dimension of amount of literacy. What we have seen from Heath's study and elsewhere is that households are part of whole communities that are oriented to literacy differently. This is not just to do with literacy but is part of the whole dynamics of the households. For the moment, it is enough to emphasize that, in Heath's Trackton, despite being unlike mainstream culture and being in many ways oral, literacy still impinges a great deal.

## WRITING AS SOCIAL PRACTICE

We are assuming that the way literacy is used in everyday life in the home and the wider community constitutes a coherent domain. It is a distinct domain in that literacy has its own uses and is sustained in particular ways; we expect to see distinctive practices that we can then draw upon to provide insights into understanding other domains such as school.

If everyday literacy is a distinct domain with its own practices, then we need to document them. In doing this, we come across several themes that provide a richer way of talking about literacy and help us identify significant aspects of the context of literacy that need to be incorporated into any theory of literacy learning. First, we need to situate people's *literacy practices* as being part of *social practices*. Next, there are particular *roles* people take and *networks* of support in which they participate. This leads on to the sense people make of reading and writing and the *value* literacy holds for them. A theme that seems very rich when discussing writing is *literacy and change*.

The last theme we will mention here is the theme of how everyday *processes* of learning are revealed in the home and community. We will examine each of these themes in turn. This is the framework used in the study by Barton and Padmore in this volume.

## Literacy Practices as Social Practices

There are common practices in reading and writing activities in any community, and membership in a community is partly defined by knowing and participating in these practices. These are literacy practices, and they need to be seen as part of social practices. People do things for a reason; people have purposes. Literacy serves other purposes. In general, people do not read in order to read, or write in order to write; rather, people read and write in order to do other things, is order to achieve other ends. People want to know what time the train leaves or how a new watch or video recorder works; they want to make sense of their lives or keep in contact with a friend; they want to make their voices heard. They need to pay the bills, to bake a birthday cake. Reading and writing can be part of these social activities. It fits in in different ways. It can be an integral part of the activity, or the relationship may be more complex. For example, it can gatekeep these activities and be a prerequisite for them. Sometimes these purposes are self-generated; at other times, such as filling in official forms, they are imposed from the outside.

Reading or writing are often one option among others for achieving a given communicative goal; to find out when the train leaves, there may be a choice between asking someone, phoning someone, or looking in a timetable—each of these involves reading and writing in different ways. Patterns of choice may vary from one individual to another; people trust these forms of communication in differing amounts. The importance of viewing reading and writing in terms of social practices is that we see the purpose behind the activities; we also see how intertwined the written word is with other forms of communication, especially spoken language.

## Roles and Networks

Who does what? There are appropriate roles and there are forbidden ones. Not everyone does everything. We can examine the asymmetry of literacy roles as well as people's assumptions about what are appropriate or pro-

scribed activities for themselves and others. "Wives write Xmas cards. . . .
Husbands write cheques." This newspaper headline (*Daily Mirror,* April 17,
1989) reporting a survey in Harpers and Queen sums up a common role
division. In couples, often women write in the personal sphere, keeping in
contact with friends and relations, while men deal with the business world.
These roles can be followed to the extent that men are unable to write a
personal letter and women do not know how to write a check. However, this
division is not a hard-and-fast one, and the roles are not always obvious.
Difficulties with reading and writing, or particular skills, can affect the roles
people perform.

Roles are much broader than just gender roles, and in any social event
people take particular roles. The importance of talking in terms of roles is
that the way people act is not just related to their *abilities* but is influenced
by socially constructed roles: People's literacy practices do not reflect
abilities in any straightforward way but are related to what is or is not
*appropriate*. People learn that, socially, there are appropriate roles and there
are inappropriate roles. To move on from describing people's actions just in
terms of abilities is a significant step in our understanding of literacy and is
a move away from overreliance on psychological or cognitive models of
learning.

Roles exist within networks. It is possible to map the social networks of
support that exist and the informal learning that takes place. These networks
have broad functions covering work, child rearing, and other areas of social
activity. Sometimes there is support, when people identify problems with
literacy-related activities. When people have problems, their roles can be
very different. In another aspect of these networks, because these networks
exist, problems do not arise; people have networks of support that help them
avoid problems.

To think in terms of roles and networks and realize that everyone has
appropriate and inappropriate roles emphasizes the relative nature of difficulties. People do not need to identify literacy "problems" to get a friend to
help them understand a tax form or to have the railway official write out some
train times. There are particular people used for support whom we can regard
as *brokers* for literacy activities. It may be a neighbor or friend who deals
with figures or fills in the forms. Or it may be institutionalized—the railway
officials who look up train times, the travel agents who fill in holiday forms
for customers.

In trying to push our understanding of literacy beyond the standard
accounts, the notion of networks is important in that it emphasizes that
reading or writing is not just an individual affair: Often a literacy event

consists of several people's contributions. Networks are also important for people's attitudes toward education and the possibilities it can provide. Outside the immediate family, other relatives can be very influential. In learning new aspects of literacy, people often rely on *learning networks* for themselves and for their children that incorporate siblings, grandparents, and other relations.

In her study of adults with literacy problems, Fingeret (1983) showed the different ways they participated in such networks. Some of these people lived in a very literate cosmopolitan world, while others lived more local lives in which there were several people who could not read or write very well. People in the latter group were treated as equals in their networks and were accepted for what they could do; they were "interdependent" and swapped skills—to the extent that for some the ability "to fix things" was a scarcer resource and was valued more than the ability to read and write. There were various ways that people with problems survived. They might be skilled at decoding particular formats, such as forms that were regularly encountered. There was a greater reliance on other media such as television and tape recorders, where this was possible. Every network contained at least one reader, and people would choose appropriate readers for specific tasks: a next-door neighbor might help with an official form, while someone might cross the city for a relative to read a personal letter. Fingeret describes only a very small number of the people she studied as "dependent" rather than interdependent. These were people who had a very basic asymmetry in their lives, and they needed to be supported without obviously giving anything back in return. She emphasizes that, in these cases, it was not literacy itself that made them dependent, although it was a part of the dependence. Literacy contributed but was not the cause.

## Values

People make sense of literacy as a social phenomenon, and their social construction of literacy lies at the root of their attitudes toward literacy and their actions. It follows from this that people's views of literacy are important in how and what they learn. A parent's attitudes and actions influence a child's behavior at school. We are trying to develop a way of talking about literacy that can encompass this. To say that literacy has a social meaning is going further than saying that there are social dimensions to it or that it exists within a social context. Literacy is embedded in institutional contexts that shape the practices and social meanings attached to reading and writing. Within these social contexts, the act of reading or writing becomes symbolic. The very act of reading or writing takes on a social meaning: It can be an act of defiance or an act of solidarity, an act of conforming or a symbol of change.

There are a range of moral and social values attached to writing. These values generate attitudes and feelings toward literacy that underlie people's practices and affect what they do. It is in practices that values are expressed. For example, people often have strong views about reading at the meal table or writing in books. If they think reading at the table is socially reprehensible, they will forbid children to do it. Values are also reflected in views about censorship of literacy materials.

In another aspect of this, values are also clearly expressed in the relative importance attached to literacy as compared with other activities, such as practical and physical activities. Sometimes reading and writing are contrasted with work, at other times they are equated with leisure. In our historical study, for instance, we got the impression that people felt it was better to be reading than to be doing nothing but it was better to be doing some "real" work rather than reading (see Barton, 1988, for example). As we can see, writing is not just a cognitive activity, feelings run through it.

## Change and Access

There are several ways in which literacy is bound up with changes in people's lives. First, in people's personal histories, they write at particular times in their lives. The demands of life change: There are times in people's lives when they need to write more and times they need to write less. These can result from changes at work or from changes in their personal lives; for example, parents may experience changing demands when their young children grow up and go to school. It is often at points like these that adults decide to return to education. People want to make changes in their lives, and reading and writing enable them to make such changes. Access to basic education classes and other forms for writing provides new possibilities for change. People vary in the extent to which they have this access to literacy. In different ways, several chapters in this volume are concerned with change and access, including those of Gardener, Gregory, and Howard.

A second notion of change traces links from the past to the present. From generation to generation, people pass on a culture. In our studies of literacy in Lancaster, we can compare different generations and see how practices are passed on from one to another. There are links with the past and with the future. Historically, there are connections with the earlier generations of people (see Barton, 1988), and, in our current study of everyday uses of literacy, we are documenting ways the people we have interviewed want life to be different for their own children. These people are passing on a culture in a changing environment, and this is an important way in which the culture and its associated practices change.

Another aspect of change is current rapid social change, where new technologies and political changes are changing the demands on people. New social practices give different possibilities, so that paying bills by installments is easier, or new systems of paying by check in supermarkets require less literacy. Some social changes increase literacy demands; some reduce literacy demands. Another example from modern technology is the choice between sending messages by mail or by telephone or, where people have access, by fax, telex, or electronic mail. The path to a choice in any particular instance is very complicated, involving availability, cost, technical ability, and reliability. These possibilities are all changing rapidly.

## Processes

Reading and writing have often been viewed just in terms of the processes involved, which have been studied in formal educational settings. However, processes are situated in a context. In home and community situations, we can see whether there are distinct processes, both in the processes of everyday reading and writing and in the processes of learning to read and write. In the Barton and Padmore study, there were several examples of everyday theories of learning, where people articulated parts of the theories of learning they were using. These were concerned with how to learn, how to remember, and how to make sense of written documents. One person hung lists of words around the house to memorize them—although reporting that it turned out to be completely ineffective. Another person wrote new words on scraps of paper, "to take them out of the jumble on the page." The theories of learning that people take to school and college to some extent come from their experiences at home with everyday theories of learning. Gardener in this volume is concerned with this link, as are Ivanič and Moss.

## PUTTING THE PIECES TOGETHER

All the above contribute to providing us with a coherent way of describing home and community literacy events, so that in any event we might see roles, networks, and values and change, access, and processes.

A brief summary of a social view of writing is that, if we are to understand writing, we need to talk in terms of "literacies," not just one literacy. These vary by social context from one domain to another and from one event to another. They are best described as *practices* rather than as *skills*. This gives a dynamic and relativistic view, where a historical perspective is essential, rather than a static model. The dominant school-based definitions of literacy and work-based definitions of literacy often are at odds with what people do in their everyday lives. Home, school, and work are different domains of literacy supported by definition-sustaining institutions. We need to continue to develop ways of talking about literacy in these different domains. The authors of the different chapters in this volume probably agree with this in outline although they are all making distinct contributions to the study of writing.

## REFERENCES

Barton, D. (1988). Exploring the historical basis of contemporary literacy. *Quarterly Newsletter of the Laboratory of Comparative Human Cognition, 10*(3), 70-76.

Fairclough, N. (1989). *Language and power.* New York: Longman.

Fingeret, A. (1983). Social networks, independence and adult illiterates. *Adult Education Quarterly, 33*(3), 133-146.

Fishman, J. (1965). Language maintenance and language shift as a field of enquiry. *Linguistics, 9,* 32-70.

Goelman, H., Oberg, A., & Smith, F. (Eds.). (1984). *Awakening to literacy.* London: Heinemann.

Heath, S. B. (1983). *Ways with words.* Cambridge: Cambridge University Press.

Heath, S. B. (1984). The achievement of pre-school literacy for mother and child. In Goelman et al. (Eds.), *Awakening to literacy.* London: Heinemann

Lave, J. (1988). *Cognition in practice.* Cambridge: Cambridge University Press.

Leichter, H. J. (1984). Families as environments for literacy. In H. Goelman et al. (Eds.), *Awakening to literacy.* London: Heinemann.

Scribner, S., & Cole, M. (1981). *The psychology of literacy.* Cambridge, MA: Harvard University Press.

Street, B. (1984). *Literacy in theory and practice.* Cambridge: Cambridge University Press.

Taylor, D. (1983). *Family literacy.* London: Heinemann.

Teale, W. H., & Sulzby, E. (Eds.). (1986). *Emergent literacy: Writing and reading.* Norwood, NJ: Ablex.

# 2

# *Because This Is Who We Are*
## *Writing in the Amish Community*

## ANDREA R. FISHMAN

"Boys don't care for writing as much as girls do. They're more interested in sports. Amish girls aren't as interested in sports as your girls are. . . . Some boys take interest in writing just like a girl . . . but mostly it's a regular thing—boys hate to write," said 16-year-old Sarah Fisher one evening while we were preparing supper for the family.

"Dad hates it [too]," 11-year-old Katie added about their father Eli.

\* \* \*

At the beginning of my study of Amish literacy, I took three notebooks to the Fisher farm so Sarah, Katie, and Daniel—their 14-year-old brother—could keep journals for me. The children were not home, but their mother Anna smiled wryly when I explained my idea.

"You're optimistic," she said.

"They could write about anything," I insisted. "Anything they did, anything that happens. . . . If Daniel and Sarah had a fight, they could write about it . . ."

"They'd never do that!" Anna interrupted sharply, then paused to change her tone. "They'll have more time now, but I don't know about this summer when we're in the field," she continued, wondering how long I wanted them to keep writing.

As it turned out, Anna gave them the notebooks, but none of the children wrote more than a single page.

\* \* \*

Swipe a piece of paper, try and find the ink. Sit and chew your pen awhile, scratch your head and think. Try to write a letter fitting to be seen, tis no trifling matter to be writing to "DIE BOTSCHAFT." Not that it's a hardship for its far from that, what gives us all the trouble is to put things pat. Hence this care and caution like nothing ever seen, tis no trifling matter to be writing to "DIE BOTSCHAFT." First you read it through yourself, then show it to your ma. Then to various other folks who don't know who you are. So take care and tear your hair and keep from being mean. You don't know who will read what you write to "DIE BOTSCHAFT." So we spend an hour or two near a smoky lamp. Ask the family for a tip and husband for a stamp. Sorry it's over for our joy was keen. Twas a thrilling pastime writing to "DIE BOTSCHAFT." Or was it?

(*"Die Botschaft"* is a "weekly newspaper serving Old Order Amish communities everywhere," according to its masthead description. Its reporters are several hundred self-selected or district-selected "scribes" who write weekly letters about news from their church districts.)

\* \* \*

Dear Readers,

We here at Die Botschaft office generally try very hard to see that no objectionable material gets printed, but once in a while we come up short. This was the case two weeks ago when an article was printed concerning a Race to Chapter 11.

Unbeknown to the staff here at the paper, some one was using us as an opportunity to make trouble and bring disparagement. The writer did not even have the decency to write his name, but instead used fictitious initials.

We wish to apologize to the people who were hurt by this article and assure you, our readers, that we will endeavor to be more careful in screening out this type of material.

It is just a very sad commentary on the times that we have people who would stoop so low as to use this method to bring hurt and humiliation to others.

We hope that all our scribes will in the future try to write constructive materials and refrain from including items which are degrading and hurtful to others.

Thank you

The Editor

*   *   *

In their own spoken and written words, these Amish writers reveal a great deal about what it means to be Amish and what it means to write. Some of these writers are teenagers, some adults; some write for a narrow private audience, some for a wider, more public one. Yet, in each situation, the writers' sense of what they do and how they do it reflects their sense of who they are—as individuals and, more importantly, as Amish.

The particular writers quoted above represent almost all the subcommunities revealed by the data collected during my ethnographic research in two settlements of this relatively closed, Old Order, Anabaptist society, which reflects its seventeenth-century Palatinate origins as much as its current American reality. As a participant-observer with the seven-member Fisher family on their farm in central Pennsylvania, I discovered five implicit communities to which the Fishers belong. These communities (described and documented more completely in my book, *Amish Literacy: What and How It Means,* 1988) include the immediate community, comprised of Amish and English (i.e., non-Amish) individuals with whom family members interact on an almost daily basis; the larger community, comprised of all Amish everywhere; the church community, comprised of those who live in the Fishers' church district; the school community, comprised of those families whose children attend Meadow Brook School; and the school itself, comprised of the teacher and students present at Meadow Brook each day.

Yet, despite the varied composition of these communities, their definitions of writing—their understandings of what counts as writing and what does not—remain remarkably consistent. And this consistency seems attributable to one unvarying factor: a shared sense of what it means to be Amish. In their actions as in their words, these writers tell themselves and each other *this is what we do and this is how we do it because this is who we are.* To each of their children they add, *you are one of us.*

## THIS IS WHAT WE DO AND
## THIS IS HOW WE DO IT

The kinds of writing done across these five communities and within the Fisher household itself may not be noticeably different from the kinds done across more mainstream contexts except perhaps in their frequency and centrality to the writers' lives. Labels and lists, letters and notes, recipes and receipts, and checks and cards are the common forms and formats of Amish writing, many of which take on a uniquely Amish quality in their actual performance.

A seemingly insignificant form of writing, labeling matters a great deal in the Fisher home and immediate community, necessitated by the size and similarities within and among families. Amish boys' and men's hats and Amish girls' and women's bonnets look essentially identical. Eli Fisher and his oldest son Daniel, 8-year-old Amos and 6-year-old Eli, Jr., and daughters Sarah and Katie are as likely to pick up each other's as their own. At family gatherings or church services where dozens of equally similar hats appear and are left in a single location, finding one's own would be nearly impossible without the initials Anna and the other women sew or mark in hatbands and bonnet linings. Similarly, cooking pots, baking pans, and food storage containers look more alike than different, especially in Anna's family, where all the women use the same manufacturer's pots and the same brand of plastic containers. On holidays, Sisters' Days, and regular visits, when everyone contributes food prepared at home, finding one's own containers after all have been emptied and washed would be impossible without the initials laundry-markered on the bottoms. Christmas and Easter require labeling too of gifts and baskets, particularly for the Easter hunt when only names distinguish hidden treasures and the rules require ignoring those found that are marked for someone else.

Businesses require another form of labeling. Many Fisher friends and relatives sell food and crafts to the general public. J and A Meats, operated by Jake and Annie King at a local farmers' market, labels its products by variety and price. Signs also announce sales and services available, including weekly specials and a call-ahead hoagie take-out service.

Amish businesses require other forms of writing too. Mary, Anna's sister-in-law, who operates Mary's Stitchery, does considerable shop-related writing. In addition to the written work any small business requires—receipts, records, licensing forms, and tax reports—Mary must advertise, particularly because of her rural location. While small signs mark the road to her house, business cards and handbills introduce the Stitchery to customers in other shops where Mary's professionally printed information sits on counters and beside cash registers. For several summers, Mary also purchased space on paper placemats used by local tourist-attracting restaurants, and she composed the text to be printed there herself.

Lists are another seemingly mundane but significant form of writing in these communities. They are the only form of writing regularly used by the church community. Because the primary church texts—the Bible and the

*Ausbund* (hymnal)—were written long ago and are seen to need neither supplement nor critical analysis, and because ministers deliver their sermons entirely without notes, extended text production is unnecessary. Writing is useful for the church, therefore, only to conduct its more secular business, that is, to produce the annual lists matching Scripture portions with particular Sundays and to list nominees during the minister selection process.

The school community too uses lists: Lists of expenses written on the blackboard at monthly school meetings, lists of nominees for school board chairman on the blackboard at the end of a term, lists of mothers responsible for various portions of the school's Christmas dinner, lists of items and prices for the school's lunch stand at a farm sale.

Lists of all kinds find their way into letters of all types also, for letters are the primary form of writing in all the communities to which the Fishers belong. All the Fishers themselves write letters with more or less regularity. Anna writes monthly in two "circle letters" and as often as she can to individual friends and relatives. Eli writes in one circle letter when Anna presses him to do so. Sarah writes in a circle letter with distant friends and writes individual letters to distant cousins, sharing her circle letter with younger sister Katie, who does not have one of her own.

These circle letters are a common phenomenon among the Amish, but I had never encountered them before I got to know the Fishers. Circle letters are written by self-selected groups of friends, relatives, former schoolmates, members of the same occupation, or any other group with shared background or interests. When a circle letter arrives, a participant adds her or his new pages and removes the pages she or he wrote for the previous circuit before mailing it to the next person.

Sarah's circle of 11 same-age girls began when she was 13. When her circle letter arrives, after reading it herself, she shares it with Katie, who is equally anxious for news about the older girls. One year Sarah's circle was broken twice by someone not doing her part. When Sarah asked her mother what the girls should do, Anna said they must figure out who keeps breaking the circle and ask her to drop out. She should not be allowed to ruin it for the others, Anna concluded.

Anna herself is part of two different circles. One is a group of women: some relatives, some friends, all approximately the same age. The other circle she shares with Eli; it is a family circle with his 11 brothers and sisters. Each couple in that group writes one page—the wife on one side of the paper, the husband on the other. "It takes Eli a half hour to write one side of a piece of tablet paper," Anna teased. "And he needs stationery with lines."

When asked what would happen to one of her circles if she did not take her turn or decided to drop out, Anna hesitated. "Why would anyone not write?" she asked. "That's how we keep in touch. You'd never hear the news if you dropped out!" In fact, to keep these circles and their news moving, anyone who keeps the letter for more than three days is expected to enclose a stamp for the next person's use as a penalty.

The four younger Fisher children do not participate in circle letters, but they do write to friends and relatives on their own. Daniel, though old enough to write more, writes only to his favorite cousin Samuel, "maybe twice a year." Katie writes to same-age cousins and to Aleesha, one of the two Fresh Air Fund children who spent two summers on the farm. Amos too writes to his cousins, as does Eli, Jr., who even before he started school, dictated his messages to Sarah and sometimes copied what she wrote down, always enclosing his own signed drawings.

In addition to writing her circle and other limited-audience letters, Anna Fisher is a *"Die Botschaft"* scribe, writing a letter each week for the extended, and to her largely unknown, audience of *"Die Botschaft"* subscribers living in Old Order settlements in 15 states and Canada.

While scribes' letters vary in length and particular content, they all follow a predictable pattern. Most begin with a salutation, from a simple "Greetings" or "Dear Reader" to the more expansive "Friendly greetings of love to all readers and writers" or even "Greetings of love to you all I send, in the name of our dear Lord and friend." From there most move to a weather and farming report, including recent temperatures and precipitation amounts, status of seasonal crops, and current chores under way (whether haymaking, tobacco cutting, manure hauling, fruit canning, or quilting).

Then, in no particular order, they describe the most recent church service, where it took place, which ministers took which parts, and what out-of-district visitors attended; they list recent births, deaths, and marriages in the district; they report who is ill or injured (often with graphic descriptions of their conditions, who is recovering, who visited whom, and any other event that seems notable (which may include runaway horses, school meetings, building of new church benches, or even recent crimes reported in their local newspapers). Sometimes scribes respond to questions or content introduced by other scribes in previous issues. In addition, scribes frequently include maxims they consider philosophically or spiritually uplifting and "upbuilding" for the community, whether from a religious or secular source. Two examples might prove useful here.

STRASBURG, PA.
Miller Street

August 15—Hello to everybody out there in Die Botschaftland.

The weather is a little cooler. We are having nice growing weather. Fourth crop alfalfa looks good.

Today Christ's Mark and Ruth Ann are here. Lydia has to stay laying with her leg elevated. She has outer blood vein trouble. She is supposed to stay off her feet one week. David B. Zook was here one part of a day to pass the time. he has a walking cast on his foot. It happened at White Oak pallet shop. A skid fell on his foot and broke his foot. But it sure did not affect his speech or friendly smile.

Last week Randy Witmore and Kenny from Dallas, Texas, were here. So I went with them 2 days. Randy bought a top buggy and a horse at Christian Weaver's. He will be in up the week of Martin's wagon sale and take his horse and buggy along home.

On Wed. the 13th, the Vocational School meeting was at Daniel E. King's with a good attendance. To be at Bish. Enos Esh's next year. It was a 1/2 day well spent to learn and hear what our forefathers did to get what we have today and hope we can all work together and keep up what they went through.

John A. Beiler


BLOOMSBURG, PA
Montour Co.

Aug. 14—Greetings to all. Looks like it might be a cloudy day although the sun was peeping a little awhile ago. We were baling hay the last 2 days, put around 1,000 bales in the barn. Hope we are thankful for the many blessings. Garden Things are so plentiful, sweet corn, lima beans, string beans, tomatoes and egg plants. And of course the weeds grow too if the other things do. I think the garden would be dry enough now to cultivate then we want to sow oats in where we can. Canned sourkraut and cantelopes this week. Now want to make ketchup yet. Dau. Susie is spending 2 days in Lanc. Co. Today is teacher's class, the other teachers from this area planned to go.

We made a call at Ike Stoltzfuses on Sun. Baby David is better again. 2 weeks ago he was not good, didn't take anything from the bottle. They fed him with a dropper. But was drinking milk again last Sun. He is 8 months old. Son Jeffs and Sam M. Stoltzfuses were here for supper.

West dist. church was at Christ Lapps. Next time to be at (Elams) Amos E. Beilers, Aug. 24. Cousin Henry Stoltzfus, David from NY was here and went with our children to church.

Christ Lapps are having their infare on Sat. for the Amos Beiler family.

We want to dig the rest of the early potatoes today and pull some weeds, also have windows to paint now that it has dried off a little.

Tobacco is being put away, cannery tomatoes picked in the neighborhood. We don't have any. Men want to haul manure.

Elam and Lydia Stoltzfus

Another form of letter writing sometimes called for in *"Die Botschaft"* is "showers." "Sunshine Showers," "Get-Well Showers," or "Birthday Showers" involve sending letters and cards to people who are unhappy, ailing or celebrating and may be requested by scribes in their letters or by others who write solely for that purpose. Whichever the case, the requesting writers explain the perceived need and supply the name and address of the proposed recipient.

Other sections of *"Die Botschaft"* not comprised of scribes' letters are reader written as well. "Ivverich un Ender," usually located in the middle of the newspaper, is "a column for the hausfrau," offering favorite recipes and household hints, some submitted in response to previously printed requests, some not. Following this "column"—which may run for several pages is the poetry section, containing reader-submitted, sometimes reader-written, poems and song lyrics, which occupy as many columns or pages as necessary. "Obituaries," "Births," an "Exchange Column," and "Classified Ads" are the other regularly occurring sections.

## BECAUSE THIS IS WHO WE ARE

At first glance, the reasons the Amish write what and how they do may seem obvious, the question almost too simple to ask. Writing is useful. It allows individuals to manage the business of their lives—to keep track of their belongings, to advertise and sell their products, to pay their bills, to organize their church services and their farm sales, to keep in touch with their families and their friends. From the perspective of mainstream society, individual purposes like these may seem paramount, and to this list of practical uses might be added other, more psychological needs: the need to identify one's self among many, the need to accomplish individual goals, and the need to achieve personal success. Certainly the Amish have such needs, and certainly writing does serve them.

But, when looking at Amish communities and Amish culture, writing becomes less an individually driven endeavor and more a socially motivated one. Seen in their sociocultural context, Fisher family writers become people not only conducting their own lives but constructing the life of their society as well. Viewed in this light, there is more to writing than meeting the personal needs of a writer; there are the ways writing reflects and shapes the society that reflect and shape the writers themselves, the society that teaches them who they are, what they value, and what they may expect from life and from each other.

Above all, the Amish are conscious of what it means to be Amish, and they value that identity. Being Amish means being separate and distinct from the English (as they call all their non-Amish neighbors) and from everyone else in the world. Being Amish means to "not be conformed to this world" (Rom. 12:2), to "be not unequally yoked together with unbelievers" (II Cor. 6:14), and to be—again in the words of the King James Version—"a peculiar people" (I Pet. 2:9 and Titus 2:14). Amish achievement of the separate identity they see called for in these passages may be marked most overtly by the clothes they wear, the buggies they drive, and the language they speak, but the desire to be separate and its manifestations run much deeper than that. Amish cultural institutions, their churches and their schools, emphatically set them apart, and so, more subtly, do their rituals and practices, from the silent grace they say before and after meals to the circle and *"Die Botschaft"* letters so many of them write and even more read.

While all these may be seen as the Amish response to the biblical commands for separation and demonstrate what it means to be Amish as opposed to being English, they are also methods of personal identification and affiliation and part of what it means to be Amish solely in terms of the community itself. What does it mean to belong to this "peculiar people"? What does this community value? And how are those meanings and values manifested in the writing?

First of all, the Amish value being part of a conforming, monolithic community. If a person is Amish—female or male—he or she is part of rather than apart from the group. Everyone has a role; everyone has a place. Everyone knows what to expect, and everyone knows what is expected of them. A young Amish girl, for example, need only watch other females in her family and community to know how to pin her dress, discipline misbehaving children, bake sticky buns, speak to strangers, or spend her time when all chores are done. And she need only look at the males around her to know how expectations for them differ from those for her.

Nor are just overtly public actions and interactions modeled by the community. Implicit expectations extend to all aspects of Amish life, even such seemingly private or personal ones as writing. It was these clear community expectations that encouraged Sarah Fisher to join a circle letter and made Katie Fisher want one of her own, and it was these same expectations that enabled Sarah and Katie to agree that "boys don't care for writing as much as girls."

And as community expectations help determine who likes to write and who does not, they also help determine the kinds of writing people will or will not do. Sarah Fisher, a girl who really enjoys writing, would not keep a journal for me any more than her brother Daniel would, despite the differences in gender expectations. Journal writing is a form not just foreign to Amish society but one that runs counter to its conformist, other-oriented expectations and values, a fact that enabled Anna Fisher to predict that none of her children would keep journals, not even to help a close friend with her work.

While community expectations like these may seem unbearably restrictive—or even punitive—to someone outside the community, Amish conformity has other, more positive, less often recognized sides. First, being Amish means being part not just of a restrictive community but of a cohesive cooperative community as well, a community that values not only life but individual lives. Sharing and helping are the norm, so caring about others more than yourself also means being cared about by people other than yourself and your immediate family.

Just as this caring translates into the communal barn raisings and quiltings of which many Americans are aware, so it translates into neighboring farmers helping with each others' harvest, neighboring women helping with each other's canning, and neighboring families helping to construct and maintain a neighborhood school. On a more global level, this same communal caring produces *"Die Botschaft"* with its scribes willing to do all the pen chewing, head scratching, and thinking necessary to produce a "letter fitting to be seen."

Because the desirability of such caring—of conforming, sharing, and putting others' needs ahead of one's own—is implicit in the modeled behavior of almost all community members almost all the time, the implicit rules governing such behavior are rarely articulated yet rarely broken. When someone does break a fundamental rule, however, the implicit must become explicit and someone—whether parent, minister, or other community adult— must address the point directly, as the *"Die Botschaft"* editor did in response to an inappropriate submission to his newspaper. His open letter to readers did not explain what "bring[s] hurt and humiliation to others," what "make[s] trouble" or "bring[s] disparagement"; it only made explicit the fact that such behaviors are unacceptable. To understand exactly what that meant, readers had to look to their community context, where such information implicitly resides.

Yet despite the apparent strength of his feelings on the issue, the editor did not feel obliged to make his own identity known by signing his open letter, for who he is makes no difference. The editorial role exists in the community as a function of communal activity; it is independent of the editor himself, so who he is does not matter. What does matter is that someone used writing for an illegitimate purpose, one neither desirable for nor tolerated by this community, which puts the communal good before all else. Because of this, someone—an "editor"—had to point that out.

Another positive aspect of Amish conformity is the universal trust and accountability it produces. As suggested earlier, people within this society are grouped according to naturally occurring, patently obvious categories of gender and age—not intelligence, ability, or any other humanly determined distinctions. When there are turns to be taken, everyone shares equally. When the group has a goal, anyone may—and everyone is expected to—help achieve that goal without regard to who volunteers most or least. This relates to writing because it produces the assumption that everyone is or will become *literate,* according to the community definition of that term. Adults and children have equal opportunity to participate in literacy events, none allowed to dominate or to demur completely. This does not deny the inclination of some individuals to be more verbal than others or of some to be less so, but, in situations with clear, shared purposes, the most assertive must make way for the most reticent, who also must participate.

From this trust and accountability accompanying conformity comes the paradox of an authoritarian society without significant hierarchical distinctions. Amish society is undeniably authoritarian, with received instruction from dominant figures an organizing fact of life. Yet authorities are not considered significantly different than other people, neither is their authoritative status overtly marked because such status accrues from without—it is neither specially merited nor intentionally acquired. Like parents, relatives, and adult friends, ministers and teachers are simply other community adults from whom children learn. They have the same credentials—the same training, the same beliefs, the same life-style—so they deserve the same attention and respect.

This fundamental assumption allows children to call all adults except their parents and grandparents by their given names without any hint of disrespect, marking their basic shared humanity instead of their superficial superior-subordinate relationships. And when it comes to writing, only in the rare instances of broken rules does authoritative statement pertain. Most of the time, people write as who they are—not what they are—claiming no authority or power for themselves, only their value as participating, caring members of the community.

All of this leads to a fourth quality the Amish value in their culture, which is its viability. The Amish cherish their ability to maintain themselves, not only in terms of their cultural identity but in terms of their economic and political independence as well. In practical terms, this means they must cooperate with the larger society from which they try to separate themselves so clearly. It means Amish dairy farmers must sell their milk to mainstream cooperatives and companies, which means using diesel-powered cooling tanks so their milk meets state health department requirements. It means they must use non-Amish modern medicine so their animals and families remain healthy. And it even means they must sell their wares of all kinds to non-Amish businesses and customers, even to the tourists who continually and often rudely invade their privacy.

When it comes to writing, this need for economic viability means that Amish children must acquire the literacy skills that will enable them to remain economically viable yet still remain Amish. They must learn to read and write English so well that their second language may become equivalent to their first. They must be able to complete order forms from mail-order seed, fabric, and equipment companies and complete other forms relating to business and government transactions of all types. They must be able to advertise their own shops, products, and services and do all the sign, label, list, and other writing businesses may require.

In terms of Amish adults, this need to ensure their economic viability by educating their children is closely related to their need to maintain political independence as well. Amish children must go to school to serve Amish purposes, but they must also go to school to comply with state law, and the state must approve the schools they attend. Of course, Amish children could attend public schools along with their English counterparts, but that would run counter to the doctrine of separation in significantly threatening ways. So the community chooses to operate its own schools, requiring that parents acquire the political and literacy skills to do so.


## THEY ARE OUR CHILDREN


The history of Amish education and of Amish political consciousness-raising is revealing here. For several generations, at least most of those born in the twentieth century, the Amish have chosen to attend school through the eighth grade, and that is what they want for their children. Despite their willingness to send their children to school, however, Amish parents are unwilling to send their children to schools staffed by outside professionals who claim to know what is best for them and for their futures. As far as the Amish are concerned now, only Amish parents and the Amish community know what Amish children need, so those parents and that community create and maintain their schools themselves, with a very clear objective in mind:

> The goal of the school shall be to prepare the child for the Amish or Mennonite way of living and the responsibilities of adulthood. In short, these standards are designed in an effort to establish the foundations of a society of useful, God-fearing, and law-abiding citizens. *(Standards of the Old Order Amish and Old Order Mennonite Parochial and Vocational Schools of Penna., p. 5)*

Yet this has not always been the case. When American public schools were small—when they retained a human scale; when each child was responsible to the group; when teachers used "old-fashioned" methods; when curriculum and pedagogy had religious components and intentions; when schools were more part of than apart from daily life—then the Amish sent their children to public schools. That was the case in the Fisher family: Anna and Eli Fisher and both sets of their parents went to one- and two-room public schools in rural Lancaster County, Pennsylvania.

American schools did not stay that way, however. As American society changed, its schools changed with it. Even before World War II, the values of intellectual achievement and technological knowledge began to replace leading a good life and acquiring wisdom as the primary goals of education. Competing for individual success became more important than cooperatively working for community welfare. Schools became more specialized, more intense, and more intensive to meet society's changing expectations, and, as they did so, those schools became potentially destructive to the Amish way of life. For these reasons, as early as the 1930s, a handful of Amish parents established their own schools.

Such aggressive activity was limited and sporadic until the 1950s and 1960s, when even the most rural public schools began to change. Then large, predominantly rural districts began consolidating, replacing their remaining one- and two room schools with big modern institutions to which farm children were bused considerable distances and to which Amish parents could not in good conscience send their children.

Legal battles ensued with public school districts trying to enforce their states' compulsory education laws by busing Amish children over their parents' strenuous objections. Some Amish parents were fined; other were actually jailed. The English who lived nearby began getting involved to support their Amish neighbors, and soon lawyers were involved. Finally, in 1972, the struggle culminated in *Wisconsin v. Yoder,* the Supreme Court decision recognizing the adequacy and necessity of Old Order schools for the maintenance and preservation of Old Order society.

After hearing "the unchallenged testimony of acknowledged experts in education and religious history," the court accepted "almost 300 years of consistent practice [as] strong evidence of a sustained faith pervading and regulating . . . the entire mode of [Amish] life." They found that "Amish religious faith and their mode of life are . . . inseparable and interdependent" and that sending Amish children to public schools posed a real and serious threat to the continuation of Amish life and Amish culture. This decision freed the Amish to establish a parochial school system coherent with the values, goals, and expectations of their society. It is a system, in Pennsylvania at least, governed by the *Standards* quoted above, a system of schools like Meadow Brook, which the five Fisher children attend.

Stepping into Meadow Brook School is like stepping into America's past. The schoolroom has a narrow-planked dark wood floor. The slant-top wooden desks and their attached chairs sit on wrought metal pedestal bases in six straight rows. A large wood stove dominates the front of the room, dwarfing the teacher's wooden desk beside it. A slanted blackboard hangs from the front wall, with print and cursive English alphabet charts above it. Student hats and coats hang from hooks along the back of the room. Light shines in through the oversized, uncurtained windows that look out on the meadows and the brook that give the school its name.

First through eighth grades meet in this one room, seated by grade but not otherwise separated. Their teacher, an unmarried Old Order woman, comes from the same kind of background they do, wears the same kind of clothes, has the same kind of eighth grade education, holds the same values and beliefs. Literally and figuratively, this teacher speaks their language. She refers to all her students as "scholars" and calls them by their first names. They refer to her as "teacher," and they call her Verna.

Verna expects her students to behave—to sit quietly, work diligently, spend their free time wisely. She expects them to be clean, neat, pleasant, and helpful, and they expect the same of her. Good manners are the norm for everyone here; bad moods are not tolerated at Meadow Brook, regardless of whose they are.

Just as Verna helps children because she is older and knows more than they do, so upper grade students help lower grade ones for the same reasons. While Verna listens to first graders reading, fifth grader Katie may give third graders the answers to the arithmetic problems they did earlier. While Verna conducts an eighth grade history lesson, seventh grade Mary Lou may respond to a second grader's raised hand. Everyone is busy, yet, when a third grade boy begins daydreaming, squirming in his seat, and gazing around at the children behind him, a stern look from an older child turns him around and back to the work at hand.

Yet while all of this activity goes on, the most striking characteristic of the Meadow Brook schoolroom is its air of concerted silence. On the last day I was there as on the first, I could hear the teacher instructing or a student reciting, but surrounding those voices was always the noticeable absence of others. There was no chatting, no whispering, no background hum, only the sounds of students getting on with the business of school. Even when assigned work was done, the silence continued as boys read extra-curricular books and girls did cross-stitch embroidery.

Because Meadow Brook has no support staff, no janitors or maintenance people, the teacher, the students, and even their parents must daily and seasonally manage the physical upkeep of the school. Each day's chores appear on the "Chore Chart," allotting responsibility for tasks—sweeping, burning trash, clapping erasers, washing the blackboard, stapling first grade papers, pulling shades, and fetching water—to upper grade students on a rotating basis. Weekly chores, like dusting, washing surfaces, and washing windows fall to upper grade girls while chopping and hauling wood, raking leaves, and shoveling snow fall to upper grade boys and to parents as well as to the teacher herself. Each year before school opens, mothers appear to help "set up" the room, and each year, whenever necessary, fathers appear to patch the roof, clean the gutters, and do any other major work the schoolhouse needs.

Parent involvement is not limited to building maintenance, however. Once each month, classes end at 1 p.m. so the "school meeting" can be held in the classroom. Conducted by the school board—these meetings are attended by the parents of Meadow Brook children and by the teacher. Finances, programs, plans, and problems are discussed, and everyone participates. Almost all parents attend these meetings just as almost all attend the annual Christmas program and end-of-the-year picnic. Most parents also visit several times a year while school is in session, bringing treats for the children and sitting in the row of folding chairs always set up in the back of the room for that purpose.

In some ways, Meadow Brook's curriculum and pedagogy are exactly what might be expected in a school created and maintained by these parents and this society. Reading, writing, and arithmetic are the core of student studies, supplemented by spelling, vocabulary, history, and geography. German is studied by the upper grades twice a week to facilitate participation in church services (conducted entirely in High German), and health is studied by those same children once a week to please the state as well as the parents.

Though hymns are sung every morning, grace said before lunch every day, and Bible verses memorized and recited once a week, religion is not taught at Meadow Brook School. Too important and too sensitive a subject, the study of God and faith is reserved for the home and the church.

The writing used at Meadow Brook also follows from what is done outside the school. Labeling, listing, copying, and letter writing all find their way into the curriculum and the classroom. All these varieties are more often modeled than directly taught, and all are used to serve the purposes not just of the school but of its homes and community as well.

Most of the studying and learning Meadow Brook students do is intended to give them a shared body of correct knowledge. Texts and teachers are seen as authoritative. To question or even discuss ideas may work against the compliant unanimity their society values, so learning involves students taking what authorities tell them and repeating it as accurately as possible, often in or through writing. The two most common forms this writing takes at Meadow Brook are workbooks and reports.

What do students write in workbooks? Primarily single letters, words, or phrases, sometimes only marks of various kinds. First graders match sounds to pictures by drawing lines or circles in their phonics workbooks. Eighth graders match definitions to words by writing the letter of the correct multiple-choice answer in their vocabulary workbooks. But neither the 6-year-olds nor the 14-year-olds are writing very differently, nor are they learning very different lessons.

Although workbook producers and client schools—whether Amish or English—seem to assume that these kinds of writing represent student learning of the information written or marked, workbook exercises teach other, less subject-related, more Amish-appropriate lessons too. Amish society teaches that there is a right answer to every question just as workbooks do. And whether in workbooks or in life, everyone must know, share, and similarly acknowledge that answer. Meadow Brook first graders and eighth graders learn to look for those single right answers to all their questions, learning to choose them from among all others that are wrong. And while eighth graders may have to use supplemental dictionaries for vocabulary lessons, adding complexity to their tasks, the focus is the same: Find the right answer and mark it the right way.

Remarkably similar in such underlying lessons are reports. Not considered composition lessons, report assignments accompany individual subjects and topics. Nature study, for example, a separate upper grade subject studied each Monday instead of vocabulary, has no text other than student-produced reports. History and geography, while primarily textbook focused, have supplementary student reports as well.

A page from Katie Fisher's Nature Study report on flowers exemplifies what all such reports are like.

Forget me knot, name given to plants of the genus Myosotis, belonging to the family Boraginaceae (q.v.). They are found in temperate zones in all parts of the world. A number of species are common in ditches and damp meadows of the U.S. The true forget-me-not, M. scorpioides, has creeping perennial roots with ascending stems bearing small sky blue flowers. The most Popular horticultural forget-Me-nots are varieties of M. sylvatica, admired especially for the brilliancy of their blue flowers. They are used extensively for ground cover in gardens and borders, and beside pools and streams. A dark blue species, the Azores forget-me-not, M. azorica, requires greenhouse cultivation in temperate regions. The romantic name is derived from the last words of a legendary German knight drowned while attempting to retrieve the flower for his lady.

                                                    The
                                                    End

Katie did what all her classmates do: She looked up her topic in the classroom set of *Funk and Wagnall's Standard Reference Encyclopedia* (1961) and copied the information she found there. Instead of finding and marking the right answers, Katie and other report writers must find and appropriately copy them. So, like workbook writing, report writing highlights what is valued and expected by the school and the community that runs it:

Students must work hard, stay within the lines, and get things right. There is only one way to do that, so everyone must do it the same way.

What keeps this Meadow Brook report writing from being plagiarism, from being illegal or immoral, as the Amish see it? First of all, plagiarism is a mainstream concept, a mainstream offense, and a mainstream problem, not an Old Order concern. No Amish student would submit a copied paper intending to defraud because no Amish student would want to claim published writing as his or her own. The ability to write like a professional—however that is defined—is not a skill valued by the Amish. New ideas, unique presentation, and fresh style conspire to make an individual noticeable, to separate him or her from other community language users. Not only is such visibility undesirable, it opposes the basic community value of group identification. Copying at Meadow Brook is a way to keep from standing out, a way to write like everyone else. Being a good report writer means not being a good plagiarist but being a good Amishman: being accurate, being efficient, and being one of a group, not one of a kind.

In addition to the studying and learning represented by workbooks and reports, writing has other uses at Meadow Brook, among them recording and reporting. Students who complete the eighth grade but have not yet reached the compulsory schooling age of 16 become "three-hour pupils," attending school only three hours a week, spending the rest of their time working at home to learn vocational skills. To demonstrate to the state that these students are actually involved in such training, three-hour pupils must keep diaries of what they do.

In her diary one September, a three-hour pupil named Arlene wrote:

MON SEPT 6    Labor Day Packed lunches. Washed the milkers then finished to wash. Went to Ed Zimmerman's for deisel fuel. Fed cows and calves.

TUE SEPT 7—Milked. Picked lima beans and string beans. Went to Lawrence Nolts for fruit then to Ike's Grocery. Trimmed yard Made supper.

In his diary for the same two days, the other three-hour pupil, James, wrote:

SEPT. 6—David Sauder came to open up the fields. Got ready to fill silo. P.M. John Shirk came and filled 10 x 50, 10 x 40, and 12 x 50 silos. Had to drive wagons.

SEPT. 7—refilled 12 x 50 silo. Got ready to fill trench put 16 loads in A.M. and 25 in P.M. one of the wagons has a cracked Beam.

Arlene's and James's entries are obviously similar despite the fact that neither was specifically told or taught what to write. Both students emphasize verbs—what they did or what was done. Explanation, description, and complete sentences do not matter to either writer because the context requires only an account of their vocational training, evidence that they are needed at home and learn necessary skills there. These students record external, verifiable facts, without evaluation or interpretation, for the purpose of a potential report to the state. They do not write for self-exploration, self-discovery, or even personal history reasons; such introspective purposes do not exist in their other-focused world.

Another recording activity produces the *Meadow Brook Gazette*. This school newspaper is printed each month on the school's hand-cranked duplicating machine and student carried to each participating household.

Throughout the year, a single *Gazette*-titled notebook rotates daily among upper grade students. Each day, it is someone's task to record a dated entry of that day's news, including absent children, visitors, interesting occurrences, changes in routine, disciplinary proceedings, and anything else the individual writer considers newsworthy. Once each month, the eighth graders use their scheduled English lesson to transcribe the notebook entries onto ditto masters. No revision marks this transcription; neither do bylines or other credits mark these pages. Even when individual student writing appears in the *Gazette,* as an occasional poem or other writing assignment might, it always remains anonymous.

The front page of one October issue looked like this:

Newspage I

Oct. 1—Arlene Martin came with a beautiful bouquet of flowers. Daniel, Richard, and Levi got prizes for leading songs. Wilma didn't get a seal for reading because she didn't know all her words. Katie F. wasn't done with her Arith. when it was time for class.

Oct. 4—Susan Hoover treated with banana's. David Nolt forgot his arithmetic book. Last night (Oct. 3) a hot air balloon landed in Edwin Nolt's field. Neighbors went down to look at it. It was big!

Oct. 5—Wilma got chicklets for starting songs. Donna Zimmerman came to visit. David had to stay in two minutes for showing a book to Mervin. Verna Burkholder set a timer for one minute and whoever was late in at recess had to stay in one minute. It was, Jakie, Daniel, David, Walter, Katie, and Melvin. Marlin, James, Walter and Melvin were whispering. They had to write their names on the board, then the teacher said she has to have glasses to read it because they wrote little. Jay got a prize for saying his timestables from 0 - 9 in 3 minutes.

Oct. 6—Today Glenn had to stay in at first recess because he told a lie. He had been showing his arithmetic around and whispering about it and someone told the teacher. Glenn said that he didn't whisper but had after all.

Corrections Oct 4 A bird flew out of stove pipe into classroom

Despite what might appear to be objectivity or formality in this anonymous first-person plural presentation, however, the *Meadow Brook Gazette* more closely resembles a mainstream newsletter than a newspaper and looks more like a rough draft than a polished product. Before the school acquired an old, secondhand typewriter, penmanship changed from page to page as all the eighth graders helped with the transcription. After the typewriter arrived, each issue still had at least one handwritten section and one was not typed at all. Sporadic editing overlooked some spelling, punctuation, and typographical errors in every issue. All corrections that were made, however, remained visible: Words and letters were crossed out rather than scraped off; new ones were inserted next to or above the blocked spaced; typewritten text was corrected by hand. Whether student or teacher written (and Verna did write open letters to parents in the paper), discarded ideas were often as visible as their replacements, providing evidence of the writer's process not usually found in published work.

The concept of multiple drafts does not seem to exist anywhere at Meadow Brook, however. Diaries, reports, newspapers, letters, and compositions (the latter two yet to be discussed) are written once, the newspaper requiring compilation but not revision. That no one writes perfectly all the time is as much a fact at Meadow Brook as elsewhere, but that fact both explains and excuses the visible corrections there. Time spent rewriting things is wasted time, especially if the unrevised version serves the writer's intended purpose. In this case, the purpose is to record and report information for a clearly defined, appreciative audience that demands purposeful activity, not some other society's definition of perfection.

It is not surprising that letter writing finds its way into the Meadow Brook curriculum, adding perhaps the most personal communication experiences these children have. One winter, for example, Verna had her upper grade girls write letters to the girls in another Old Order school, this one in Indiana, and once again, Katie Fisher's work may represent all of theirs.

Dear Emma Schwartz,

Hi, Greetings from far and near. How are you hope fine thats how you would find me. I'm in the fifth grade and eleven years old. I go to Meadow Brook School. My teachers name is Verna Burkholder. I have a cat and a dog of my own. We live on a farm. We have forty-five cows to milk. I sometimes help milk evenings not always mornings. What do you always do at your place? My birthday is Feb twenty eight. You did not write when your birthday is?! Write Back and tell me. I have a friend Emma in Lancaster. She went to my school when we still lived in Lancaster. We have seven in our family with Mom and Dad. Well am about out of news. Write Back!!!

HERE IS OUR FAMILY

|       |            | Age |
|-------|------------|-----|
| Dad   | Eli B.     | 38  |
| Mom   | Anna S.    | 34  |
|       | Sarah Ann  | 15  |
|       | Daniel Jay | 14  |
| Me    | Katie Mae  | 11  |
|       | Amos Elson | 9   |
|       | Eli F. Jr. | 5   |

Here's my address Write me then and give me your address then i will write you back.

Katie Fisher

c/o Eli B. Fisher

(town), (state) Box 345

(zip code)

I will be looking for your letter!!

Loads of Love

Katie M. Fisher

Where did Katie learn to write letters like this? Verna did not have to teach her how. Her home and community already had.

What might be considered formal composition does have a place at Meadow Brook, but it is a relatively minor one, occurring irregularly, most often replacing vocabulary in the regular schedule. Composition is strictly an upper grade subject, but composition is never taught. No explicit lesson precedes, accompanies, or follows the writing. Verna's assignments either model her expectations through compositions she actually writes herself and then reads to the class, or they point to appropriate models in newspapers or sale handbills, or they structure the task to create an almost unavoidable model, as these two compositions by fifth grade Katie and eighth grade Daniel illustrate. Though Katie and Daniel are of different ages and have different abilities and interests when it comes to writing, Verna's assignment is clearly apparent in both of their compositions.

REX (by Daniel)

He is brown and black mixed. He is about six feet tall. I have him around half a year.

His good habits are he doesn't kick and his bad habits are he tries to bite you. He doesn't follow me arround. I din't have him long enough to see how he got along with other horses.

The future of him is Rex and I are going to live together in an old shack.

"MY DOG" (by Katie)

My dog is little. He's mostly black but has a little white.

He's not to old yet. His name is Rover. He is a fat puppy!!!!!

His good habits are, he braks when people come. He does not run away. He is not scared of people He runs up to them and bits them.

His bad habits arc, He runs after cars, trucks and other things, He follows us to school. He gets Moms things. He likes to chew on soft things. When I go out to milk He comes and likes to chew on my shoe strings.

"The End"

What had Verna told them before they wrote? Write about one of your pets, she had said. In the first paragraph, describe the animal; in the second, give its good and bad habits; and in the third "give its future." Katie and Daniel did exactly that to the best of their individual understanding and ability.

So what can be said about the role of composition at Meadow Brook and its relation to writing? Composition, per se, is of minimal importance. Taught when Verna feels "inspired," it has no place in the regular schedule; neither does it have a place with other subjects on the students' report cards, appearing in the second section between "Rank in Class" and "Neatness." Instead of having its own identity, composition becomes what report writing, newspaper writing, letter writing, and all other writing are not. At worst, it is an academic exercise Meadow Brook students tolerate because their homes and community support what their school requires. At best, composition is an additional opportunity to practice thinking and writing in socially approved ways and to transmit cultural lessons about what is appropriate for public consideration and what is not.

## CONCLUSION

It seems evident then that, like all other Meadow Brook School activities, the writing students do derives from and in turn reinforces the homes and the community that create and maintain the school. While Meadow Brook writing in particular—and Meadow Brook pedagogy in general—may seem limiting or even abhorrent to mainstream educators (despite its frightening similarities to what actually goes on in many mainstream schools), it is crucial to realize that such abhorrence stems from the discontinuity between Amish culture and the more academic one, not from anything inherently "wrong" with either.

While Amish schools, homes, and communities are obviously discontinuous with some, more mainstream varieties, they are strictly continuous with each other. Yet their continuity is not a matter of home and community aligning themselves with school (as many public educators would demand in their own domains) but of home and school aligning themselves with community. In fact, it may be the presence of a separate, identifiable community that enables this group of homes to create one school and to remain continuous with it. Instead of remaining two potentially opposite poles, home and school become two sides of a three-sided relationship, their triangular equilibrium more stable than any two-sided interaction. Nor is the triangle equilateral; instead, the two sides of home and school depend on the third—community—to keep their balance.

It seems important to point out, however, that this set of relationships did not just happen. The Amish chose to create these relationships, doing so only after realizing that public schools were becoming significantly discontinuous with their homes and their community and posed a serious threat to both. The continuity observed in this study seems the result of this realization and of subsequent conscious decisions to control and ensure their cultural survival by charging home, community, and school with the responsibility for Amish-appropriate literacy transmission.

To achieve this goal, schools like Meadow Brook were created not as highly specialized organs but as direct reflections of Amish homes and communities in terms of their values, expectations, and methods. As the examples here reveal, definitions of what counts as good writing do not change significantly from home to community to school. Based on this shared understanding of what it means to write, each context can comfortably assume some responsibility for fostering the literacy all find necessary. And each can also be sure that, rather than mixed or crossed messages, students will consistently understand that *this is what we do and this is how we do it because this is who we are.*

## REFERENCE

Fishman, A. R. (1988). *Amish literacy: What and how it means.* Portsmouth, NH: Heinemann.

# 3

# *Bilingual Written Language Use by Low-Education Latin American Newcomers*

## CECIL KLASSEN

**In 1981, Shirley Brice Heath** wrote (in reference to the United States):

> There is almost no systematic description of the functions of writing in the society as a whole or in special groups and subcultures which differ among themselves and from school culture in their uses of writing and their attitude toward it. (Heath, 1981, p. 44)

Communities of newcomers (I avoid the term *immigrant* because it does not technically include the many individuals who do not yet have official immigrant or refugee status) form one category of such groups in North America. Minority language groups formed by newcomers face a bilingual, and more frequently a multilingual, reality as they adapt to a new society. Little attention has as yet been paid, however, to the uses newcomers make of written language in their mother tongues and in the majority language as they attempt to manage their new living situations. Studies that look at language use in multilingual settings tend to focus more on minority language groups in developing countries (e.g., Hamel, 1984; Shaw, 1983) or on aboriginal and native groups in North America (Burnaby, 1985). These existing studies are often linked to government or development organization attempts to determine effective language policies for literacy and basic education programs for marginalized minority language adults who have not previously had access to extensive schooling. The rationale for such studies, therefore, has been largely pedagogical: to help minority language adults learn literacy skills. Adult educators and literacy scholars tend to start from the premise that learning is best facilitated when the knowledge or skills to be learned are immediately useful in, and articulate well culturally with, the everyday reality of the adult learners (relevance to the learner emerged, for example, as one of the primary themes in the Persepolis literacy conference; Bataille, 1976).

This challenge of providing learning opportunities that are practically and culturally relevant is not, however, an approach that is useful only to rural, minority language groups in Third World countries. The challenge also exists in urban centers of North America, where significant numbers of adult newcomers from Southeast Asia and Central America arrive with little formal schooling from their own countries. American and Canadian studies have found that low-education adult newcomers tend to benefit very little from conventional second-language classes and are thereby often excluded from entry into the kinds of training programs that provide the credentialing necessary for semiskilled and skilled employment opportunities (d'Anglejan, 1983; Tollefson, 1985; Weinstein, 1984). This problem with learning entry-level majority language skills (English or French) challenges educators to find reasons for this lack of success and to find approaches that better serve the learning needs of low-education adult newcomers. The place to start, according to current learner-centered approaches in education research (as Szwed, 1981, eloquently argued almost a decade ago), would be to determine how to make learning opportunities relevant to the learners. But little systematic knowledge exists about the everyday uses that any given group of low-education newcomers have for literacy skills. There is clearly a need to conduct studies that describe the functions of written language in the everyday lives of, in Heath's (1981, p. 44) words, "special groups and subcultures," in this case, various groups of low-education adult newcomers. In this chapter, I report a study I conducted in Toronto that looked at ways in which written language articulates with the everyday experience of low-education Latin American adults.

## SOCIOLINGUISTIC LITERACY THEORY

Scholars in many fields are interested in the phenomena of written language. A number of authors have argued that the field of literacy studies, partly because it is an interdisciplinary area of interest, lacks theoretical coherence and uses a terminology that is confused and imprecise. Graff (1979, p. 3) observes, for example, that discussions of literacy "are confused and ambiguous. . . . Vagueness pervades virtually all efforts to discern the meaning of literacy." Literacy's "sprawl across several disciplines," according to Levine (1986), "results in identical issues being discussed in quite separate contexts with different vocabularies," (p. 6), and some of the controversies in literacy research, he writes, "reflect the fact that we are dealing with a complex amalgam of psychological, linguistic, and social processes layered one on top of another" (p. 22).

An approach that has begun to provide a reasonably coherent theoretical framework across disciplines is the sociolinguistic approach suggested by Heath. It is based on the descriptively useful and tangible foundation of the everyday uses for written language in a specific locality. Researchers in a number of related applied fields such as second-language learning, bilingual education, language planning, and comparative adult education have turned to similar sociolinguistic perspectives. In literacy studies specifically, as Graff (1986) points out in a review of recent literature, a shift has taken place away from quantitative studies of large populations to smaller-scale ethnographic studies of specific groups and subgroups. He writes that many scholars in literacy research have adopted a qualitative approach because they have come to recognize the need for "much sharper contextual grounding in clearly delineated localities" (Graff, 1986, p. 126). A new conceptualization of contexts, he concludes, "offers both new and better cases for study, opportunities for explanations, and approaches to literacy's variable historical meaning and contribution" (p. 127).

There are a number of theoretical developments that have come out of this "third generation" of literacy research (as Graff describes it). One development (as a result of a focus on written language use in specific localities) is the growing conviction that literacy is *not* essentially the same phenomena wherever it is found. Rather, literacy changes from place to place. Scribner and Cole (1981, p. 132), for example, concluded from their study with the Vai in Liberia that

> although many writers discuss literacy and its social and psychological implications as though literacy entails the same knowledge and skills whenever people read or write, our experimental outcomes support our social analysis in demonstrating that literacies are highly differentiated.

Similarly, Levine (1986, p. 43) argues that literacy must be redefined, and the first step would be "to discard an albatross of an idea—that literacy is a single unified competence—and to begin to think wherever possible in terms of a multiplicity . . . of literacies."

In discussing how literacy practices vary from group to group, various authors have argued that the differences between literacies are not primarily technical (contained in language or script differences, for example) even though different scripts and script-use practices can be observed from context to context and from culture to culture. The differences, authors such as Graff (1979), Heath (1983), and Street (1984) have argued, are more fundamentally due to the cultural practices, values, or, as Street (1984) argues, the "ideologies" from within which written language is given roles in any particular context. Street challenges earlier theories that viewed literacy as a neutral set of skills that produce the same positive intellectual, economic, and social effects in any given context. Instead, he argues,

> What the particular practices and concepts of reading and writing are for a given society depends upon the context; that they are already embedded in an ideology and cannot be isolated or treated as "neutral" or merely "technical." . . . The skills and concepts that accompany literacy acquisition, in whatever form, do not stem in some automatic way from the inherent qualities of literacy . . . but are aspects of a specific ideology. (Street, 1984, p. 1)

Heath (1983) has shown that even neighboring English-speaking communities in the United States can socialize their members into distinct cultural patterns and habits of using oral and written language.

When this sociolinguistic perspective is used to explore the multilingual reality that newcomers experience, such as in the study I conducted, a complex language mix must be described. Minority language individuals bring with them their own cultural ways of using and giving roles to written language. They also encounter the ways in which the new society uses and values written language. How newcomers come to manage this written language mix in the various domains of their everyday lives in a new society is the general context of this study. When the focus is narrowed to low-education adult newcomers, a very specific language use reality can be observed.

## RESEARCH METHODOLOGY

The research approach I used focuses on describing how written language is actually used in everyday contexts, an essentially ethnographic methodology. The study I conducted, however, cannot be considered a true ethnography because it is exploratory rather than comprehensive; it explores rather than exhaustively catalogues ways in which written language operates in the everyday lives of a specific subculture in Toronto. For data collection, I relied almost exclusively on interviews rather than on participant observation, although I conducted many of the interviews in the context of bilingual literacy classes in which I participated over a period of almost a year. During that time, I recorded conversations with most of the nine low-education Latin American adults who make up my sample. In those conversations, I explored how each individual experiences and manages the print and print-related practices she or he regularly encounters in Toronto. This, of course, included investigation of print use in both English and Spanish.

The nine individuals I interviewed had had little or no previous formal schooling. Four were men and five were women, the men having on the whole slightly higher levels of schooling. The literacy skills in the group ranged from a virtual lack of coding and decoding skills, even in Spanish, to various levels of Spanish and English reading and writing skills. All but one came to Toronto with less than a third grade level of schooling, four having had no schooling whatsoever. Two who could read and write in Spanish well enough to read Spanish newspapers and write letters home said they had learned to read and write Spanish mainly outside of school, one because of the regular Bible reading that went on in his home, and the other because of magazines and comics that she learned to read after having two years of schooling as a child.

I started gathering data (in Spanish) by diagramming my informants' daily schedules and by mapping the *domains* (a term I borrow from Wagner, Messick, & Spratt, 1986) that each person regularly entered in the course of their daily lives in order to capture the variety in their regular experience. With the schedules and maps as a basis, I then asked each informant to describe the kinds of print materials that she or he encounters, domain by domain. I then moved to questions about use (users, uses, and importance of the uses). I included questions about how the informants themselves interact with the print and the problems they have as a result of the print. The final topic of conversation in each round of interviews centered on feelings and opinions not only about the print that is encountered but also about the ways in which print is managed.

## RESULTS AND ANALYSIS

As in most qualitative studies, the data collected were narrative and extensive. To summarize the main themes that emerged from the analysis of the data, I will discuss the findings in three parts: (a) kinds of written language encountered in the various domains of everyday life, (b) print-managing practices used to deal with the print encountered, and finally (c) ideological dimensions of print use. Throughout the discussion, I briefly illustrate the themes that emerged with examples that are representative of other data collected. I also refer occasionally to what other authors have found and argued in order to place my findings in the context of other studies. The names of people used in this report are, of course, pseudonyms.

## DOMAINS

The domains that emerged over and over again in the data fall roughly into the categories of the home, streets, and stores; bureaucracies; places of work; schools; and church. The brief summary that follows of the kinds of written language used in the various domains of everyday urban life reads much like the account Kozol (1985) gives of the kinds of print that English-speaking non-literates must deal with in urban America.

All the domains tend to merge in the first category, the home, which is the center from which individuals venture out into other domains. Written language encountered in the home falls roughly into the following overlapping categories: household paperwork, correspondence, school work, and religious and leisure print. The household management activities in which written language is used include shopping (advertisements, shopping lists) and cooking (recipes); remembering appointments (calendars) and prescription schedules (dosages); managing bills, notices, forms, and documents; and overseeing schooling arrangements for children. These activities primarily require managing English written language. Letter reading and writing, on the other hand, is almost exclusively a Spanish language activity. Similarly, use of written language for religious purposes (Bibles and religious literature) and leisure (newspapers, magazines, novels, children's stories) also primarily involve Spanish print. Other English written language encountered in the home is used by sons, daughters, and husbands who are students (school-books and English newspapers, used only because teachers gave assignments to read newspapers).

In the streets, my informants reported using the numbers and names of buses, streetcars, and subway stations to help them find their way around the city. Several of the less literate mentioned jotting down these numbers or the first two or three letters of bus and bus stop names to help them get around the city. Other public print, such as the writing on billboards, posters, and street signs, is apparently ignored. In stores, several of my informants reported finding their way around by learning the layout, by knowing, for example, that a bright display with colored posters or balloons meant sales and specials. Price tags, expiration dates, and logos and pictures on packages are important whereas other print on packages tends to be ignored.

In the bureaucratic domain—in banks and in government, medical, or school offices—written language that my informants reported using includes notices (hearing dates, appointments), forms (applications, withdrawal and deposit slips, checks, unemployment report cards), and documents (pass-ports, visas, social insurance cards). I found, much as Rockhill (1987) did in her study with Latin Americans in Los Angeles, that the women, not the men, tend to take care of much of this kind of family paperwork. This was true, I found, even when the men or children in the household had schooling and knew English.

The written language in places of work, if used at all, tended to be minimal, such as that involving paychecks and letter or number codes or colored labels for identification of boxes of products or containers with supplies. Various authors (Graff, 1979; Heath, 1983; Levine, 1986) have made similar findings about the minimal use of written language in many places of work. Juan included safety posters, warnings, and instructions in his list of written language that he encounters at work, but he said that, because he knew his job, he had no need to read them. Only Angela, who can read Spanish, described depending on books as part of her job. She used the pictures, however, rather than the print in recipe books to help her improve the look of regular dishes she made at a university cafeteria. She used recipe cards, which her daughter translated into Spanish for her, only on rare occasions to help her make out-of-the-ordinary dishes (for a Christmas banquet, for example).

The two remaining domains—the school and the church—were reported to be the most difficult to manage. Schools, I was told, require use of both

Spanish and English reading and writing for the purpose of learning new vocabulary, understanding grammatical structure, doing exercises, and using reference books. Church participation, on the other hand, involves only Spanish written language in the form of prayerbooks, hymnbooks, and Bibles, and often, as in schools, written language on posters and blackboards, in book indexes, and on program schedules.

## PRINT-MANAGING PRACTICES

My informants must somehow manage the Spanish and English print they regularly encounter in Toronto. One way print is dealt with, as was briefly referred to earlier, is by simply ignoring it. This reflects Levine's (1986, p. 38) point that print "is an incidental and auxiliary feature of a great many social situations and settings. There are many substitutes for it and, for those that need them, strategies for circumventing it." Two strategies that emerged in the data I gathered, which allow my informants to ignore a certain amount of the print they regularly encounter, are reliance on memory and learning by experimenting (rather than learning by reading). Rebecca, for example, said she seldom gets lost because she is able to remember streets and buildings she passes on buses and streetcars. Similarly, all of the women I spoke to depended on their memory for cooking. They learned from others orally, from family and friends. Rebecca, for example, told me, "I would ask them the first times I needed to make something, 'How many teaspoons should I add?' Then they would tell me and I didn't forget."

Related to memory is the strategy of experimenting. María and Doña Ana, for example, said they learned the city by trying a new route, getting lost, and then retracing their steps until they learned the route. All the informants, even Juan and Pedro, who can read and write some English, described doing their shopping by experimenting with small quantities of unfamiliar products until they found what they liked and then buying in larger quantities. Juan said that, even though he could sound out much of the print on package labels or menus, most of the vocabulary was meaningless to him, and, therefore, it was a waste of time to try and read them.

Written language, however, is not always ignored. I found that, even though five of the nine people in my sample had virtually no word-level coding and decoding skills even in Spanish, all of them actually "use" some of the print they encounter. Thus it became clear to me very early in the investigation that the ability to use much of the print encountered daily does not require well-developed reading and writing skills in Spanish or in English.

One frequently used written language strategy that emerged in the data involves very elementary yet useful forms of literacy such as personal memory codes, logo and format recognition, and various levels of limited print and number literacy. Authors such as Fingeret (1983), Heath (1983), and Kozol (1985) have also described these practices. These elementary literacy skills allow people who cannot themselves decode the majority of the words on bills, notices, forms, calendars, and lists of frequently used addresses and phone numbers to effectively manage these pieces of paper in what Fingeret calls a "formulaic nature," allowing them to ignore the majority of the print on the forms. Much of the reading and writing requires learning only the format of a particular form and then "copying" an address or a social insurance number from other pieces of paper, then signing and being able to recognize and present the proper information or document to the appropriate secretary or bureaucrat.

María, the least literate of those in my sample, is a good example. She manages to take care of much of the banking, immigration, insurance, and hospital bureaucratic needs of her family with only limited copying skills. She recognizes the telephone bill by its look and knows where to find the charge and how to pay it at the bank, she told me, without having to ask her husband for help even though she cannot read any of the writing on the bill. She remembers appointments by drawing onto a calendar a prominent letter or logo symbol she finds on appointment cards given to her at a doctor's office, for example, and then matching what she has painstakingly drawn onto the calendar with the correct appointment cards. She could neither tell me the names of the letters she drew nor decode the words in which she found them. She simply copied meaningless letters to use as symbols to be matched to aid memory. She has found that, as long as she can present the correct pieces of paper in places like banks and government offices, and can copy addresses and her signature, she can take care of much of the paperwork. What is involved, she told me, is time: time to make multiple trips to offices to make contacts with sympathetic people, to learn what is required, to arrange appointments and spend hours sitting in reception areas often followed by trips to other offices. She believes that it makes more sense for her than for her schooled children or husband to take care of this business because they need to spend their time bettering themselves by studying English.

A second strategy demonstrated above by María's search for sympathetic people is finding people who are willing, trustworthy, and sympathetic enough to become part of one's network of helpers. Fingeret (1983), referring to nonliterates, and Rockhill (1987), referring to Latin Americans in Los Angeles, both discuss the way social networks that function in terms of reciprocal exchange serve to give access to many of the kinds of help needed for management of most of the print encountered from day to day. I found that all of my informants rely on family members (although children often are not trusted) or friends or other professional contacts for dealing with a wide range of kinds of print such as letters to and from family, dosages on medicine bottles, applications and forms, and personal address books and calendars. Angela and Carlos, for example, both mentioned always going to the same teller at the bank because, in both cases, the teller knows Spanish, is sympathetic, and knows what help is needed.

What these strategies suggest is that, in terms of basic functioning, many low-education Latin Americans are able to manage a majority of the everyday domains of life in Toronto with only minimal literacy skills in Spanish. As mentioned earlier, however, it is important to note that there are domains where this is not true. Schools and churches are particularly difficult to manage regardless of the print-management strategies described above. Some of the reasons for these difficulties will be discussed below.

## IDEOLOGY OF LITERACY

That the people I interviewed manage most domains of everyday life with minimal literacy skills does not mean, however, that they place no value on literacy/schooling. On the contrary, they place a high value on it, as suggested by María's decision to be the one who wasted time sitting in offices so that her husband and children could get the English schooling required to succeed in Canada. The issue that authors like Graff (1979), Heath (1983), and Street (1984) raise about the ideologies, social values, or cultural meanings in which use of written language takes place begins to emerge at this point. The significance of this ideological component in literacy makes it important to go beyond a simple description of print-use practices (as I described them above) to the meanings and values that become attached to print. Although I did not attempt to conduct an in-depth study of the meanings or values the people in my sample attach to print and print-use practices, definite indications of an ideological dimension to literacy emerged in the conversations. The ideological themes that emerged can be divided into two groups: (a) the positive functions of literacy—or the uses written language is deemed to have in everyday life—and (b) the negative aspects—or the way in which the perceived lack of abilities to use written language brings problems and negative experiences into the everyday lives of those I interviewed.

The benefits that come from reading and writing, or the uses of literacy, that my informants identified fell roughly into four categories: (a) managing everyday tasks, (b) communicating, (c) being informed, and (d) learning. The first use, managing everyday tasks, seems to contradict the way my informants effectively manage most everyday tasks with little literacy. They told me, however, that reading and writing are useful for aiding memory (calendars, shopping lists, vocabulary lists), following instructions (recipes, warnings, directions), locating places and objects (maps, signs indicating location of offices or products or items on sale, product labels), and managing bureaucracies (understanding bureaucratic mail, filling out applications, and managing appointments). The ability to use written language for such purposes is desirable, I was told, because it allows more "direct" access to information—recognizing, for example, a cut or variety of meat at a butcher shop by a sign or label attached to it rather than simply by its looks. The label somehow, Rebecca insisted, gives one more trustworthy and immediate information than the ability to recognize the items. She told me, "But notice—it takes more effort for someone who doesn't know [how to read] than for one who knows because the person who knows can go directly to read the labels, but the one who doesn't know must go through more."

An important distinction emerged in conversations about the usefulness of written language skills for managing everyday tasks. This distinction was one in which English literacy—considered very difficult to attain—was immediately disregarded because it was not a realistic alternative to consider, whereas Spanish literacy was in the realm of the possible. María, for example, when asked what she would be able to do if she were able to read and write in English that she cannot do now, told me, "My God, how different my life could be" and then immediately switched the conversation to what was, in her mind, actually possible—achieving Spanish literacy to improve her ability to manage English print. She told me that many Latin Americans in Toronto manage well by "delettering" English words using Spanish literacy skills. "If I knew how to read in Spanish," she told me, "I could manage to follow the letters that are written in English, even if it's the wrong pronunciation, but one would at least understand." Others made similar statements, which reveal a belief that Spanish literacy gives Latin American newcomers adequate skills for managing much of the English written language they encounter daily.

Communicating with others, especially letter writing, was one of the most frequently mentioned uses for reading and writing, which reveals the importance that correspondence with friends and family in the home country has to newcomers. As mentioned earlier, letter writing involves Spanish literacy exclusively. Note writing was also identified as important for communication: notes of instruction to family members, notes to friends or Spanish-speaking corner store owners, and notes between teachers and parents. Again, most kinds of note writing involve Spanish literacy skills; even schools, on request, send notes to the home in Spanish. This way, the message could be understood "directly" rather than through the children's translation (indirect and not as trustworthy).

A third use identified for reading and writing is to "be informed"—to stay informed, for example, about what comes in the mail (bills, paperwork, advertising, notes from school, news from home), about what appears on notices and bulletin boards (cars for sale, announcements, job openings), and about the many kinds of information in newspapers. Rebecca, Angela, and María all commented on the usefulness of newspapers because, unlike other media (radio, television), newspapers contain not only more trustworthy information that is more "directly" accessible but also a wider range of useful information such as special advertising and classified sections. Toronto-based Spanish papers are preferred to English papers because they contain news from Latin America, notices of local Latin American social events, and advertisements by Spanish-speaking tradespeople, shop owners, businesses, and so forth. English newspapers are used only for two things—the special advertising sections (pictures and prices can be easily decoded), and, much like school texts, for school assignments (ESL teachers sometimes assign regular newspaper reading at home).

One additional reason that was given for staying informed is having something to talk about. The majority of the informants referred to the importance and enjoyment of talking with others about the major stories in the newspaper. Doña Ana, for example, who can read very little in Spanish, said, "I like very much to be aware of things, of whatever story from the previous day, so that I can talk about it, in order to have a base to talk from." This concept of "knowing" or being seen as one who "knows" is a prominent theme that will emerge again in the discussion below.

The fourth major category of uses for reading and writing is "learning." Several of the women described watching their young children play with books and newspapers, learning their letters or English through play. But most of the discussions about learning were in terms of formal schooling. Spanish schooling, my informants told me, more than any other factor, helps

Latin Americans learn quickly (*rápido se aprenden*). This is especially true for learning English. Latin Americans, I was told, who have the school-learned skills to take notes, read, do written drills, and use dictionaries learn English quickly, not only in class but also at home, because these skills make learning accessible. Very similar comments were made in relation to the church domain. Six of the informants referred to the importance of reading and writing for benefiting from religious instruction both in public worship and in private religious devotion and study. One other learning-related use for written language was the ability to oversee and help children do homework. Four of the women who have or had school-aged children talked about not being able to help their children with their schooling, of sitting helplessly trying to make sure their children did their homework but not being able either to help or to ensure that the proper work got done.

In summary, what these task-specific uses for literacy reveal is that my informants tend to perceive reading and writing skills as giving more power of memory, more control over details, and more direct access to information, learning, and self-betterment. And it is important to note that it is Spanish literacy, not English literacy, that is seen as most immediately useful to low-education adults for day-to-day functioning in Toronto and as essential in the long run for any successful chances in the arduous task of learning English (as will be discussed later).

These "positive" uses for written language were not, however, the only ideological themes that emerged from the interviews. More abstract "negative" themes also became evident, which suggested problems of access to socially acceptable employment and cultured or civilized ways of thinking and acting. This more abstract dimension is most clearly seen in negative experiences and perceptions that result from not having literacy skills. Unlike the discussion above about the demonstrated capacity to accomplish many everyday tasks with various strategies in Spanish, at this more abstract level, the discussion reveals feelings of helplessness and exclusion due to the lack not only of reading and writing skills but also of Spanish language schooling. The ideology of literacy that they encounter and to varying degrees have internalized becomes apparent in three negative themes that emerged from the data: (a) a sense of personal inadequacy, (b) experiences of exclusion or lack of access, and (c) strong feelings of stigma.

My informants frequently expressed strong feelings of inadequacy in spite of the successful management of many of the literacy problems they faced. This echoes Graff's (1979) account of literacy in nineteenth-century urban Ontario in which he points out a contradiction between the limited ways in which people actually used reading and writing in their everyday lives and the high value they placed on it. My informants frequently expressed negative emotions in relation to the print-managing practices they reported using. This was true especially of the strategy of asking other people to read and write for them. Rebecca, for example, said it sometimes made her cry with frustration to always have to ask people to read or write something. One of the main reasons she was having friends help her learn to read and write in Spanish, she told me, was so that she herself could correspond with family back home because "that way I don't have to always be pleading (with my children), 'please write a letter for me.' " Even María, who seemed to have no hesitation asking for help, always used the word *molestar* (to bother) in reference to asking someone to read or write for her. And Carlos and Pedro gave examples, from shopping to dealing with immigration counselors, of how they would avoid seeking help, preferring to learn by experimenting because, in Canada, they said, unlike in El Salvador, people do not like to waste words explaining things.

Some annoyance was occasionally expressed as well in relation to other strategies that were used to manage some of the written language regularly encountered. Rebecca, Pedro, and Carlos all commented about wasted time and wasted products because of their inefficient way of experimenting with products or of not being able to get information directly from print. They perceive schooled individuals to be more efficient or direct. Such comments reveal a sense of themselves as inept and bothersome, which leads to embarrassing dependency and results in a feeling of lack of control over the details of their lives, requiring extra effort or personal and emotional cost (the words *me cuesta mucho* were used frequently in the conversations), which literates presumably do not experience. The contradiction between how well I found these low education adults manage most of the domains they regularly encounter and their sense of inadequacy suggests that these individuals have internalized pejorative standards that brand them as non-functional individuals.

As mentioned earlier, however, one domain in which inadequacy is actually corroborated by an inability to manage is the school. Because of the adult education and pedagogical rationale for this study, this issue is crucial. The interviews clearly revealed that one particularly difficult domain to manage is the ESL classroom. As I briefly mentioned in the introduction, various authors (d'Anglejan, 1983; Tollefson, 1985; Weinstein, 1984) have described the same problem. Other authors (Fingeret, 1983; Heath, 1983; Szwed, 1981) argue that the ways language is often taught and used in classrooms are different from the ways minority culture individuals are socialized into using language. The reason my informants gave for the difficulty they have in the classroom is not just their lack of Spanish reading and writing skills but their lack of Spanish schooling, the belief being that Spanish schooling makes language learning accessible.

I asked in the interviews what specific problems each person encountered in classrooms. Angela, who is basically unschooled yet literate in Spanish, said that she had never gone back to an ESL class she once started because the teacher embarrassed her by asking her about things she had never learned before. María and Doña Lucía described spending their time in class "drawing" letters and words they could not understand while everyone else read the words and learned. María said she left class knowing no more than when she first came (*me quedo igual*). Doña Ana said schooled students could note what they heard, but she could not do that: "It's that nothing stays with me. I just sit and listen. All the others write what they're hearing." Rebecca and María pointed out that ESL students who had been schooled in their own countries could not only write translations of new vocabulary to help them remember, they could also study at home from notes and books. Pedro and Rebecca both said that, because they did not "know Spanish" (meaning that they did not know proper "schooled" Spanish), they could not understand ESL teachers' explanations about grammar, especially verbs. Pedro also gave the example of problems nonschooled Latin Americans like himself had with dictionaries. He said that the main problem is not that he must skim through the entire dictionary to find words that start with the same letters but that he does not know the right form of the word to look for (the root) or whether the word he wants is proper Spanish or rural "dialect." This illustrates a general theme that emerged in the interviews—a sense of extreme handicap in ESL classes, largely due to lack of Spanish language schooling.

A second negative theme is exclusion. Outright exclusion is most strongly felt in two related contexts—ESL classes and employment. ESL and employment are related because the successful completion of higher level ESL courses is understood to be a prerequisite for entry into training courses, which in turn are required for access to better paying jobs. This reflects the distinction Levine makes between job literacy and employment literacy, the former being the reading and writing needed to perform a job, the latter being the reading and writing requirements required in personnel offices to get a job (Levine, 1986, p. 139). It is significant to note that, when my informants referred to the inadequacy of their literacy skills, it was rarely in reference to the workplace. On the contrary, they perceived of themselves as good workers, all of them having worked for most of their lives. A number of them commented on the unfairness of the Canadian system because they felt the exclusion they experienced from better paying jobs was based not on whether they could do the job but on whether or not they have Canadian credentials and work experience. Rebecca, for example, despite five years of work experience in the food catering industry in the United States, is required, she told me, to take training courses to get the kind of work in a cafeteria or restaurant that would pay enough to raise a family of four. But she cannot get into the higher-level ESL courses that are prerequisite to training courses because of her low-education/nonliteracy.

This reveals a feeling of exclusion as well from English classes. Doña Ana and Doña Lucía, for example, experienced the classroom as a place where teachers isolated them from other students (devastating, as Fingeret, 1983, suggests, for people accustomed to operating in social networks) and then avoided them or even referred them to other classes to get rid of them. Similarly, Rebecca described being advanced (because she understands English quite well) from the basic beginner level to a third level only to be immediately returned to the first level because she could not do the reading and writing in the higher level. Consequently, she spent her time in the first level helping schooled Latin Americans learn the basic English she already knew and then watching them quickly transfer to the higher levels while she remained behind. Whether or not such practices regularly occur, the perception my informants have is that lack of Spanish schooling creates an unscalable obstacle to access to the higher level English classes that are prerequisite for entry into job training programs.

Stigma is the third negative theme that emerged from the data. Expressions of inadequacy and exclusion, as described above, often included an implicit link between Spanish schooling and Spanish culture. This theme in the interviews recalls Paulo Freire's (1970) emphasis in his approach to literacy training, which he developed out of a South American context, on helping nonliterates gain a sense of having a legitimate culture of their own. Suggesting this same issue, my informants frequently contrasted themselves negatively to *los que saben* (those who know). Schooled people, they implied, have culture because they "know," can learn, and are informed. Also implied was the opposite, that the nonschooled have no legitimate knowledge, cannot learn, and do not have access to information. Contrasts my informants made between themselves and schooled Latin Americans frequently contained pejorative terminology that characterizes nonliterates as nonschooled, rural, Indian, and nonhuman—in opposition to those who are schooled, urban, Spanish, and human—all of which imply a distinction between civilized and savage.

This stigma was described especially in reference to the home. Rebecca and María (with tears) expressed anger and humiliation when their children equate them with Indians because of the "mountain" Spanish they speak. Doña Ana and Angela both remarked that they continually try to avoid contact with less cultured people and to improve their language and bearing (under their children's tutelage) to keep from embarrassing themselves and their children in front of the more educated and cultured Latin Americans at school, at church, or at other social gatherings. In this same context, Doña Ana told me she wished to "be informed" as part of her attempt to act as "one who knows." For this same reason, my informants continually expressed their need to learn "Spanish," by which they meant proper, schooled Spanish, not only to be able to operate more directly and effectively in everyday activities, and to gain access to English learning, but also to reduce the stigma they feel because of their lack of proper Spanish culture. Rockhill (1987) identifies a similar theme in her study with Latin Americans in Los Angeles. The women she interviewed based their talk about their dreams for getting ahead in life on the passionate desire for schooling. Their dream, however, remains perpetually unrealized because of many factors in their lived experience that keep schooling out of reach, such as their seclusion in the household due to their responsibilities as mothers, to jealous husbands, and to dangerous neighborhoods where public transportation systems are poor.

This passionate desire for schooling, coupled with the stigma that comes from not having schooling, are themes that clearly suggest that, for the Latin Americans I interviewed, the use of written language is very much tied up in an ideological system in which nonliteracy becomes linked to inadequacy in everyday task specific functions (which contradicts their successful management of many of those tasks), to exclusion from ESL/training/employment opportunities, and also to a lack of culture/civilization/status both at home and in their larger social world.


## CONCLUSION


As I suggested in the introduction, the rationale for doing this study was pedagogical, related to providing low-education newcomers with skills (presumably language and literacy skills) that would help them adapt to and effectively participate in the new society in which they have come to live. A study such as this of the uses made of written language as well as of the values and meanings attached to those uses by a specific group of low-education newcomers gives rise to a number of pedagogical implications. Because the study was exploratory and deals only with Latin Americans, the implications are both speculative and cannot be generalized to other immigrant groups. One implication is the pedagogical usefulness of findings about the ways written language is used in everyday life. The different ways literacy is used in the home, for example, such as the use of calendars, of formulaic paper management skills for dealing with bureaucratic paperwork, of personal lists of addresses and phone numbers, and of the skills for reading dosages on medicine bottles, suggests relevant needs and incipient skills to build on and extend. The usefulness of Spanish literacy for participating in the English world, such as for managing many of the everyday print-related tasks and for benefiting from ESL classroom learning, provides important pedagogical reasons for providing opportunities for mother tongue nonliterate Latin Americans in Toronto to learn Spanish reading and writing skills. Perhaps more significant, the need for Spanish literacy for a range of other personal purposes, from correspondence to participating in church services, suggests another kind of relevant use of written language that can and should be built on if the literacy skills of low-education Latin American newcomers are to be extended.

This implication reflects the "functional literacy" approach that has become dominant in literacy movements. Much of the interest around the world in providing literacy programs for minority groups comes out of the desire to bring marginalized groups into the mainstream of a developing society. The literature on literacy has focused over many years on the degree to which nonliterates can "function" in society (e.g., Goody, 1977; Unesco, 1965). There has been understandable criticism of this preoccupation with the economic and public implications of functional literacy because of its ethnocentric, political, and assimilationist overtones (Bataille, 1976, Levine, 1986; Rockhill, 1987; Street, 1984). But the question of how well nonliterates "function" continues to be an issue. Kozol (1985), for example, argues that depictions of nonliterates as ingenious and resourceful do more harm than good because this picture hides the reality of exclusion and paralysis many nonliterates and semiliterates experience (Kozol, 1985, p. 11). He argues that nonliterates face insurmountable difficulties at home, at work, and in the city and that "most illiterates are virtually immobilized" (p. 126).

Other authors, however, argue that the nonliterate's experience is not so simply rendered because evidence suggests that many nonliterates do effectively manage most domains of their everyday lives. Levine (1986, p. 38), for example, argues that it "is very hard to identify a set of social transactions which can only be carried out via writing and which are absolutely necessary to adequate functioning, however this is defined."

Fingeret (1983) incorporates both sides of this debate into a continuum that ranges from complete paralysis and dependence at one extreme (the "local" pole) to resourcefulness and effective management of one's economic and social world at the other extreme (the "cosmopolitan" pole). This continuum suggests that both sides of the spectrum help explain the nonliterate's world. To emphasize only one side of a continuum, only the ability to manage effectively, or only total paralysis, is to reify the experience of semi- and nonliterates. Both sides of the continuum need to be addressed in learning programs.

And out of this focus on adequately accounting for the nonliterates' experience of everyday contexts comes the second and perhaps the more basic implication for studies such as this—the ideological dimensions of literacy. In her study, Fingeret goes on to point out that the primary obstacle that many nonliterates encounter and must overcome if they are to participate more in other unfamiliar contexts of society is *not* so much their inability to read and write as much as the social definition of themselves as deficient, incompetent, and dependent (Fingeret, 1983, p. 145). In the study I reported above, the themes of exclusion, stigma, and inadequacy, which are directly linked to a school-based literacy ideology (the Spanish schooling/ESL training/job training sequence), are grounded in both psychological and institutional reality. The desire to become schooled is immense, a desire that is fed by both a Latin American version of an ideology of schooling and a Toronto-based ESL and job training system that is based on levels of schooling. The challenge, therefore, is multiple: There is a need not only to provide low-education newcomers with the opportunities to acquire immediately useful written language skills so that they may be able to participate more in a new society, for example, but also to alter the psychological and institutional reality that contributes to their feelings of exclusion and stigma. This, once again, makes Freire's (1970) approach of coming to terms with culture to deal with literacy so appropriate for low-education Latin American adults.

## REFERENCES

d'Anglejan, A. (1983). Teaching marginally literate immigrant and refugee learners: A case for specialized teacher training. In J. E. Alatis, H. H. Stern, & P. Strevens (Eds.), *Georgetown University round table on languages and linguistics. Applied linguistics and the preparation of second language teachers: Toward a rationale* (pp. 124-132). Washington, DC: George-town University Press.
Bataille, L. (Ed.). (1976). *A turning point for literacy.* Oxford: Pergamon.

Burnaby, B. (1985). *Promoting native writing systems in Canada.* Toronto: OISE Press.

Fingeret, A. (1983). Social network: A new perspective on independence and illiterate adults. *Adult Education Quarterly, 33,* 133-134.

Freire, P. (1970). *Pedagogy of the oppressed.* New York: Seabury.

Goody, J. (1977). *The domestication of the savage mind.* Cambridge: Cambridge University Press.

Graff, H. J. (1979). *The literacy myth: Literacy and social structure in the nineteenth-century city.* New York: Academic Press.

Graff, H. J. (1986). The history of literacy: Toward a third generation. *Interchange, 17*(2), 122-134.

Hamel, R. E. (1984). Socio-cultural conflict and bilingual education: The case of the Otomi Indians in Mexico. *International Social Science Journal, 36*(1), 113-128.

Heath, S. B. (1981). Toward an ethnology of writing in American education. In M. F. Whiteman & W. S. Hall (Eds.), *Writing: Vol. 1. Variations in writing* (pp. 25-45). Hillsdale, NJ: Lawrence Erlbaum.

Heath, S. B. (1983). *Ways with words: Language, life, and work in communities and classrooms.* Cambridge: Cambridge University Press.

Klassen, C. (1987). *Language and literacy learning: The adult immigrants' account.* Unpublished master's thesis, University of Toronto.

Kozol, J. (1985). *Illiterate America.* Garden City, NY: Anchor, Doubleday.

Levine, K. (1986). *The social context of literacy.* London: Routledge & Kegan Paul.

Rockhill, K. (1982). *Participation in ESL by working-class immigrants.* Unpublished manuscript.

Rockhill, K. (1987). Gender, language and the politics of literacy. *The British Journal of Sociology of Education, 8*(2), 153-167.

Scribner, S., & Cole, M. (1981). *The psychology of literacy.* Cambridge, MA: Harvard University Press.

Shaw, W. D. (1983). *The choice of a language for adult literacy programs: A guide for decision makers.* Unpublished doctoral dissertation, University of Massachusetts. (University Microfilms No. 8310334)

Street, B. V. (1984). *Literacy in theory and practice.* Cambridge: Cambridge University Press.

Szwed, J. F. (1981). The ethnography of literacy. In M. F. Whiteman & W. S. Hall (Eds.), *Writing: Vol. 1. Variations in writing* (pp. 13-23). Hillsdale, NJ: Lawrence Erlbaum.

Tollefson, J. W. (1985). Research on refugee resettlement: Implications for instructional programs. *TESOL Quarterly, 19*(4), 753-764.

Unesco. (1965). *World conference of ministers of education on the eradication of illiteracy, final report.* Paris: Unesco.

Wagner, D. A., Messick, B. M., & Spratt, J. (1986). Studying literacy in Morocco. In C. A. Ferguson & S. B. Heath (Eds.), *Language in the USA* (pp. 145-174). Cambridge: Cambridge University Press.

Weinstein, G. (1984). Literacy and second language acquisition: Issues and perspectives. *TESOL Quarterly, 18*(3), 471-484.

# 4

# *Roles, Networks, and Values in Everyday Writing*

## DAVID BARTON
## SARAH PADMORE

**In this chapter, we want** to make sense of people's everyday writing. We will do this by investigating a particular group of adults: documenting what writing they do and finding out what value it holds for them, examining what they do if they experience problems, and seeing how writing fits into the rest of their lives.

The research reported in this chapter is just one part of a larger study in which we are building a general a general picture of the role of literacy in people's everyday lives in Lancaster, a small city in northwest England. As part of the study, we have carried out 20 interviews of local people. We are now carrying out more detailed case studies of a few families going about their everyday lives. We have observed how their home uses of literacy fit in with the demands of children at school, differing literacy demands at home and at work, and what people do when they identify problems of reading and writing. We are carrying out general observations of reading and writing in the local community; finding out what people read and write in shops, the post office, the hospital, and so on; and examining the "visual environment" of advertisements, street signs, notices. Finally, we are collecting recorded data on access points for literacy: the history and use of libraries and bookshops in the city, provision of adult literacy tuition, school records, and so on. We aim to build up an overall picture of the significance of literacy in

AUTHORS' NOTE: This research has been supported in part with a grant from the University Research Fund of Lancaster University awarded to David Barton and in part with a grant from the Economic and Social Research Council R000-23-1419 awarded to David Barton and Mary Hamilton. The interviews were carried out by Sarah Padmore. We are grateful to Mary Hamilton, Roz Ivanič, and Brian Street for comments on earlier drafts of this chapter.

people's lives. Elsewhere, we intend to write more extensively about other aspects of literacy, about the general background of Lancaster, and about the significance of this for adult basic education. In this chapter, we concentrate on information from these interviews and particularly on the significance of *writing* in these people's lives.

Most studies of literacy are concerned with children and with educational settings. Only a few studies have begun to examine the role of literacy in people's lives, including adults' actual uses of reading and writing and their attitudes to the awareness of literacy. Three key studies in this area are those of Heath (1983), Street (1984), and Scribner and Cole (1981). Briefly, Heath (1983) developed close ties with three Appalachian communities in the United States over seven years and used ethnographic and sociolinguistic methods to provide detailed descriptions of people's uses of reading and writing in the home and in the community. Street (1984) studied Islamic villagers in Iran; he lived there as an anthropologist and carried out ethnographic field work. As part of this, he observed two literacies being used side by side in the community, one he terms "commercial" and the other "*maktab*"—that of the traditional Koranic school. He documents how commercial literacy emerged out of skills developed in the traditional context of religious education. His concern is to describe different literacies rather than putting the usual emphasis on a single school-based model of literacy. Scribner and Cole (1981) have studied literacy among the Vai of West Africa, using a battery of cross-cultural psychological tests along with interviews and observations of the community. They provide detailed descriptions of forms of literacy that are learned informally and that exist outside the educational system.

There are other, smaller studies that contribute to this approach. Fingeret (1983) in the United States has studied adult literacy students and the social networks they establish, paying particular attention to different social roles people have. Moll (1989) is studying how networks act as funds of knowledge. Rockhill (1987) and Horsman (1987) have examined literacy in women's lives. Fishman (this volume) has examined literacy in an Amish community. Klassen (this volume) has examined the uses of literacy in bilingual communities. Similarly, Reder (1985) has worked with Inuit and Hispanic communities. Levine (1985) has studied people with low levels of literacy and the problems they have encountered in obtaining work. Taylor (1985) and Taylor and Dorsey-Gaines (1988) have used ethnographic methods to study literacy within the family. Other examples of research in the United States using ethnographic approaches are described in Schieffelin and

Gilmore (1986) and in Langer (1987). Studies focusing on writing outside of educational contexts, referred to as "nonacademic writing," include Doheny-Farina and Odell (1985), Faigley (1985), and Stotsky (1987).

Two recent studies we have carried out in Lancaster provide further background to this study. First, we examined oral history data of working-class people born around the turn of the century in northwest England, drawing together what they said about reading, writing, and education and using their words to build up a composite picture of the significance of literacy in their culture (see Barton, 1988). We have information on the extent of their literacy, what they used reading and writing for, and their attitudes and expectations related to literacy. To give one brief example of the findings: Literacy was given a moral value by them, it was a "good thing"; what people read was often religious in nature; and there was moral censorship of what children were allowed to read. These findings can act as a starting point for examining contemporary attitudes to and beliefs about literacy. If we turn to the uses of literacy in the Lancaster community today, we find, for example, that the moral attitude toward literacy and the censorship of what children read still exists but that it seems to have a less explicit religious basis.

Second, Hamilton (1987) analyzed data from a large-scale longitudinal study of a sample of the population of Britain (the National Child Development Study), focusing on reported difficulties in reading, writing, and arithmetic. The study provides a national overview of reading and writing problems that people encounter in their everyday lives. Its breadth provides a useful context for the detailed ethnographic approach proposed here. In this study, there were far more people who expressed problems with writing than those who said they had problems with reading. This imbalance is probably not reflected in adult literacy provision: Most programs emphasize learning to read, although now often more stress is laid upon developing writing.

## THE INTERVIEWS

Lancaster is a city of 47,000 people, a few miles from the coast in northwest England. It was formally a mill town. The collapse of the manufacturing industry has left a legacy of unemployment. Most people who have jobs work at one of the large Victorian hospitals, at the power station, at the university, or in the retail trade. Lancaster is also an ancient market town, serving a large rural area, and is developing as a tourist center.

The adults we interviewed were all people who had been educated locally in Lancashire, mostly in Lancaster itself, who had left school at the minimum age, 15 or 16 years. They had all left school with no qualifications, although some had since gained qualifications. Most of them had identified problems with reading and writing at some time in their adult lives and had attended the local literacy program. Thirteen were currently attending basic education courses at the literacy program; five of them had gone on from basic education courses to other courses. Further details of the twenty people interviewed together with some indication of their levels of literacy are given in the Appendix.

Our intention when designing the interview was that it should be like an oral history interview. There were topics we wanted to cover but we also wanted to allow for the possibility of issues arising that we had not thought of beforehand. The topics to be covered came initially from our own research (such as Barton, 1988), from that of others (such as Heath, 1983), and from our experience of working in and talking to people in basic education. We added questions and dropped others after trying out the interview and going through it with participants from a research methods course.

In the end, the interview contained 160 questions, several of which had subdivisions. They were divided into groups, roughly following the sections we use to discuss the results below. We should emphasize that we did not keep rigorously to these questions in the interviews. The aim of each interview was to encourage people to talk freely about the part literacy plays in their lives. The topics were not covered in any particular order and the interview schedule was used by the interviewer to make sure that the topics we were interested in were discussed.

Each interview lasted around two hours and all but one of the interviews took place in the local adult education college, which was familiar to all the people interviewed. Everyone interviewed had met the interviewer previously, and most knew her well; she had been a teacher at the local literacy program for the previous six years. Some people were interviewed twice. In the second interview, we were able to pick up on information we had not covered in the first interview or to pursue topics we wished to know more about, we also found that the interviewees had thought more about the topics in the intervening time and, having had time to mull them over or discuss them with relatives, would arrive with further information for us. They all seemed to enjoy the interview process and welcomed the opportunity to talk about themselves and reflect on their lives with an attentive listener. No one seemed surprised at the interest we were taking in everyday details of their lives. The interviews were tape-recorded and later transcribed.

## WRITING

There is not a straightforward way to analyze and bring together qualitative data from 20 intensive interviews. We have analyzed our data in terms of several themes. They provide a rich way of identifying significant aspects of the context of literacy that need to be incorporated into any theory of literacy learning. The set of themes comes from the view of literacy as a social practice: Some themes were implicit in our interview questions, others came from our analysis of the interview transcripts. This framework is discussed in more detail in Barton (this volume). In this chapter, first, we document what people actually write in their everyday lives, including what, where, when, and with what they write; we situate these activities as part of *social practices.* As components of these practices, we examine particular *roles* people take and how writing varies in importance as people's roles change. We then move on to the *networks* of support in which people participate. This leads on to what *value* literacy holds for them. We will examine each of these themes in turn, documenting the role of writing in these people's lives.

### Social Practices

In our interviews, we obtained a great deal of information about what people write in going about their day-to-day lives. Much of the writing they reported consisted of memory aids for themselves or of messages for others, helping them to organize themselves and their households. All these categories overlap because a note on a notice board, for example, can act as a memory aid and a message at the same time. We refer to this area of writing loosely as *writing to maintain the household,* and we will deal with this first. Another general area, which we will deal with next, is *writing to maintain communication,* and a third area we observed in our data is *personal writing.*

We asked people questions about their household record keeping. One or two people ringed dates or wrote down appointments on wall calendars; one of them, Liz, wrote on a calendar in her own "personal shorthand." (We will use pseudonyms throughout when referring to the people we interviewed.) Five others stuck reminders straight to the wall or pinned them to a notice board. But a third of those questioned about appointments and reminders said that they never wrote any down at all.

Very few people used appointment diaries although several owned them, and two, Pat and Ruth, used out-of-date diaries for other purposes: Pat recorded how well he had done at clay pigeon shooting or made notes about his physical training courses in an old and unused diary of his daughter's, and Ruth used a childhood diary to write shopping lists until someone suggested that she was "spoiling" it. Neil started using a diary for the first time when he went to work at a chain store, "A diary reminds you where and what you've got to do" he remarked, but on another occasion he talked of finding his own notes difficult to make sense of, and it is not clear whether he actually did have more to remember in this job than the jobs he had had in the past.

Seven people said they had notice boards in their homes, although two were not using them—Paul's was lying in the cellar and Lesley's was lying on top of a wardrobe. Those who used them mentioned doing so for appointments, messages, lists of tasks needing doing, and the like. People's uses for notice boards varied considerably; Cath, who lives alone, had at least two notice boards. Her initial response was "Yes, millions of them!" On her downstairs notice board, she listed domestic repairs that needed doing, "but the bedroom one's more for pleasure" and that had more personal displays and lists of local entertainment. There were also two notice boards in Pat's household although neither had anything to do with him: one displayed things relating to his wife's work as a nurse and the other was in his daughter's bedroom: Pat remarked, "She probably needs it more than us because she forgets things." Rita's simply had dental and medical appointments and the occasional card from a friend, and Ruth's had great lists and timetables, mostly relating to her children's many hobbies and activities.

Pat is a good example of someone who said he led a very busy life but never felt the need to write himself reminders of dates and times. He had a full-time manual job at the local power station and a part-time evening job as a "keep fit" instructor. He had various hobbies and interests that involved him in different clubs and organizations. He also did odd jobs for a number of elderly people in the community and had a reputation for being someone who can find out things—someone to go to if you have a problem. Although Pat was not unique in having the ability to "keep them in me head"—good memories and literacy difficulties can go hand in hand—there were others in the interview who identified both problems with literacy and with memory. Ruth, who also led a busy life, suggested that it was so important for her to get appointments written down that she would write on anything that came to hand; it was not uncommon for her to write on a paperback book if she had one in her bag.

In some households, written messages of some sort or another were common and would be left in a set place known to family members, such as stuck to the fridge with magnets. But in other homes written messages were virtually unknown. Whether or not people left messages for each other did not appear to be indication of the amount of other writing done in the home. In addition, everyone interviewed appeared to keep writing materials in their homes. People could often identify a place in their houses where they could always find scrap paper for messages, and they said that they also had pens and pencils lying around. Each person's answer was slightly different. Often the paper was old envelopes kept in a particular drawer or scraps of paper or a memo pad kept by the telephone.

Most people made shopping lists of some sort, although they did not necessarily use them. There seem to be many ways to use a shopping list, and our informal observation of the local market and supermarket suggests, maybe surprisingly, that people do not tend to consult a shopping list while actually shopping. Julie remembers watching her mother making shopping lists as a child; this was the only writing she recalls her mother ever doing. One or two people made daily plans of "things to do that day." Andrea reported that she regularly wrote out shopping lists twice and suggested that she got on everyone's nerves with her perpetual list making. Her mother still criticized her for needing to make lists at all: "Can't you remember things!"

Turning to *writing to maintain communication,* several people did some regular writing, such as writing letters to friends or relatives who do not live nearby. Rita commented that she had no need to write letters to family or friends "because we all live local." Liz, who had friends and relatives living away from the area, said she wished she could write letters more but did not feel able to: "It's the spelling." However, she did have one friend with whom she corresponded: "Dilys makes me 'cos she knows [about Liz's literacy difficulties]. She knows and she accepts it so it's not too bad." More common was keeping up relations with people by the regular sending of cards. Several people reported keeping a Christmas card list and/or a list of people's birthdays and anniversaries. Other people also reported having corresponded with relatives at times when they lived away from Lancaster. When writing letters, 12 people said they sometimes wrote drafts or rough copies of things they were writing, which included personal letters, and only two of them mentioned letters of application for jobs. We were left with a general impression that rewriting is not an uncommon literacy activity in the home.

A third area of everyday writing we identified was *personal writing,* something people did for themselves and not for communicative purposes. We cannot get a feel of how common personal writing is in this community, and, because they were contacted via a college, the people we talked to are unlikely to be representative in this respect. Nevertheless, in this group of twenty people, we were surprised at the number who do some personal writing in their everyday lives. This took various forms, including poems, diaries, and stories. As adults, at least nine of those interviewed had written at least one poem that had nothing to do with their college work; some wrote poems or "short pieces"; three people, Roger, Cath, and Julie, talked about writing down their thoughts; two, Lesley and Dick, had kept personal diaries for around a year.

During the period when we were interviewing, we came across two men, not included in our interviews, who composed poetry but did not write it down. One of them, an older man, had been composing poems in his head for several years, which, because he was unable to write, he had been dictating to his daughter; he came to college specifically to learn to write down his poems himself. Both men performed their poems informally in the community. These do not seem to be isolated instances.

People keep all sorts of records of themselves and their lives. Although keeping a personal diary seemed quite rare, there were people who at some point in their lives had kept a diary. Lesley had written a diary for 12 months after the birth of one of her children; Andrea and Frances had kept diaries when they were children; and Andrea was currently keeping a monthly record of her infant niece's development. Andrea's childhood diary had been a fictitious record of day-to-day life at a stables.

People had definite places for keeping personal writing, and there is a sense of secrecy about much of it. Julie saved hers in dated envelopes and put them away in a box; as a teenager, she recalls hiding secret writings in a Tampax box, a private place. Roger kept his writing in a file as well as keeping other spoken thoughts on cassettes; Dick had given his personal diary to his ex-wife and told her, "This is for when I'm gone." He had apologized for sounding melodramatic but was serious and trusted his wife not to open it. Andrea stored no writing apart from college work, but, in the past, when she had an office job, she sometimes used to read the thoughts and bits of conversation that she had typed on the end of spoiled letters aloud to the other women in the office before throwing them in the bin. Cath has been storing her own personal writing under her mattress since she was an 18-year-old, but she did once send a poem of her daughter's to a magazine. Finding a place to keep writing relates to other social practices to do with personal space—both mental and physical—that people have within the household; we hope to return to this in later work.

We asked people questions about where and when they wrote, and these were accepted as reasonable questions to ask. People tended to have a regular time and place for writing: Mark always did any writing he needed to do in his bedroom directly after tea; Cath always wrote letters at around 6 a.m.; Val always got her writing done right after breakfast or at night; Lynne wrote in the afternoons. People often wrote in a place and at a time when they could be by themselves, and, although several talked of needing quiet, four reported writing in the living room in the evening while other people were watching television.

People often identified a particular type of pen and special paper. Half of those questioned about paper said that it must be lined; two felt the quality of paper was important; and one, Andrea, had strong feelings about color. Only three, Pat, Neil, and Liz, expressed no special interest in the paper they used. Most people cared about pens too and were able to describe why they had a particular preference and how different pens affected their writing; everyone had something different to say about pens.

Finally, there is a problem in trying to make generalizations about people's literacy practices, and there is a limit to the extent to which we can do this. The overall frequency of the practices we have described is hard to ascertain in most cases but we do know that Andrea, Ruth, and Cath chose to sit down and write every day; Ruth's writing was personal creative writing; the minimum that Andrea and Cath did each day was to chart the following day's activities, writing out things to get done. Another difficulty when trying to ascertain general patterns is that everyone seemed to have their own practices, something unique about the way they used writing. To give some examples, Lynne had recently written a poem for a neighbor going into hospital, to let her know that someone cared for her and was thinking of her. Paul regularly left joking messages for his partner, for example, a note saying "empty" in the bottom of an empty tea tin. Andrea, going through a difficult period with her partner, was communicating with him almost solely through messages left around the house. Julie said she had "pinched" bits and pieces of published poetry to put in love letters; Rita had composed a poem for the first time in her life when separated from a boyfriend and sent the poem to him in a card.

## Roles

When people talked about the writing they did within the household and beyond it, it was often in terms of roles; they referred to themselves as parents, relatives, workers, neighbors, friends—each role making differing literacy demands upon them. One clear role differentiation that was apparent within the household was that between men and women. Usually this followed the common division of women writing in the personal sphere while men dealt with the official world (see Barton, this volume). We had many examples of this. If we take the example of dealing with household correspondence, everyone interviewed played some part in this but in most homes, other than wholly male set-ups, letter and card writing tended to be seen as the woman's responsibility, while dealing with forms and bills was the man's.

Two factors we observed that could affect these roles were problems with literacy and employment. An example of someone with literacy problems was Dick, who left everything to do with money to his wife when they were living together. He said that this was because she was "a good manager" while he was a "spendthrift." However, we noticed that, even in partnerships where the woman found all aspects of literacy easier than the man, and in cases where the man could barely read or write at all, he would still have a definite role to play in dealing with anything of a financial nature; even if, as with Neil, this amounted to was asking the bank to pay bills directly, or like Bob, who said firmly, "I'll sort them out, who to pay, and she'll write them."

Arranging the payment of the bills was typically done by the men. This may have been connected with the man being the main breadwinner. When the woman was the main breadwinner, the roles sometimes changed, but when Bob was out of work and his wife was employed, for example, he continued to be responsible for organizing bills, even though anything involving literacy was quite difficult for him and both partners must have realized that Frances would have been quite capable of sorting the bills herself.

In Paul's male household, correspondence appeared to be similarly divided; Paul was the card sender and left bills to his partner, who provided the main income. Andrea also mentions her lack of personal income as the reason for playing no part in bill paying. In his childhood home, Paul recalls that his father dealt with the bills: "Well, he would leave bills that weren't paid by standing order for my mother literally to take money in the book to be paid, but I think he'd brief her very carefully on something like that."

These literacy practices can be situated as part of broader gender roles in personal relations and relate to power in the home. Paying bills or organizing their payment is not just any household task, it would seem to represent something far more significant. To some extent, it seems to be a measure of how important such activities are perceived to be. This is true of family finances. It depends on whether they are regarded as a crucial part of negotiating with the outside world or, to use Rockhill's phrase, whether they are seen as being "part of the housework."

## Changing Roles

Roles are not static. We saw examples of how writing played a part in people's changing lives. For example, coming to college seemed to affect people's roles. It was not simply a question of people coming to college in order to change their lives deliberately. Rather, there seemed to be a complex interaction of people coming to college and, once there, discovering new possibilities for themselves, realizing from the new opportunities they came across that things could change.

We can see this best by looking at one example in detail. In Lynne's home, male and female roles were starting to change as Lynne developed her writing skills at college. When she had started there three years before, she had often asked her husband, who apparently had no difficulty himself, for help and guidance; at first, he was encouraging but, as her "hobby" developed, he became less supportive. At first, she used to read her stories to him; but the more involved she became, the less patience he had with her writing and the "willing ear" of the early days finally closed altogether. Rockhill has discussed this, commenting on how literacy can become a threat when the learning skills become education. Secretarial roles are encouraged, while creative writing is a threat.

Lynne expressed some sympathy with her husband's feelings and was very sensitive to the possibility of his feeling "shut out"; she said that she rationed the amount of course work she did when he was at home and, presumably because this had caused friction in the past, avoided retiring upstairs to get on with her writing, although this was something she would have loved to have done. We can contrast this with the attitude toward other activities such as tending the garden, which Lynne also spent a lot of time doing: Gardening was seen by both partners as something that would benefit the family as a whole, whereas writing was seen as something of a threat, encroaching as it did on family activities, such as sitting down together, chatting, watching television, and threatening family members' relative status.

Lynne's husband had started asking her to deal with his correspondence, such as filling in tax returns. She said that she could hardly believe that she was now working sums out for her husband. At his request, she had started drafting letters for him to copy. It was unlikely that either of them would have dreamed of suggesting this several years earlier; so, although Lynne still tended to defer to her husband's needs and decision making, their literacy roles were changing significantly.

Another example of change in people's lives is children going to school. People's roles changed and this was often the time when they decided to go back to college as adults; also, several of the people we interviewed wanted life to be different for their children. Both Cath and Julie articulated this strongly, and it was also expressed by other people with children. Cath left school with no qualifications. She was drawn into education while bringing up her children. She made a great effort to get her children to read, choosing books for them and helping them with their homework. Her husband appeared to have played no part in this. She saw it as "the only way out of the poverty trap for the children," and, in fact, both her children had gone on to university education. Julie expressed herself as being desperate that her children should have the benefits of education; education had "opened up a new world" for her, different than the one provided by her mother. She was concerned about her grandchild as she did not feel her daughter was "doing enough with books."

## Networks

In our data, we can see clearly that social networks of support exist for people. These networks are part of everyday life whether or not people have problems. Sometimes there was support for people who identified problems. Often it was within the family. Neil, Paul, and Bob all mentioned getting help from their partners. Mark took writing problems to his sister, while Duncan relied on his parents. Liz got help from her husband and her daughter as well as from a friend who worked 40 miles away. Sometimes particular people were chosen for help; Julie's mother would approach an uncle "because he worked in an office"—one of several examples where work skills extend into the home. When Sally got married, she found that there were many everyday tasks she could not deal with, and she turned to her mother to help her learn the new writing tasks.

These networks of support extend out into the community and include asking for help in post offices, shops, and banks. Most people we interviewed reported having seen people receiving help in the town center, and our own observations back this up. When we asked people if they knew people in the neighborhood who provided support, there were examples. Leslie's mother-in-law worked in a news agent's shop and was known to help customers writing greeting cards. These would be regular customers, often elderly people. She would help them choose cards, read the messages to them, and sometimes write the cards for them. To these customers, she was acting as a literacy broker. Although we did not particularly ask about skills exchanges, there were examples in which the people we interviewed helped others with literacy as a part of some other strength they had to offer. We will give two examples in which the people interviewed were used for support, even though they did not have particularly high levels of literacy. Julie said that people came to her for emotional advice and literacy:

> Neighbors, when their marriages were in trouble, they would come to me and then the forms would follow on the problem. Or filling in forms for kids for school holidays or, how to get money for free school uniform or bus passes. I was quite well known for being able to sort out that kind of thing. It's because I'm a bit of a busybody really.

While Cath, who had always painted as a hobby and had a long history of enjoying writing for writing's sake, recalled how her "copying" was the neatest in class when she was a child and was now quite often called upon by people in her local community to make signs or posters for them; she was also well known locally as someone to go for do-it-yourself advice. Neither of these women felt totally confident about their own literacy skills but Julie felt quite confident in handing out advice and Cath felt quite confident about her "do-it-yourself" and her artwork.

Pat, like Julie, had become someone who people turned to for literacy help. People did not come to his house for advice, but in tea and dinner breaks at work he often assisted people with filling out forms or making sense of public service information documents. He also got information for them. He said that he was good at finding out things because there were not many situations that he had not been through himself. Pat confronted people with their literacy difficulties. He said that it was not so much that they confided in him but his ability to tell, just by talking to people, whether they had problems. At the age of 31, Liz became a store detective despite difficulties with the writing needed for the job, and a friend gave her some help writing her reports. The friend explained that the reports were basically written to a formula, and she showed Liz how to rely on a few stock phrases and sentences. A slightly different form of support was mentioned by Val, who took phone messages for her sister who lived round the corner and had no phone; similarly Sally's mother took phone messages for her.

It is important to emphasize that often, because these networks exist, problems do not arise. People live within these networks and go about their lives without particularly identifying problems with reading and writing. Often it was when these networks were disrupted that people were confronted with problems, and this was sometimes given as a reason for coming to basic education classes. Lesley, for example, had lived near her relatives for some time outside Lancaster. She reported that several of her relatives had problems with reading and writing but that they supported each other. Her description of her life then is what Fingeret (1983) refers to as an "interdependent" life. It was only when she moved to Lancaster itself, away from her network of relatives, even though it was a fairly short move, that Leslie felt the need to improve her reading and writing. When she moved outside of her established social network, in many ways her life turned to being more of a "dependent" life in Fingeret's terms.

## Values

When people talked about writing, everything they said was imbued with values and attitudes. They evaluated themselves and others and talked about the power of writing, its pleasure or its difficulty.

First, we can look at how they see themselves. Neil, for example, was a section manager at a branch of a food store chain and had great difficulty writing. He was sent to courses in which he trained with people who had passed all sorts of examinations. He didn't understand how he could talk and work so easily alongside these people who could produce pages and pages of writing effortlessly while he struggled to make a sentence. When discussing writing letters to the newspaper, two people, Pat and Bob, suggested it was laziness on their part that prevented them from writing such letters; Roger, on the other hand, said, "It seems such a long, laborious task to write it out and then send it and then see if they're going to write it out," implying the fault was in the process rather than himself. It is interesting that Bob commented, "I must be a lazy sort of person" because his typical response to questions about writing was that he couldn't write. Like Pat, he was orally articulate and cared passionately about local and national issues.

Several people referred to "people with problems"—meaning other people, not themselves. Val, for example, had never really thought of herself as having literacy difficulties at all; she enrolled in a basic education course in the hope that she would increase her vocabulary. In her parish work, she found she was mixing with other church people who talked in a language she could not understand; she said that all the long words they used were making her feel inadequate and this was the main reason for her joining classes. Liz reported a change over the years in her attitude to writing and, looking back, appeared surprised by her past courage in applying for jobs and dealing with problems. A few years earlier, she was apparently unconcerned by her difficulty but now even refuses to write a shopping list because she might drop it and someone might discover it.

Two out of twenty people interviewed commented that they got no pleasure whatsoever out of writing, and several others expressed negative attitudes. Neil and Bob did not get any enjoyment from writing; for them, the process was too laborious and they were frustrated by what they saw as the inadequacy of their written work. Pat wrote only out of a sense of duty: "I feel I should, you know. . . . I don't like it 'cos I'm not that good." Liz echoed Pat's words, saying she did not enjoy writing because she could not do it. Duncan also sometimes found writing "a pain," when he knew what he wanted to say but could not find the words to express it. Like Pat and Sally, he preferred reading to writing. Three people felt they could express themselves better writing than speaking: Lynne, Dick, and Andrea. Dick also said he took "comfort in writing down things instead of saying them." This was in contrast to Andrea, who usually wrote down things in order to say them. Lynne is perhaps closer: "I can write things down what I feel or want to say but can't say verbally because I'm embarrassed."

Lesley and Roger definitely preferred writing to reading. Perhaps, as Pat commented, "That's like most people—what they're good at they like, what they're not good at, they don't." Lesley had always enjoyed writing. She was adamant that she really enjoyed writing before she was able to make any sense of reading and, in fact, still struggles with reading: "Mmm, I'd scribble on and on. Some of it didn't make sense 'cos spellings weren't right and stuff, but I knew what it were all about—I love writing." And Roger, who avoided reading because he found it difficult, spent a lot of his spare time recording personal thoughts and answered "definitely" when asked if he enjoyed writing. Frances said that she enjoyed writing for herself but not for other people, and at work it worried her when she was expected to write letters.

Only four of the people questioned about writing processes, Liz, Neil, Pat, and Paul, did not mention the look of handwriting or neatness as being important to them; possibly in their cases other considerations such as spelling and self-expression simply overrode any thought of presentation. Although Neil wrote drafts and top copies, it was the content of the top copy he mentioned rather than the look of it, "I still know it doesn't make sense to a lot . . . what other people will think. I've always known that."

People's awareness of the value of writing was apparent when they talked about writing to the newspaper. Seven of the eight people who commented on whether they had ever written or thought of writing to the newspapers or television about anything said they had thought of it and gave examples of the kind of things they would like to write in about. Pat was angry about a local environmental issue, a meat processing business that wafts nauseous smells across the city: "If we all wrote, we'd probably get something done," he suggested. But in this belief he was unusual; the power to effect change through letter writing was not a belief that was typically expressed: more often, they voiced a fatalistic view of the world. Some, however, managed to discover power for themselves in writing.

Lynne was very aware of the power of writing. Recently, an item in the news about an incident in Ireland had made her furious. She felt a tremendous urge to vent her anger in a letter to a newspaper, but she didn't write it: "You'd be scared of what you might write. . . . Once it's written down it's recorded." Lynne said that this news item was the first thing she had ever wanted to write to the papers about: "The first time I'd ever felt I would want to write something down and voice my own opinion." Writing was also used as part of acts of resistance. At one time, when Andrea had an office job, she used to find she was adding paragraphs of personal writing, often commentary on things that were happening in the office, to letters she was supposed to be copying for her boss, or, if she was in a bad mood, she would express her fury in angry type print. She always threw away these writings, which she referred to as "doodles."

Lesley had difficulty writing; neither she nor her husband had ever written a note to school about any of her three children. The only letter she could remember writing was to complain about a family holiday because "it weren't same as it said in brochure"; it is very unlikely that, at the time she wrote this letter, before starting basic education classes, she could actually have read what it said in the brochure herself. Since the interview, she has begun to discover the power of writing. She wrote a letter of appeal to the local education office pleading for her eldest child to be given a place at the secondary school of her choice, and she won her case. She reported that she was very pleased with the result of her letter.

Again, when we examine values, we can identify common attitudes as well as see individual ways of incorporating literacy into people's lives. Two people expressed opposite views on the relation between writing and personal problems. One person, Dick, used writing to cope with changes in his life, involving illness, unemployment, and separation, and he kept a diary for 12 months. "It was putting in a diary, putting on paper what I couldn't say. It was a good idea . . . but it drained me . . . mainly private thoughts." It was the first time since leaving school that he had written anything except applications for jobs. On the other hand, another person, Rita, had the opposite reaction to the role of writing and personal problems: "You can't read and write when you are going through a bad time." When her husband left her and her mother died, she felt she was living on her "nerves" and she never picked up a book or a pen.

A third person, Ruth, talked of excessive personal writing actually having contributed to a relative's mental breakdown and said she had to limit herself in her writing, not so much because she was afraid of the same thing happening to her but because she felt the family might start watching her anxiously. This contrasted interestingly with Andrea's personal use of writing when she was angry or worried; Andrea wrote down what she was going to say before an argument or tricky confrontation precisely because she was scared of what she might say. Writing provided a safety valve for her, a means of careful rehearsal; she felt safe when she wrote.

Two people, Ruth and Andrea, wrote continually, every day; Ruth sat down each evening and wrote for an hour or two, doing personal writing; she also mentioned poetry going round in her head in the middle of the night, which she would love to have jotted down but didn't because she was always too tired. Andrea made daily lists and plans and enjoyed "rabbling on" to friends in letters.

## CONCLUSION

We are partway through our work; nevertheless, we have something to say about writing in our local community: In a group of adults, many of whom have experienced problems with writing, there are identifiable uses of writing. Writing has a place in maintaining the household and in maintaining communication, and a proportion of them did some regular personal writing. In situating their literacy practices as part of social practices, there were clear roles with respect to literacy that people took, and these roles existed within established networks of support. People expressed attitudes about the power of writing and the relative value of writing compared with other activities. They also held strong conceptions of the nature of language and literacy and of the differences in function between spoken and written language. We intend to pursue this work, relating what we have found out about writing to other aspects of literacy and using other sources of data to build up a fuller picture of the role of literacy in people's everyday lives.

# APPENDIX

Here we provide details of the 20 people who were interviewed, with some indication of their levels of literacy.

(1) *Cath:* aged 47, separated, two grown-up children, lives alone, works part-time, in a dairy; at time of interview was attending WEA women's group; reads broadly and writes for pleasure but asks for help with forms.

(2) *Roger:* 32, single, lives with parents; unemployed; has attended basic education classes since 1981; some difficulties with spelling and punctuation; recently started writing for pleasure at home; avoids reading.

(3) *Julie:* 45, separated, two grown-up children and one grandchild; lives alone, unemployed, attending WEA women's group at time of interview; reads broadly and writes for pleasure; sometimes turns to children for advice.

(4) *Ray:* 33, single, lives alone, works part-time as a cleaner and has attended basic education classes for a number of years; likes support when writing unless copying but is more confident about reading.

(5) *Lesley:* 34, lives with partner and three primary school age children; works part-time as a cleaner/child minder; has attended basic education classes for two years; enjoys writing but dislikes reading.

(6) *Val:* 42, single, lives with elderly relative, unemployed at time of interview but doing voluntary work for the church; has attended basic education classes for two years; reads quite broadly and quite enjoys writing.

(7) *Lynne:* 34, lives with husband and three children, works part-time (cooks, cleans, and serves in fast food shop); attends basic education classes; enjoys both reading and writing.

(8) *Mark:* 20, single, lives with parents, works in a printers; has attended basic education for two years, now about to go to Art college; dislikes writing because he has difficulty spelling but has just started to enjoy novels.

(9) *Duncan:* 24, lives with parents (at time of interview), single, unemployed; attends basic education classes; some general writing difficulties but enjoys computer work and medical books; went to a special school.

(10) *Liz:* 39, lives with partner, two grown-up children; unemployed at time of interview and attending basic education classes; reads newspapers and novels but has some real problems with writing.

(11) *Sally:* 25, separated, lives with brother; unemployed and attending basic education classes, some writing difficulties but reads widely; came to college to take mind off physical condition—rhematoid arthritis.

(12)  *Rita:* 37, separated, lives with teenage daughter, part-time cleaner/caretaker, attends basic education classes; some writing difficulties but reads novels occasionally; came to classes for social reasons.

(13)  *Pat:* 44, lives with partner and child by previous marriage; full-time manual worker; has attended basic education classes in the past; taught himself to read after leaving school, now reads broadly but avoids writing.

(14)  *Neil:* 26, lives with partner and primary school child; full-time supermarket worker; attends basic education classes; can read but has real difficulties writing.

(15)  *Dick:* Around 40, separated, one child; lives in room in another family's house, unemployed due to physical ailment; presently attends open college classes (ex-basic education student); reads broadly and has enjoyed writing.

(16)  *Ruth:* 36, lives with partner and three children; unemployed and attends basic education classes as a step to other classes; wants to become a nurse; writes for pleasure everyday, has some writing difficulties.

(17)  *Paul:* 25, lives with partner, has attended basic education classes for several years; took access courses and is now on a degree course; reads widely and enjoys writing "short pieces" for pleasure.

(18)  *Bob:* 36, lives with partner and two children; full-time builder, has attended basic education in past and has real difficulties with reading and writing but doesn't worry about them.

(19)  *Frances:* 35, lives with partner and two children; full-time clerical worker, has attended basic education classes in the past; no obvious problems but doesn't read much; enjoyed creative writing at college.

(20)  *Andrea:* 32, lives with partner and one child (primary school); unemployed at present, attends basic education classes; can type, enjoys reading, and loves writing; talks of herself as a compulsive writer.

## REFERENCES

Barton, D. (1988). Exploring the historical basis of contemporary literacy. *Quarterly Newsletter of the Laboratory of Comparative Human Cognition, 10*(3), 70-76.

Doheny-Farina, S., & Odell, L. (1985). Ethnographic research on writing: Assumptions and methodology. In L. Odell & D. Goswami (Eds.), *Writing in non-academic settings* (pp. 503-535). New York: Guilford.

Faigley, L. (1985). Non-academic writing: The social perspective. In L. Odell & D. Goswami (Eds.), *Writing in non-academic settings* (pp. 231-248). New York: Guilford.

Fingeret, A. (1983). Social networks, independence and adult illiterates. *Adult Education Quarterly, 33*(3), 133-146.

Hamilton, M. (1987). *Literacy numeracy and adults*. London: Adult Literacy and Basic Skills Unit.

Heath, S. B. (1983). *Ways with words*. Cambridge: Cambridge University Press.

Horsman, J. (1987). *Something in my mind besides the everyday: Ill/literacy in the context of women's lives in Nova Scotia*. Unpublished doctoral dissertation, University of Toronto.

Langer, J. A. (Ed.). (1987). *Language, literacy and culture*. Norwood, NJ: Ablex.

Levine, K. (1985). *The social context of literacy*. London: Routledge & Kegan Paul.

Moll, L. (1989, September). *Creating zones of learning: An ethnographic approach*. Paper presented at the EARLI Conference, Madrid.

Reder, S. M. (1985). *Giving literacy away*. Unpublished manuscript.

Rockhill, K. (1987). *Literacy as threat/desire: Longing to be somebody*. In J. S. Gaskill & A. T. McLaren (Eds.), *Women and education: A Canadian perspective*. Calgary: Detselig.

Scribner, S., & Cole, M. (1981). *The psychology of literacy*. Cambridge, MA: Harvard University Press.

Street, B. (1984). *Literacy in theory and practice*. Cambridge: Cambridge University Press.

Schieffelin, B., & Gilmore, P. (Eds.). (1986). *The acquisition of literacy: Ethnographic perspectives*. Norwood, NJ: Ablex.

Stotsky, S. (1987). Writing in a political context. *Written Communication, 4*, 394-410.

Taylor, D. (1985). *Family literacy*. London: Heinemann.

Taylor, D., & Dorsey-Gaines, C. (1988). *Growing up literate*. London: Heinemann.

# 5

# *Self, Education, and Writing in Nineteenth-Century English Communities*

## URSULA HOWARD

**Learning to write** was part of the lives of many working-class people in England long before it was generally accepted as an economically or morally desirable skill for all social classes. The desire to learn to write, and especially to be a writer, involved moving against powerful material and psychological obstacles. Among "superior" classes, it was not widely expected that working-class people would develop reading and writing skills or practices to anything beyond the basic measurement of literacy, which was the ability to sign the marriage register rather than mark it with an "x." Remnants of low expectations survive. In 1987, one historian wrote that "the working classes . . . had less need to practice literacy skills" (Stephen, 1987, p. 4). The teaching of reading was widely accepted and promoted in the early years of the century. But, before the 1840s, writing was a contested subject. It was banned from many Sunday schools as unsuitable for the Sabbath: It was secular and provided skills that encouraged the growth of subversive publishing, inappropriate aspirations, and the crime of forgery.

This chapter is about some of the ways working-class people learned and used writing before the coming of state elementary education after the 1870 Education Act as well as some of the currents that flowed with and against their energies. The growth of a reading and writing public, and the impact of widespread literacy on society and popular culture in the nineteenth century, have become the subjects of important historical research, quantitative and qualitative in emphasis (recent work includes Stephen, 1987, with useful bibliography, and Vincent, 1989). It has been established that the biggest quantitative increase in literacy was in the period before, not after, the education acts of the late nineteenth century. Recent research has emphasized the complexity and diversity of ways of learning. An extraordinary fluidity of groupings, associations, schools, and institutions existed working both in alliance and in competition, some surviving for short and others for longer periods and changing under pressure from inside and outside forces.

My focus is on the processes and meanings of learning and using skills and knowledge, and the interaction between individual learners and the communities from which they formed "learning associations." I will draw mainly on autobiography. The first part of the chapter looks at popular images and assumptions about "self-educated" working-class learners; the second part concerns learning and writing from the writers' experience, focusing mainly on two writers with examples from others. The third section is about people living away from home and the role writing played in their lives.

## SOLITUDE, PAIN, MASCULINITY

Any version of individual autonomy which fails to recognize, or which radically displaces, the social conditions inherent in any practical individuality, but which has then, at another level, to reintroduce these social conditions as the decisive "practical business" of the everyday world, can lead at best to self-contradiction, at worst to hypocrisy or despair. It can become complicit with a process which rejects, deforms, or actually destroys individuals in the very name of individualism. (Williams, 1977, p. 194)

Among popular images and vocabulary in historical and fictional writing about working-class learning, three have been significant in shaping attitudes. The first is that of the solitary learner. The central experience of the "autodidact" is seen to be the nights of study after long working days, with little guidance beyond the possibility of support from the family. In this version, the working *man* laboriously practiced letter formation in copy books; he engaged in a relatively unstructured program of reading, ranging from *Pilgrim's Progress* and Latin grammars to Burton's *Anatomy of Melancholy*. Excitement, frustration, and depression were experienced successively. Success of any kind signaled a triumph of determination over circumstances. A basis for this view of learning can be found in contemporary journals, in novels, and in the writers' own life stories; but the same sources provide evidence that suggests complex, community-based, and structured learning patterns.

In *The Country and the City* (1975), Raymond Williams explored the meaning of autodidacticism when he questioned a contemporary literary critic's assertion that George Eliot, Hardy, and Lawrence, whose fathers were a bailiff, a builder, and a miner, respectively, were "our three great autodidacts." Yet each, in addition to independent learning and reading, had a solid secondary education; Hardy also had a professional qualification, and Lawrence went to Nottingham University. Williams assesses the statement as "one of the sharp revealing moments of English cultural history," because

> it is not only that by their contemporary standards these levels of formal education are high; it is also that they are higher, absolutely, than those of four out of five people in contemporary Britain. So the flat patronage of autodidact can be related to only one fact: that none of the three was in the pattern of boarding school and Oxbridge which by the end of the century was being regarded not simply as a kind of education but as education itself: to have missed that circuit was to have missed being "educated" at all. In other words, a "standard" education was that received by one or two per cent of the population; all the rest were seen as "uneducated" or as "autodidacts"; seen also, of course, as either comically ignorant or, when they pretended to learning, as awkward, overearnest, fanatical. The effects of this on the English imagination have been deep. (Williams, 1975, p. 208-209)

The level of formal education is made to bear directly on the appropriateness of a person's ambitions and choice of occupation. It is true that the social background and education of autodidacts and working-class writers is often as strong a focus of attention as the writing itself. Of John Clare, the poet who was also a Northamptonshire agricultural laborer, it has typically been asserted that, although "refreshing," and "he compares favourably with his better-known contemporaries. . . . He remains, however, a minor poet, and his case is one of only partial victory over circumstances" (Klingopolous, 1982, p. 72). It is hard to imagine in what more suitable circumstances he could have been placed to write pastoral poems or over what circumstances he would have sensed victory in writing his most acclaimed poem of alienation and loneliness "I Am" while shut away in a lunatic asylum. "Circumstances" appear to relate simply to his lack of formal education and his status as an agricultural laborer, assumed to be necessarily working against creativity.[1]

The vocabulary of autodidacticism often centers on an unproblematized notion of "self," illustrated by expressions like *self-education, self-taught,* and *self-improving*. These terms are bolstered by a range of characterizing key words: *solitary, aspiring, enthusiasm, effort, scholar(d), striving, struggling, sincere,* and so on. Then there is another commonly used set of terms that, despite obvious contradictions, is often used interchangeably with the first set: *unlettered, untaught, unschooled, uneducated, peasant* (poet), *groping, simple, ambitious, unsophisticated,* (literacy) *pretensions, rudimentary, smattering* (knowledge), and so on. Both sets of defining terms use the image of the solitary learner. They also reflect the language of patronage toward autodidacts.

The second problematic area is the imagery of pain, struggle, and awkwardness that is attached to people in manual labor learning to read and write. This is exemplified in an inspector's report to the Committee of Council on Education, which asserts that good writing was beyond "the fingers of the rural labourer . . . the boy that can hold a plough cannot grasp the more delicate handle of a pen" (quoted in Horn, 1978, p. 128).[2] Attitudes like this were often expressed by nineteenth-century writers, as in George Eliot's description of a village night school in *Adam Bede:*

> These three big men, with the marks of their hard labour about them, anxiously bending over the worn books, and painfully making out, "The grass is green". . . . It was almost as if three rough animals were making humble efforts to learn how they might become human. (Eliot, 1960, p.228)

The equation of literacy as the measure of fully human status, the sense of an anthropologist observing an alien people and the assumption that the attempt to learn the skills normally practiced by a more powerful class would be approached "humbly" with little likelihood of significant success are indicators of the distance between the sets of meanings attached to education and culture by "educated" and "uneducated" writers. And this is from a writer who herself has been described as self-educated.

The third area is gender bias. This is highlighted by the identification of "autodidact" with "self-taught working man" in many accounts. One assumption has been that women learners and writers were the exception rather than the rule. The sexual division of labor and the double burden of paid and domestic labor certainly made time for learning throughout the nineteenth century more difficult for many working-class women. They had less access to or time for mutual learning, and less access also to benefactors, and were relatively rarely published. Far less women's writing has, therefore, survived. Despite the male-oriented stereotype, the nature of their lives made women, ironically, more likely to be isolated learners than men.

Working-class writers have to some extent endorsed all three sets of images and assumptions, as in this passage from the autobiography of the Chartist activist and writer Thomas Cooper:

My first poem—for it was sure to come, sooner or later—seemed almost to make itself, one evening as I walked in the valley below Pringle Hill. I give it here, be it remembered, as the first literary feat of a self-educated boy of fifteen. I say *self*-educated, so far as I was educated. Mine has been almost entirely self-educated, all the way through life. From that time forth I often struck off little pieces of rhyme, and made attempts at blank verse; but all such doings were really worthless, and I kept no record of them. (Cooper, 1873, p. 43)

Elsewhere in his book, he made it clear that he was far from solely "self"-educated, and here he described writing as coming to him so naturally it could "make itself."

The use of texts and emphases has been selective. Broad generalizations about working-class culture by writers of a different class have served to encourage generic views about working-class writers at the expense of exploring differences between writers in terms of individual experiences, gender and cultural differences, conditions of production, preoccupations and style. The blending of the dominant images of pain, humility, and unnaturalness, on the one hand, and ill-directed solitary learning by working men, on the other, has favored the perpetuation of oversimplified versions of working-class learning practices.

In his autobiography, Charles Shaw, a potter from Tunstall in the Black Country, described his experience of solitary learning. It is worth quoting as one of the fuller examples of the kind of writing that has led to the familiar image of working-class learners:

We had in our house a small room over "an entry." This entry afforded a passage from the street to the backyards of the cottages. This room was about three to four feet wide, the widest part being a recess near the window, the other part of the room being narrowed by the chimney. I got a small iron stove to warm the room on cold nights, and I fixed up a small desk against the wall, and two small shelves for my few books. I don't know what a university atmosphere is. I have dreamt of it, but I know when I entered this little room at night I was in another world. I seemed to leave all squalor and toil and distraction behind. I felt as if I entered into converse with presences who were living and breathing in that room. I had not read many authors then, but such as I had seemed to meet me with an unspoken welcome every night. My life there was strangely and sweetly above what it had been during the day. It was often from nine o'clock to half-past before I could enter this room after walking from my work and getting my tea-supper, the only meal since half-past twelve at noon.

But, usually, as soon as I entered that room, I was as a giant refreshed with new wine. Its silence was as refreshing as dew, and exhausted energies seemed refilled with vigour and pulsed along with eager ardour. Unfortunately, I never acquired much in the way of knowledge. As I have since found out, I was on the wrong track and had no-one to guide me. But what I failed to get in acquisition I got in inspiration and communion with some of those "sceptered sovrans who still sway our spirits from their urns." I made the mistake of climbing trees for golden fruit when I should have been digging and delving in the soul. . . .

I look back pensively and gratefully, however, upon what I did in my little room. I might have done much more in much less time if I had had a guiding mind. Sometimes I read and wrote on till two or three in the morning. (Shaw, 1977, pp. 224-225).[3]

Charles Shaw described how, on six days out of seven, he got up to go to work two and a half hours later; on Sundays he was active at a Sunday school.

The interest of this passage lies not only in its corroboration of the stereotypical working-class adult learner. The celebration of "a room of one's own" as a prerequisite for creativity, away from "distraction," prefigures Virginia Woolf's argument that the lack of solitude, together with lack of (unearned) income, were the chief explanations for women's apparent inability to write. The phrases of humility and confessions of misdirected efforts that are familiar in autobiographical and historical accounts are countered by the hint that his small room was equal to the imagined other, dreamlike world of university. He invested this experience with the happier qualities of a fairy tale, "strange and sweet," and he himself is a "giant" refreshed to superhuman strength, who met with spirits, climbed trees for golden fruit, and made books come literally to life. This extract contains not only the language of earnest and humble self-improvement but also that of fantasy and the investing of learning with a romantic aura. Nor is this vision of magical solitude the whole picture of Charles Shaw's learning life in his hometown.

The vocabulary of autodidacticism lifts learners out of the connecting social relationships and learning associations in which their lives were embedded. They are not seen as part of anything solid, so that the associations and organizations they were supported by cannot be given legitimation as any kind of system. We need to use the whole context of complexity and ambivalence that emerges from the recorded experiences of learners and users of literacy to understand the perpetuation of myths, to understand why they were partially internalized by working-class writers, who had no vested interest in a system of "flat patronage" and public undereducation. We also need to notice what else they were saying and questioning about learning methods, about writing and creative expression, about definitions of knowledge, and about "progression" (to borrow modern jargon) during a period when multiple and diverse forms of education were being reshaped and channeled into state- and middle-class directed conformity and hierarchy. To aid an understanding of what was lost as well as what was gained by the advent of a state education system, we need to place the idea and practice of "self-education" in the social relationships and communities that were its context.

The term *autodidact* has recently been interestingly defined by Logie Barrow (1986) to mean "persons who were making their education their own affair, irrespective of social superiors."[4] His definition assumes not that people literally learn alone but that what they learn is not systematized by an outside authority. He focuses his argument on concerted attempts in the nineteenth century by what he called "English Plebeians" to create their own, democratic, definitions of knowledge, a "democratic epistemology." This definition of *autodidact* allows for mutuality and cooperation. It encompasses even those more structured kinds of collective self-education like the one that Robert Colls (1976) described in a northeast England mining community in the 1830s. In this period, education was a part of trade union and community activity, organized by and for the workers and their families.

Most learners began with the resources of knowledge and language held in common by the communities around them. Starting points for learning writing—for example, the strokes making up letters of the alphabet—had a set of names that related to everyday life: "pothooks" and "ladles," "tar-bottles," "sheephooks," and so on (see, e.g., Clare, 1983, p. 4; Rushton, 1907, p. 23). Writing was learned primarily by copying. First, strokes would be drawn, then letters, followed by moral lines and homilies, proverbs, poems, or psalms. The Bible, which vast numbers of households owned, was used to teach reading. It provided a mixture, in a sense, of a graded reading scheme, with the tenth chapter of Nehemiah as the summit of achievement (see, e.g., Lawson, 1887, p. 45) and a "Real Book," whose stories and meanings were a central part of life and literature for adults and children. Readers then advanced to the learning of texts that were also a living part of a common culture—*Pilgrims Progress, Paradise Lost, Robinson Crusoe*—as well as sensational literature, poetry, and the range of books available at the libraries established by Sunday schools, cooperative societies, Mechanics Institutes, and other organizations that provided education for working people.[5] Stories, myths, and legends were learned through oral traditions, for example, from neighbors, family, friends, itinerant workers, and visitors. Thomas Cooper remembered the tales told him by the peddlers and beggars who stayed at a local lodging house.

It is not surprising that writing by people who had learned this way reflected their range of reading. Reading for many working-class learners was the direct inspiration to write themselves. For others, like the Cheshire farm laborer and silk-mill worker Adam Rushton, the seemingly deadening exercise of copy writing was the source of inspiration to write for themselves. The closeness of new writers to the sources of their inspiration was not perceived by them as a problem. Their work was not clouded by self-conscious fears of plagiarism or lack of originality. There is a sense of surprise in much writing at the fact of its being written at all, which includes a celebratory use of the material of their intellectual development. However, working-class writers and poets are often criticized for the transparency of the sources from which their writing was derived. John Clare's reading of eighteenth-century verse is said to show in his writing, which is also flawed by repetition of the same word within a poem. *Derivative, repetitive,* and *overambitious* are some of the critical adjectives attached to working-class cultural production.

These views of working-class writers and autodidacts have managed to separate people from their communities and culture as individualized learners and simultaneously to lump them together as a genre, as writers who find an individual creative voice only with great difficulty.

## LEARNING ASSOCIATIONS IN THE COMMUNITY

In this section, I will concentrate on two writers, to draw out some of the forms of learning and writing that existed within communities, where learning associations with people and institutions were physically accessible.

Charles Shaw was born in 1832, and grew up in Tunstall, Staffordshire, a pottery town with a population he estimated at between 7,000 and 8,000 during his youth. His childhood was marked by one terrible shadow: In 1842, the family were sent to the workhouse as paupers. This apart, his experience is not, externally, untypical of working-class life in a small industrial town.

His formal schooling began at the age of 3 or 4 at "Old Betty W's" day school. He left at age 7, when he had "finished his education." At Betty's he learned to read, spell (which meant sounding out, syllablizing words, a method that did not use writing), and knit stockings, at the time an important skill that contributed to the family economy that Betty taught both boys and girls. Writing, as in many private working-class schools, was not included in the curriculum.[6] This was in contrast to the National and British and Foreign

Society schools, where reading and writing were often taught simultaneously. In many private schools, writing and arithmetic were taught later, often in specialist Writing Schools, like the one attended by the autobiographer John Castle (n.d.), where "I filled only two copy books." Attendance at such schools may have been frequently brief, for many people left school able to read but not to write. Betty's school was fairly typical of the private working-class schools of the period, although many accounts of similar schools are not so glowing, and Charles Shaw may have romanticized it in his memory. In his estimation, she laid the essential foundation for the next possible stages of learning:

> She and her class did two things—they made night schools possible for those who wanted to go further, say, to learn writing and arithmetic; and they made it possible for Sunday School teachers to have less elementary drudgery.

Like many other "little workers," his "childhood" was brief.[7] Anything more sophisticated than a school such as Betty's was out of reach for most people, and the next stages of education had to be acquired in an increasingly secularized Sunday school curriculum. By the age of 6, before leaving Betty's, Shaw had progressed to an advanced reading class at Sunday school, a Bible class, by which time he notes that he could "never remember any difficulty in reading or spelling except, of course, very exceptional and long words in the Bible." The credit for his success is given to Betty's "method of teaching." The two institutions, day and Sunday school, are seen as the source of a flow of possibilities: "The former soon ceased to flow directly, but never indirectly, while the latter, Nile-like, has spread its fruitful waters over all my life."

He described a defined and hierarchical learning process, which he recognized as a foundation of essential learning from which to build. From this basis, other options followed. In a chapter called "The Pursuit of Knowledge Under Difficulties," he provided a "description of the methods of my own educational development." He did not mean "on his own" but the processes of continued learning with many other providers and colearners. The first, William Leigh, was another potter from a better-off family:

> He found out, from seeing me reading at nights when he came to our house, that I was fond of reading, and up to the time of going to the workhouse he regularly supplied me with books, and these were as precious as the bread he gave us. It was he who first opened to me the great world of literature and from that day I have known "the world of books is still the world."

At Sunday school, Charles Shaw mentioned by name three people who took his education further than the bare bones of the official curriculum: the first was the school's superintendent Daniel Spilsbury, who heard him read, "smiled pleasantly upon me, and stroking my hair . . . said the Bible I had read from . . . I could take home as a present. Sunday school prizes had not then come into fashion." Ralph Lawton was the Sunday school teacher whose "tender interest" in Shaw, as well as his quality of "unspeakable serenity," is still so vivid to the writer Shaw that "sixty years after the vision of his ecstasy would be like a 'bright cloud' hanging over an old scholar's life, at once an inspiration and a joy." He became strongly attached to Ralph Lawton because of his attempts to reintegrate the Shaw brothers into the class after they came back from the workhouse, "branded" because they were wearing a parish "brat," or apron, and rejected by their school fellows. After a miserable period of taunting, Charles and his brother walked out of the school. For several weeks, he hid at home but eventually his "passion for the Sunday School" led him to try another school. As they stood against the wall of the chapel outside, they were approached by a young man with a "gentle face" who invited them to join the school. His name was George Kirkham, and "in his hands I was as a plant carefully tended, nurtured and watered. He lent me books. He gave me counsel. He breathed his prayers for me." He is remembered for the care and love he provided for six years after that. The description of George Kirkham's intervention is colored by the religious imagery of the moment of conversion from "shame and fear" to hope, from darkness to light. Shaw's religion was education and his "saintly" guide worked the miracle of "giving him a dawning interest in a larger world . . . like the blind man in the Gospel, I had begun to 'see men as trees walking.' " When he died suddenly, "I felt a loneliness which chilled me." He experienced a sense of bewilderment at the loss of guidance to deal with the "many questions whose dimness spurred my interest in them." This "perilous interval" where Shaw feared losing everything he had learned was survived by his continued work at the Sunday school and his developing friendships with some young men "a little older than myself." Together they formed a learning association, which became central to the next phase of his education.

William Leigh, Daniel Spilsbury, Ralph Lawton, and George Kirkham were significant figures for Charles Shaw. They were represented as more complex figures than teachers. They provided love, including physical affection, and a feeling of being recognized, valued, and able to learn. From the number of autobiographies in which comparable relationships feature, there is clearly a significant dimension of growing up, to learning within a community, not answered by family or school, which has multiple meanings for the emerging sense of self of the learner/writer. This offers one way of looking at community in this period. These guiding friends are sometimes strangers encountered at moments of crisis. They are sometimes familiar figures from social networks around the locality, home, or workplace. They are prominently, repeatedly named (if they have known names). The repeated writing of names often appears to have a ritual significance in autobiography.

In a world where "real" parents or older siblings were hard-pressed to provide material essentials for life, other adults, met sometimes apparently by chance at moments of crisis, came to fulfill, for a period of time, the roles of guide, counselor, or spiritual, intellectual, and more uncomplicatedly loving "parent." They were often succeeded serially by another, allowing each to remain romanticized, part of another world and unaffected by the constraints and compromises of long-term close associations. In some accounts, significant figures are constructions of an undiluted goodness, intellectual strength, and heroic, saintly, almost magical qualities. In other versions, the structure of feeling is closer to the idea of solidarity, usually associated with organizational, public forms of working class life. The sense of solidarity in these writings is more of mutual support between individuals and small groups, wishing each other well, sharing scarce resources, and providing safe environments to explore knowledge away from the imagined contempt of the well educated.

In many autobiographies, the tone of the writing about intellectual parents and learning associations is in stark contrast to the descriptions of family, which are often noticeable for their brevity, phrases of bland praise, or abiding resentments at outright conflict or obstruction such as that experienced by John Clare, who felt forced to pretend to his parents that the poems he read to them in the hope of helpful criticism were not his but simply ones he had practiced his writing skills on by copying out—something his parents, like others—thoroughly approved of, as a way to better paid work. "She'd be bound, I should one day be able to reward them with my pen, for the trouble they had taken in giveing me schooling" (Clare, 1983, p. 4). Family conflict, especially around education and learning to write, is more often openly explored in women's writing.

At a narrower, self-conscious level, "parent" figures are represented as knowledgeable, sometimes inspiring teachers offering systematic guidance and method to the learning process. They might offer a prescribed course of reading, reading with discussion, or exercises in writing. A great deal of the learning of skills generally was remembered as underpinned by conversation on questions about particular subjects, or on knowledge itself, as posed by the learner. There was no hierarchy of appropriate levels of questioning or areas of knowledge.

George Kirkham provided the "assistance and stimulus" to Shaw's reading. The choice was limited to the Sunday School library. He began with *Robinson Crusoe,* Rollin's *Ancient History,* Dick's *Christian Philosopher, Paradise Lost,* Klopstock's *Messiah,* Pollock's *Course of Time,* and Gilfillan's *Bards of the Bible.* Of these, he concentrated his efforts on the *Christian Philosopher:*

> Scientific matters were put before me with such new vividness and interest, I felt far more interest in this than in Rollin's *History.* Nature, from sods to stars, became to me a temple. The religious tone of the book entranced, and the sublimities of the heavens which it unfolded awoke in me imaginings which thrilled my soul.

Looking back, he saw this as a "strange assortment." But it was not a selection of his own choice. George Kirkham had no resources beyond the library, so "they just happened to fall into my hands." But this was more than desultory reading, and, beyond the tone of devout humility, three things become clear from his account. First, he repeatedly drew argued comparisons between the relative merits of particular volumes; second, he deliberately chose more difficult texts because the "more elementary and educative books . . . could not have moved passion in me which these other books did"; and, third, his course of reading began to generate a desire to write:

> I began to feel a desire to express myself about the things I read, and certain forms of expression lingered in my ear as well as entranced my eye. This I imagine, was the first movement of a literary instinct.

Ready to learn to write, he initially began by himself, unaided, using materials typical in his situation. These were chosen largely on grounds of price. In his case, he worked with the least baffling:

> I remember my first efforts at composition were made on a slate. I could better manage a slate pencil than a pen. I tried a pen and a copy-book now and then, but the exercise proved a weariness to the hand and an irritation to the mind.

Writing materials were in any case a luxury. In another learning association with curiously ironic circumstances, Thomas Cooper earned the money for his writing paper, lead pencils, and water colors from his letter carrier uncle, who could not read and paid his nephew to give him directions (Cooper, 1873, pp. 20-21). A quill pen needed a sharp knife. There was a tax on paper. Slates too were beyond the means of many people, and, in one Yorkshire village, bits of broken pot or chalk were used on stones, causeways, and doorsteps (Lawson, 1887, pp. 40, 45).

The limitations of learning alone without guidance prompted Charles Shaw to find a teacher in "a well read man, and one who thought deeply on many subjects, as I thought then and have known since." His teacher, for the next two years, was "an old friend," a boot and shoemaker. The lessons were officially writing and arithmetic, but, because the exercises themselves progressed "slowly and irksomely," the conversation often became so absorbing that "both teacher and pupil forgot the more mechanical work on which I should have been engaged." Charles Shaw stopped his writing lessons able "only to scrawl a little" and "inside the range of vulgar fractions," but with the benefit, as he saw it, of wide-ranging discussion sessions.

Ideas for writing were generated by reading, by discussion, and by the political activity he witnessed and reflected upon (a whole chapter of his book is devoted to Joseph Capper of Tunstall, leader of the 1842 riot in the town, and to an analysis of the political consciousness of the potters). The wish to formulate his ideas in writing, to compose, was the impetus to learning the mechanical, transcriptive skills. His lack of mechanical literacy skill did not prevent his later becoming a journalist and author. For others, it was the opposite process. Adam Rushton, a tenant farmer's son who worked in a silk mill, remembered how ideas would come to him by copying out hymns and poems that "greatly excited" him and prompted him to read (Rushton, 1907, pp. 24-25). Both chose their own pace and sequence of learning.

Charles Shaw began a course in "recitation" with his companions that was so enjoyable, and working together provided such "mental uplift," that together they became part of a wider group that formed a Young Men's Mutual Improvement Society. It was this group's work, and the demanding preparation for their meetings, that stimulated Shaw to settle himself into the study room described at the beginning of this chapter. It was for this group that he read and wrote there. His description of the process of their education exposes his ambivalent attitude toward the gains and losses of "these more disciplined days" of universal elementary education. "We never dreamt," he writes, "of any *elementary* pursuit of knowledge" (italics added). "We met to discuss and criticize all things in heaven and earth, and sometimes even a far deeper province of the universe." They read, met on Saturday nights, listened to the essay one had prepared, discussed it, and decided the next subject to ensure variety. They discussed "as if the fate of a nation depended on that night's debate." The group grew and was amalgamated with another society. Shaw belonged to it for four years. It was typical of untold numbers of informal study groups over the period, with meetings based around writing on the essay/discussion model. The Mutual Improvement Society to which Thomas Cooper belonged set up an Adult School to teach reading and writing, which was not untypical of the way those active in educational and cultural ways took initiative or became involved in the many interacting or parallel groupings and organizations.

Criticism of government and municipal negligence toward working-class education runs through Charles Shaw's narrative. He did not consistently romanticize the past. He described the 1840s and 1850s as primitive times, celebrating the achievements of the Empire. But his view of progress was presented with an unmistakable sense of misgiving, confused by what appears to be faltering confidence to write down and make permanent his enduring anger that Betty W. was providing school for "a pittance" when "our rulers were squandering the resources of the nation in less useful ways." His rebuke of the "powers" for "lethargy and paralysis" was accompanied by a strong sense that, since "the schoolmaster has been abroad," it had by no means been all gain. When he wrote of "these more self-conscious days," when the world would sneer in "wonder and amusement" at the essays produced in the Mutual Improvement Societies, he was not unequivocally hailing the new structures as progressive. He was at least as much concerned with the loss as with the gain. His text at one level constitutes a working through of the value of his own experience in an era that had no time for informal learning, which saw self-education in Logie Barrow's sense as the bad that went before the change for good. Despite his ambivalence, and his belittling of his own efforts down to "simplicity and sincerity," even blundering, what he actually celebrated was the "audacity" of people of his class in those times to attempt to create a knowledge of their own. Thomas Cooper, whose book is likewise full of learning friendships and associations, explored with those around him a wide range of subjects including a serious interest in astrology. Their spurning of the "elementary" grew out of an entirely different approach to knowledge, as Shaw describes:

> We could expatiate about the universe when an examination in the geography of England would have confounded us. We could discuss astronomy (imaginatively) when a sum in decimals would have plucked us from our soaring heights into an abyss of perplexity. We could discuss the policies of governments and nations, and the creeds and constitutions of churches, while we would have been puzzled to give a bare outline of our country's history.

The mood of the text is one of speaking to an audience incapable of understanding or valuing those methods. The new system, "by examinations and even by "cramming', has scared away all such lofty flights." He knew already that their efforts to work through reading, thinking, writing together, toward their own understanding, could only be seen as "bombastic pretence." He was thankful that the " 'essays' were not published," saving him and his friends from the humiliation of a "great misunderstanding." He was decidedly against a "hardening and narrowing respectability," which he saw as one explanation for the defeat of the democratic movements of the 1840s. The new education system as he saw it suffered from some of these defects. It was inadequate reparation for past neglect. And it had caused the loss of mutual associations for self-directed learning.

Logie Barrow argues that there was real loss and that, even now, possible outcomes from education are perceived by many people as narrower than nineteenth-century independent learners' hopes for themselves:

> What is lacking is a confidence that knowledge, once gained, may enable you to do, discover or help decide something important. However seldom nineteenth century plebeian autodidacts were potentially in such a position . . . we shall hardly find them believing invincibly in their own stupidity or rather . . . in their own pointlessness or lack of qualification. Not them: on this score, they—or at any rate those who fill our sources—were decidedly optimistic.

> One reason for their optimism may, with some, have been that however great the social and political barriers against acquiring many types of knowledge—the situation was sometimes more open than today. We only have to think of very famous examples such as Faraday (Barrow, 1986, p. 152)

George Bourne, a writer from a working-class rural community in Surrey, criticized the new education for similar reasons:

> It was sterile of results. It opened to him no view, no vista; set up in his brain no stir or activity such as could continue after he had left school; and this for the reason that those simple items of knowledge which it conveyed to him were too scrappy and too few to begin running together into any understanding of the larger aspects of life. . . . no English history, no fairy-tales or romance, no inkling of the infinities of time and space, or of the riches of human thought; but merely a few "pieces" of poetry, and a few haphazard and detached observations (called "Nature Study" nowadays) about familiar things—"the cat", "the cow", "the parsnip". . . . And what could a child get from it to kindle his enthusiasm for that civilized learning in which, none the less, it all may have its place? (Bourne, 1984, p. 131)

His view of the new technical "night schools," aimed mainly at young adults, was similarly dismissive as unlikely to set up any "constructive idea activity." Looking back, some working-class writers felt that the new system was more of a jumble of bits and pieces than the old. Writing, which they had learned in order to compose what they wanted to say, was now regimented into a hierarchy of technical skills, with the carrot of the composition lesson (remembered by many working-class writers even now as the only space for creative, imaginative work in their schooling) held out for years, until Standard VI, as the reward for years of "parsnips."

For working women in the mid-nineteenth century, public forms of association and companionship were less easily accessible. Earning a living through writing (in either the clerical or the creative sense) usually remained a fantasy, except to the extent women could become teachers and later office workers, in significant numbers. The yearning and longing to write, for women, were born in even deeper conflict with outside pressures than was the case for men. The process of overcoming fundamental opposition sometimes meant forcing underground the whole learning process until such time as it could bubble up again as a completed fact. As long as it caused no disruption to the needs of the family or employer, it might even be permitted to flow on to lucrative rewards or improved status for the family. Pride in a girl's achievement as a clerk or teacher could then be happily shared, without having incurred risk or sacrifice to anyone's comfort but her own.

Church organizations were perhaps the most common route for girls and women to find the human contact they needed for learning. Marianne Farningham (a pseudonym; the family name was Hearn) was born in 1834 in Farningham, Kent. Her father was the village postmaster, and both parents were teachers at the Baptist Sunday school in Eynsford, the nearest village, which was one mile away. There was no school in Farningham, so, as soon as she could walk the distance, she started Sunday school at Eynsford with her four brothers and sisters. The nearest "dame school" was also at Eynsford. Apart from a brief spell there, she was taught to read, with the Bible as lesson book, by her paternal grandmother, "who thought beautiful thoughts, and expressed them in beautiful language" and who wrote poetry (Farningham, 1907, p. 13). Early in her life, her father became an abstainer after hearing a temperance orator, and Marianne Farningham's first remembered act of writing was signing the pledge. Her father guided her hands as together they wrote her own name.

Writing was not part of her education. She insisted on it. It was the first outright demand she records making in her reconstruction of herself as an insubordinate, willful child:

> My first attempt at rhyming was an epitaph on a dead toad which we found in
> the garden, and which we put in a match-box and buried with great solemnity.

I could not write the epitaph, for in the matter of writing I was quite behind the other children of my age. My ignorance in this respect was a sore burden to them with my continual cry, "Teach me to write."

The desire to write became the vehicle for turning transgressive negative energies into constructive activity. She eventually realized that her desire to learn was as transgressive and challenging to her allotted place in the family as her earlier disobedience had been, although at first her demands were met. Up until that time, her family had provided all the teaching she had had, and it is likely that they could only write a little themselves. A cousin, Isabella Rogers, also a Baptist, heard of her "childish desire" and offered to teach her. Her father assented under pressure and "took great pains with a little box in the shape of a book, which he made to hold my copy-book, pen, ink, ruler, and pencil, and which I proudly carried under my arm when I went to receive my writing lesson."

The process of learning to write was closely connected, in her memory, with her own wish to write rhymes. The link is reinforced by passages describing an "awakening" of the soul that immediately followed the account of her determination to learn writing. In a copy of *The Sailors' Magazine* (hers was a seafaring family), which she was leafing through while minding her baby brother, she found a poem, expressing "strange, sweet emotions," titled "A Better Land," a utopian vision of "coral strands", "sands of gold", and "secret mines". She felt "overcome with faintness" and rushed to the door for fresh air but was soon recalled to her "duty" by the baby's "loud cries." The tension she felt between the wish to follow her dreams, to be with nature and play with other children, and the constant duties her mother exacted of her as the oldest daughter tumble out in passages exulting in the pleasure she found and indulged as "Nature claimed me" and she "spent hours . . . leaning against the wall and looking out into the world of summer." But "I was never allowed to stay long enough to satisfy me." In tones of subdued anger she remembered how her mother's "cheery voice" recalled her to child care and domestic chores. Playing with her brothers and sisters was acceptable within limits, but reading and solitude were discouraged. "I am afraid she was grieved at my evident love of standing still and gazing." Reading required self-centeredness and permission to take time for oneself. In this period, as Florence Nightingale wrote bitterly in "Cassandra," girls and unmarried daughters were expected to be occupied in socially available ways for most of their waking hours: middle-class girls, with social activities, crafts, and accomplishments, and working-class girls, with domestic labor and family duties. For girls to move against this because they wanted something different for themselves was almost inconceivable.

Selfishness, detectable in many forms of behavior, including excessive reading or enjoying being alone, was an unacceptable characteristic for girls. One punishment Marianne Farningham was given for talking to herself was to repeat the cleaning task she had just finished. Eventually, books were forbidden until after the day's work was done. Her longing to attend school was, therefore, a fantasy of freedom, promising release from housework and the constant fear of incurring displeasure. When a new school was built in Eynsford by the British and Foreign School Society[8] in 1843-1844, described in her book as a triumph for the Nonconformists, Marianne Farningham and her siblings were among the first pupils. Her memories of school are dominated by stories of her willfulness and bad behavior. It was a brief respite from adult responsibilities. In 1846, her mother died, which changed the daughter's life fundamentally. It was the end of regular formal schooling. (It is interesting that her mother wrote, or had written for her, a will dividing up her few possessions and providing a spiritual legacy entrusting her children's goodness and well-being to God; Marianne kept the "pathetic document" all her life.)

Her mother's death, when Marianne was 12, was a schismatic break from a "normally" difficult, spirited childhood into an adult life whose unending responsibilities exhausted her: "My father often said that I never had a girlhood, but grew at once from a child into a women." The family were poor. Marianne became the unwilling substitute mother to her siblings. She prayed for a stepmother to release her from her duties.

The tension between her longing and the exacting claims of the family became explosive. There is a detached defiance in her record of that time, written 60 years later:

> I still think it was a bad time for a girl to pass through. Reading was my consolation, and I had not much time for that. My father gave us two monthly magazines . . . the "Teacher's Offering" and the "Child's Companion." In one of these was a series of descriptive articles on men who had been poor boys, and risen to be rich and great. Every month I hoped to find the story of some poor ignorant *girl,* who, beginning life as handicapped as I, had yet been able by her own efforts . . . to live a life of usefulness if not of greatness. But I believe there was not a woman in the whole series. I was very bitter and naughty at the time. I did not pray, and was not anxious to be good.

She sought and found support outside her own family. She felt drawn to the Sunday school teacher, Miss Eliza Hearn (her namesake) who also taught at the British School. Miss Hearn became her mentor. She resumed attendance at school, erratically, "that I might be with her." Her interest in writing seems to have become suppressed at this time, although one outlet was helping her father to sort letters: "Whenever there was an address in a particularly good handwriting, I copied it and tried to imitate it." She was later criticized for having no individual style to her handwriting.

Perhaps it was the constant tension that made it impossible for her to concentrate for the long periods remembered by, for examples, Charles Shaw. She was emphatically less inhibited at exposing the conflicts in herself and her family relationships. (Intergenerational conflict is more commonly addressed in the autobiographies and testimony of working women than in writing by men and significantly so around the issue of permission to write.)

Although her "ignorance was a constant burden," she found it impossible to concentrate on lesson books. Like Charles Shaw, she did not enjoy them. One summer she got up at 5:00 every morning and sat in the woods or meadows, trying to concentrate and failing. In any case, her father expected her to be at work long before 7:00. She too "tried hard to burn the midnight tallow." Sent to bed at 10:00, exhausted, she kept herself awake by the "immoral device" of drinking strong tea that she kept back from the afternoon's brew. She was overwhelmed by feelings of guilt at her deception. She also feared her studying would stir up her father's disapproval and anger. After a short time, she was discovered when a customer in the post office asked about the bedroom light shining after midnight. The evidence she was ordered to produce exposed the gap that she felt separated her reality and aspiration: "Some cheap copy-books with badly written pages, full of descriptions of the places that I had dreamed about, and never hoped to see."

Her father criticized the "dishonourable" act of saying goodnight under false pretenses, thus setting a bad example to the others. He "did not think such knowledge would ever be of much use to" her. Through the mundane world of geography lesson books, Marianne was still exploring the poetic fantasy world of the "Better Land." But usefulness for her, as her father saw it, meant usefulness to others, which he would have seen as the center of her life's meaning, expressed in the moral and religious absolutes of duty and service. The study of ideas and skills beyond those needed to prepare women for occupations that reflected the class, gender, and economic relationships of her time and place would have been unlikely to occur to many parents in the 1840s and 1850s. More ambitious aspirations reached dangerously beyond a working woman's place. Marianne Farningham expressed her knowledge of these boundaries in language that suggested her writing and studying was sinful. But she had already developed too strong a sense of her own needs, through learning, to be dispersed into other-centeredness, and eventually "yielded to temptation once more." She wrote and read at night, often falling asleep inadvertently, waking at 6:00 with all her clothes on and the candle burnt out. One night she woke to find her room on fire. Her father calmly extinguished the flames.

After the fire, there was a shift in relations between Marianne Farningham and her father. He "began to consult with me" about a return to school. The compromise was half-time work as a shoe binder and half-time school, with contributions from her for board and lodging. From this time, her study and writing activities took precedence and she worked with a series of teachers, all of whom were connected to local Baptist networks and through whom she studied a range of religious and scientific subjects, including astronomy. Her education moved from solitary learning within a conflictual family relationship to participations within local circles of teachers and friends around the Baptist church, which provided the setting around which working-class cultural and educational life clustered. The series of remembered names and places, subjects and debates, the draw of religion, the sense of belonging saturate the pages of her book as she draws away from family and into a public world. In comparison with Charles Shaw's narrative, with its unproblematized sense of gratitude to guides and companions, fateful coincidence, and luck alongside his hard work, Marianne Farningham lays claim to her own sense of agency in moving against opposition, proving herself through solitary study and stubborn opposition before she could get access to networks of people to steer her learning.

During her years as mother/sister, she had "written rhymes for friends' birthdays and other local happenings." Now she, and others, became influenced by Reverend J. Whittemore, Eynsford's Baptist minister and a writer: "His talk about books and newspapers and publishing matters generally quickened in the minds of several young people a latent desire to write." He also gave her a copy of *Jane Eyre*, "a book, my girl, which is thrilling everybody." His impact on her was strong. First of all, he was suggesting she read fiction, which she had been taught to think of as "wicked." Second, in encouraging her education and engagement with literature, he was suggesting a challenge to her accepted position in life. He replanted in her mind the ambition to write with " 'if you can write like this you will do something'. Alas! I only wished I could, and have been wishing it ever since." But authority and gender conflict were present in her interaction with Whittemore, although it was in a different form than previously. He confronted her with bullying and sarcastic criticism of her writing. He read her poems out loud, pointing out their weaknesses with "most aggravating scorn in his voice." She became afraid of his opinion and again turned to secrecy, working alone to improve her style and incorporate his criticisms. Some time later, however:

> A little girl, connected with our family, died, and I wrote some verses and sent to the child's mother, a lady of fine intellectual ability. She wrote a short account of her daughter and put my verses in it. Mr. Whittemore read this account during his funeral sermon. There was no name attached to the verses and he, believing them to have been written by the lady herself, said before reading them, "I do not know the author of these lines, but they are very beautiful." I was quietly sitting in our pew at the back of the chapel, with my father, and I had a moment of keen joy, not unmixed with pride, for I knew that nothing would have induced him to speak thus had he known the words were mine.

This second phase of learning to write resembled the first in the experience of humiliation as a motivation for persistence. There is nowhere a sense of self-doubt at her ability in her autobiography. She was not afraid to be different. Her feeling at the funeral scene was not humble gratitude for recognition from someone she revered but triumph that she had forced the recognition due to her, by both hard work and a necessary degree of deception and secrecy.

She continued to write poetry while she was at school and made a positive choice to leave home to become a teaching assistant in Bristol. When she returned home to look after a sick sister, she experienced it as the end of all her "best prospects in life." Eventually she became a teacher, a member of the Northhampton School Board, and gave lectures all over the country. Independently of Whittemore, she found her first publisher. When he asked why she had bypassed the journal he edited, she was confident enough to confront him with his destructive criticism and collaborate on a more equal basis. In 1867, she decided to write for a living. She wrote a biography of Grace Darling and appreciations of Harriet Martineau, Charlotte Brontë, and Elizabeth Barrett Browning, a fictional story arguing for the abolition of capital punishment, and her autobiography. Like many working-class auto-biographies, her narrative is punctuated with incidents that bring together her early steps in learning to write with her status as a published writer: acting as scribe for other people, noting changes in writing materials, referring to spelling, and quoting from early poems.

In her choice of subjects, Marianne Farningham showed her identification with other women writers whose lives had been difficult or isolated or who had rebelled against the weight of duty, which contributed to the legend of the neglected, tragic heroine. She also wrote about other working women writers. In a critical appreciation of the Blackburn factory worker and poet Ethel Carnie, she argued that her poetry was more likely to have been positively influenced by her factory work, against the idea that working-class circumstances are not fitting for creative work. Ethel Carnie often quoted from the article. One of her best-known poems describes experiences that Marianne Farningham shared: "I draw the blind and light the lamp/and in the world of books I go" (Carnie, 1907).[9]

Throughout her childhood and early adult life, writing was the means by which Marianne Farningham developed a sense of agency and permission to voice herself. She was more literally self-taught than Charles Shaw, Thomas Cooper, or other working-class men. Their learning experiences seem to exemplify learning through association and mutual support. She moved through situations of conflict, measuring herself against powerful authorities, into a position of strength, where she could work with others and use organizational groups, particularly around the nonconformist church, as sources of enjoyment, friendship, and companionship as well as education. She needed confidence in equality before she could collaborate with others such as Whittemore. She refused to accept the submissiveness and passivity expected of her in family life and tried to live up to others' ambitions for her outside it. She was able to learn independently, and she yearned for an independence she eventually won. Like Charles Shaw and Thomas Cooper, learning was a passion because it was experienced not only as earnest self-improvement but as pleasure, a source of enjoyment and a way of moving with the fantasy of "A Better Land."

## SEPARATION AND
## COMMUNITY WRITING PRACTICES

There was one postal delivery a day and towards ten o'clock the heads of the women beating their mats would be turned towards the allotment path to watch for "Old Postie." Some days there were two, or even three letters for Lark Rise; quite as often there were none; but there were few women who did not gaze longingly. This longing for letters was called "yearning." . . . "No, I be-ant especting' nothing, but I be so 'yarnin' " one woman would say to another. (Thompson, 1939, p. 101)

Separation from family and friends was part of the pattern of life in rural and urban communities in the nineteenth century. The notion of nineteenth-century villages or small towns as tight units fixed in time with little movement is far from true. Autobiographers and other writers witness the coming and going of migrant workers, itinerant people, domestic workers, circus people, and day laborers. They also describe long journeys to work to escape poverty or unemployment, to seek fortunes, or to take part in the activities of social and political movements. Decades of radical change connected to the Industrial Revolution affected everybody's lives: moves and journeys were commonplace; immigration and emigration were part of the pattern of life. Separation was a strong enough reason for people to learn to write.

The need for communication between families, lovers, friends, and political allies made writing and sending letters a key feature of nineteenth-century life. The significance of literacy in general, and letter writing in particular, is clear from life stories, magazines, journals, parliamentary papers, and other historical sources. Nineteenth-century novelists used literacy in many ways as a metaphor to underline class divisions or as the mechanism for representing social and economic mobility. It was a common device of short story writers in popular magazines, but also in major novels, to make the plot turn on a letter. Popular images often depicted the arrival of a portentous message or fateful letter. In autobiography, letters emerge as one of the most important forms for practicing literacy.

Letters, often anonymous, also had a role in the culture of public political and religious movements. In the actions of the machine breakers and rick burners, letters sent as threats or left behind as marks of their work signed, for example, Ned Lud or Captain Swing, have the feel of talismans, part of a ritualizing function that dramatized the protest. In the culture of religious organizations teaching literacy, such as Adult Schools, letters describing the conversion to literacy and sobriety were used and sometimes published in their journals. In sensationalist journalism, as well as in radical newspapers like the *Northern Star,* letters telling the true story or last-minute repentance of doomed criminals were fairly regular features as was correspondence between political prisoners and their families and supporters. Through newspapers, views were exchanged on many topics by letter, sometimes for months, and by people who may have had access to no other form of debate or discussion.

Private correspondence eased the pain of separation and brought longed-for news. It also had a practical value. One witness to the Select Committee on Postage in 1839 (pp. 261-262) emphasized the value that working-class people placed on the exchange of information, more likely to be trusted in written form, about wages, labor, and the availability of work in different parts of the country. This could have been more readily available if published material had been cheaper to receive, but information could also be transmitted through letter writing from people working away from their own communities.

The absence of letters was as significant as their arrival, because the regular visits of letter carriers had to be endured whether or not they had something to bring a person waiting for news. The sense of loss and absence was kept acutely present by regular deliveries of mail. It was more sensitive when letters brought bad news. The arrival of post was a very public affair, especially if a reader was needed. For people with relatives, friends, and lovers away, receiving letters, and the ability to write them, were associated with loss and longing but also with status and the power to overcome acute isolation.

Both writing and receiving letters was a social as much as a solitary activity. There were many ways of writing to people, and, in small communities, there were still unofficial scribes. In a family, one person was often responsible for correspondence. After the 1890s, it was common for a Board School educated child to be the scribe for older family members who did not have literacy skills. Awkward feelings between generations made this a source of family conflicts (see, e.g., Thompson, 1981, pp. 69-70, 91-95). Earlier, when the educational balance between generations was not so loaded, family relations around writing may have been less problematic. Joseph Arch's mother, who taught her son to write, "was a splendid hand at writing letters. A great many of the poor people who had children and relatives away from home, but who could not write to them, used to come to my mother and ask her to write their letters for them. She did it with pleasure" (Arch, 1966, p. 22).

The introduction of the prepaid Penny Post in the 1840s greatly improved the opportunities for writing letters. Before that, complicated systems of avoiding the prohibitive costs of *receiving* letters had to be found. One witness to the Select Committee on Postage (1839, pp. 261-262) remarked that, when people began their letters, as they often did, with the phrase "having obtained an opportunity," they meant a way had been found of avoiding the cost. The opportunities for alternative carriers were not always available, and the number of letters people could send was thus limited. Cost was a more significant constraint on communication than difficulties with literacy. Another witness, an educational publisher of elementary books, reported:

I have in service several people, male and female; I know one who has seven or eight brothers and sisters scattered all over the kingdom; I put the question to him the other day, How many letters do you receive from your relations? Not above one in six months, and hardly that. I said, if the postage were 1d or 2d, how many would you receive then? He said, we should be happy to receive one a week and to send one a week; some of them do not receive a letter in a twelvemonth. (Select Committee on Postage, 1839, p. 278)

The significance of letters was heightened by the conditions under which they were produced. The difficulty of the process is part of the painful consciousness of the absence of the person to whom one wrote. The following account from the biography of Will Crooks describes the joint letter writing efforts of his mother and one of his brothers and illustrates the way in which separation, ironically, became a focus for those left behind to work together to produce a piece of writing.

[They] spent nearly three hours one evening preparing a letter to a far-away sister, the mother painfully composing the sentences, the lad painfully writing them down. The glorious epistle was at last complete, the first great triumph of a combined intellectual effort between mother and son. Proudly they held the letter to the candle-light to dry the ink, when the flame caught it and behold! the work of three laborious hours destroyed in three seconds. It was more than they could bear. Mother and son sat down and cried together. (Haw, 1907, p. 18)

Another cost-related form of writing letters was to send blank letters. Before 1840 and the passing of the bill that introduced the Uniform Penny Postage, Samuel Taylor Coleridge recorded how he witnessed the postman deliver a letter to a woman at a cottage door in the Lake District and saw the woman refusing to pay the postage, which was one shilling. Coleridge paid (reluctantly), but, when the carrier was out of sight, the woman revealed that his money had been wasted. The sheet of paper was empty. She had an agreement with her son, who thus "wrote" to let her know he was well (quoted in Birkbeck Hill, 1880, p. 239). Various kinds of invisible ink were also used, witnesses reported to the committee, and notes were written on the sides of newspapers and printed material, which were carried more cheaply. The practices used to subvert the old systems were formidable and speak of a determination to stay in communication against all obstacles in the only way possible.

In small communities, the post office was an informal advice and social center oiling the wheels of working people's lives. Flora Thompson wrote of her work as a postmistress in North Oxfordshire, writing letters home for itinerant Irish harvesters who came in to send postal orders to their families. The postmaster or mistress, or the postman, read letters out loud to people who could not read. A mischievous version of this practice was described by

John Bedford Leno, Chartist and poet, in his autobiography. He became a postboy in Uxbridge and enjoyed the power "to create smiles and draw forth tears." He enjoyed the dependence of adults who could not read as he could. He relished "the possession of secret knowledge" he gained from reading the many letters sent without the luxury of sealed envelopes (Bedford Leno, 1892, p. 8). When a letter arrived safely, it had to be paid for, according to its contents and the distance covered, and "it was common to see the working people going from door to door, trying to borrow the postage" (Lawson, 1887, p. 40). The postmistress was also well placed to observe changes in writing practices. Flora Thompson noticed that the practice of sending "lace bedecked" sentimental Valentines, an old practice, changed in the nineteenth century into an outlet for comic cruelty and obscene abuse.

Buried under the detail of getting letters written and, if necessary, smuggled through a prohibitive system were the feelings of loneliness for people who had no choice in leaving home. This would be especially true of girls and women in service, but many others living in enforced isolation, such as prisoners, learned writing to communicate. Longing for contact with home could lead to a crisis without writing, if there was no one to help compose and transcribe thoughts onto paper. For those who could write, letters were relief from the isolation of life in large, empty, silent houses or in solitary kinds of agricultural work, for many girls, a stark contrast with the familiarity and noise of home, family, and village life. Ruth Barrow's letters to her future husband express her depression: "I am almost ashamed to say it, that I feel very dull and I cannot away with it at all. . . . It is such a great chaing, a chaing that can only be felt by those who have felt what it is to leave all they hold dear and have sought a home amongst straingers" (Horn, 1986, p. 105). Middle-class commentators were very alive to the moral dangers awaiting isolated women in their employer's houses. One witness to the Select Committee (1839, p. 258) warned of the problems when servants' "affections are obstructed" by not being able to afford postage.

The early life of Janet Bathgate, daughter of a poor agricultural laboring family, illustrates some of the issues involved in writing home. In the mid-to late 1830s, as a 12 year-old farm worker with five years of domestic service behind her, she could read just a little but could not write at all. She had been taught to embroider a little by her employer, "Peggie." Her job was to mind sheep, which involved long hours daily on her own "with no one to speak to, no one to give her a lesson" (Bathgate, 1894, p. 71). When her employer gave her a piece of cloth and some thread, she decided to embroider a "map" of the lakeside where she sat each day. Her family would have had no photographs or any way of visualizing how she was "placed"—her physical environment, her relationship with her employers, her health, her own sense of herself separated from her family without friends or peer group. Once she finished work on her sampler "map," she had no means of delivering it. She had no holidays and could neither write nor afford postage.

In the immediate confrontation between the inflexibility of the external world and her own needs, she focused on teaching herself to write as the means of action. She moved from despair at her own powerlessness to a discovery of the possibility of her own agency. She rediscovered in her pocket a letter from her father to her employer asking after his daughter's welfare. She had kept it to use as her lesson book for reading. She tried to copy the letters she was sure of, to shape her own words from those to write a letter home. She also possessed a religious book, *The Single Question,* which she read with difficulty but also used as a source of letters to form words. Her task was harder because she had no writing materials. Each letter was marked out by pricks with a pin head, written on a blank corner cut off her father's letter. Below is the text. Its received meaning can be read in the actions that followed its delivery: "My dear father and mother I am well thank God Peggie is kind to me I hope you are all well God bless you Your daughter Janet."

The way she organized the dispatch and delivery of her letter illustrates other obstacles to communication between separated working families. Her letter was tied in rag, unaddressed, and given to the letter carrier with verbal instructions to deliver it to the baker in the village closest to home, avoiding postal charges. Her parents could not understand the letter or the sampler. They were deciphered by a middle-class young woman who had been making "friendly visits" to the family. Her parents read in their daughter's letter both the call for help and the wish to learn. Janet was brought home and sent to school. It lasted only two weeks, before she had to start work to bring in money, but it was enough to make use of her next employer's offer to help her with reading and writing.

Her letter initiated a long chain of changes in her relationships with family and friends. Eventually she became the teacher at the local school. The distance she had traveled since her first piece of writing is signaled in her autobiography: "She would laugh when she remembered her first letter and the green map."

The crisis that activated a need and a desire to write brought about a change in her material circumstances and in her sense of self. The act of writing was a watershed between two versions of self. When she could not write, she experienced herself as the object and victim of other people's choices. From early childhood, brief and desperate opposition had given way to passive acceptance. The self who wrote the letter and developed into a writer has a positive subjectivity and sense of agency. Her autobiography registers this watershed. The middle chapter, titled "A First Attempt at Letter Writing," marks the divide.

For nineteenth-century working-class autobiographers, the first act of writing, as for Janet Bathgate, was often remembered as significant, particularly if it was linked to a major change, such as previously unimagined kinds of work or public prominence. Thus, like Thomas Cooper, "first attempts" are often reprinted. George Edwards, who could not read or write until taught as an adult by his wife, later became a union leader and MP. In his autobiography, he reprinted in full a letter he wrote on the subject of victimization following a strike action. The first pieces of writing, whether letter, poem, epitaph, or article, are the first links made in a connecting chain of experiences and events of which literacy is a crucial factor. To remember the first time is to remember the coming into life of the self who now writes, as defined by the act of writing, as well as the self who could so easily not have written.

The motives of Parliament and the Select Committee on Postage in the late 1830s reveal a web of social, moral, and, above all, economic preoccupations in relation to education and culture. Their questioning of witnesses on working-class writing practices focused on the question of whether the drastic reduction of postal duties would be financially compensated for by an increase in writing—and whether that in itself was morally and politically desirable. Thanks to people's ways of subverting prohibitive postal costs, we have no exact way of knowing how much people were able to write to each other. Tiny amounts of private writing have survived. It can be argued that autobiographers were exceptional—certainly published ones—and that men like Charles Shaw were a small minority. Evidence of how much people wrote to each other, whether in "real" writing or in the kinds of codes unearthed by Select Committees, is scanty. It seems likely that the large numbers of people affected by separation, the availability of supportive community networks to help write and deliver post, and the extent of the visual and literary references to letters meant that writing was a far more widespread activity than has usually been granted. Some examples have survived that express the complexity of people's lives, perceptions and feelings, as well as a dexterity and imagination with varieties of written English. They invite literary criticism more than patronage or genre classification. Below is one example. It is part of a love letter, written on September 9, 1868, from a *daily* correspondence between David Jones, a grocer's assistant in Rhymney, and his lover Mary Ann, who worked as a shaper in the hat trade. The spelling is as reprinted in Thomas Jones's *Rhymney Memories* (1938, pp. 36-37):

Last night no place to go put bed to comfort myself and soon as I got to bed my mind was running over the mountains towards the viaduck of Crumlyn and the heart of yours. Somehow it wouldn't sleep put it was telling me that the mind was lonely and no moonlight to accompany us both. Bed by myself but after all my eyes was still with me to I have nothing to do put try and look through the window and there I was listening to hear if I could see something but before long I could see the Bird in all colours come and told me you have a friend and the last word she said tonight after prayers was that she have a friend in Rhymney has a plant of love in his heart for which I wish you to comfort him before dark.

## CONCLUSION

This chapter is part of a wider study of working-class reading and writing practices in the nineteenth century that, by bringing out diversities and differences as well as shared experiences and circumstances, aims to work against the generalizing principles that are often used to label cultural and educational activities.

The split between the individual and collective modes of action, including learning, has been perpetuated from widely differing perspectives. Analyses on the left have placed organized collective action and radical education initiatives on one side. The autodidacts were situated on the other side (sometimes even the same people as the radical educationists but at a different time in their lives). They were self-improvers, Smilesian "self-helpers," seeking respectability and upward mobility, at worst "selling out." The nineteenth-century Tory view, demonizing collective activisms, scorning and belittling "self-education," has transformed itself and merged into a more traditional liberal view that romanticizes the individual learner-writer as a heroic figure but patronizes "him" as one who can never quite win. The autodidact is admired and contained at once in a consoling fantasy about working-class life. What left and right versions leave out is community or, rather, communities. Within communities, even if full-blown autobiographers were rare (which is doubtful on the evidence of present-day practices), writers in a broader sense were not. Writing was needed and practiced widely. The ways people learned writing and the circumstances in which they wrote and studied were enormously varied. But they were practices within communities or in relation to communities. They involved forms of solidarity and support unattached to "movements." They were real associations and, therefore, also involved a range of emotions and qualities, from anger and pain, vanity and confidence, and stubbornness and determination, little understood outside their learning communities and their class.

Although self-education is better understood as a social, rather than an individual, process, there is a sense in which the notion of self-education can be retained. It is the way in which articulation and extension of the idea of oneself were facilitated by writing. The writers above were people who knew that the self who lived without a signature and without a voice in a lettered world was a different self than one who could write.

The desire to write was created by the insistent presence and power of literacy around them and by a recognition of the denial of their real capacity. It could only be realized by persistent demands, by confronting conflict and the fear of disappointment, by activating allies, and by endless resourcefulness. They lived the difficulty and the empowerment of moving through to a different self-consciousness.

## NOTES

1. See Williams and Williams (1986). Their introduction reassesses the relationship of Clare's life and work to literary criticism of Clare's poetry.

2. Pamela Horn quotes an inspector as complaining, in 1845, that he often encountered the belief that education "unfits for manual labour," including the fear that "instead of plodding, hard-working peasantry, who do their labour much as the animals they tend, we shall have an *effeminate* class of persons" (Horn, 1980, pp. 135-136, italics added).

3. All subsequent Charles Shaw quotes are from his (1977) autobiography.

4. See Barrow (1986, especially chap. 6) for his concept of democratic epistemology.

5. It is still stated that there was little "culture" in working-class homes. Mingray (1977, p. 162) wrote of children that "they came from homes where there was rarely a book or any thoughtful conversation and their parents might be almost, if not quite, illiterate." To counter this view, see Vincent (1982, especially chap. 6).

6. See Gardner (1984, pp. 112-113). He notes that, although writing was more often taught to boys, and the teachers were more often men, it was not as overwhelmingly the case as has been thought.

7. See, for example, Pamela Horn (1981, pp. 528-529), where she wrote of the persistence of "the old attitude which saw the child as a small adult" and she quotes a Huntingdon man reporting of the late 1870s that "after I were about nine years old, I got real ashamed o' going to school when other folks went to work. . . . I used to get into the dykes and slink along ouiyt o' sight in case anybody should see me and laught at me."

8. The British and Foreign School Society was founded by Joseph Lancaster at Borough Road School in 1798. Throughout the period, it rivaled the National School system founded by Bell.

9. Marianne Farningham's review in *The Christian World* is quoted in Carnie's Preface to *Rhymes from the Factory* (1907).

## REFERENCES

Arch, J. (1966). *The autobiography of Joseph Arch.* London: McGibbon & Kee.

Barrow, L. (1986). *Independent spirits: Spiritualism and English plebeians 1850-1910.* London: Routledge.

Bathgate, J. (1894). *Aunt Janet's legacy to her nieces: Recollections of humble life in Yarrow at the beginning of the century.* Selkirk.

Bedford Leno, J. (1892). *The aftermath: With autobiography of the author.* London.

Birkbeck Hill, G. (1880). *Life of Sir Rowland Hill KCB and history of the Penny Postage.* London.

Bourne, G. (1984). *Change in the village.* London: Penguin.

Carnie, E. (1907). The bookworm. In *Rhymes from the factory.* Blackburn.

Castle, J. [born 1819]. (n.d.). *The diary of John Castle* (manuscript held in Bishopsgate Institute, London).

Clare, J. (1983). *Autobiographical writings.* Oxford: Oxford University Press.

Colls, R. (1976, November). "Oh happy English children": Coal, class and education in the North East. *Past and Present,* pp. 75-79.

Cooper, T. (1873). *The life of Thomas Cooper. Written by himself.* London.

Eliot, G. [Mary Ann Evans]. (1960). *Adam Bede.* London: Dent, Everyman's Library.

Farningham, M. (1907). *A working woman's life: An autobiography.* London.

Gardner, P. (1984). *The lost elementary schools of Victorian England: The people's education.* Beckenham: Croom Helm.

Haw, G. (1907). *From workhouse to Westminster: The life story of Will Crooks.* London.

Horn, P. (1978). *Education in rural England 1800-1914.* Dublin: Gill and McMillan.

Horn, P. (1980). *The rural world.* London: Hutchinson.

Horn, P. (1981). Country children. In G. E. Mingay (Ed.), *the Victorian countryside.* London: Routledge.

Horn, P. (1986). *The rise and fall of the domestic servant.* Gloucester: Alan Sutton.

Horn, P. (1986). *The rise and fall of the Victorian servant.* Gloucester.

Jones, T. (1938). *Rhymney memories.* Newton: Welsh Outlook.

Klingopolous, G. D. (1982). The literary scene. In B. Ford (Ed.), *The new Pelican guide to English literature* (No. 6, From Dickens to Hardy). London: Penguin.

Lawson, J. (1887). *Letters to the young on progress in Pudsey during the last 60 years.*

Mingay, G. E. (1977). *Rural life in England.* Dublin.

Select Committee on Postage. (1839). In *Parliamentary papers.* London.

Rushton, A. (1907). *My life as a farmer's boy, factory lad, teacher and preacher.* Manchester: Manchester University Press.

Shaw, C. (1977). *When I was a child, by an old potter.* Firle: Caliban Books.

Stephen, W. B. (1987). *Education, literacy & society 1830-70: The geography of diversity in provincial England.* Manchester: Manchester University Press.

Thompson, F. (1939). *Lark Rise to Candleford.* London: Penguin.

Thompson, T. (1981). *Edwardian childhoods.* London: Routledge.

Vincent, D. (1982). *Bread, knowledge and freedom: A study of 19th century working class autobiography.* London: Methuen.

Vincent, D. (1989). *Literacy & popular culture, England 1750-1914.*

Williams, M., & Williams, R. (1986). *John Clare: Selected poetry & prose.* New York: Methuen.

Williams, R. (1975). *The country and the city.* St. Albans: Paladin.

Williams, R. (1977). *Marxism & literature.* Oxford: Oxford University Press.

# 6

# *Community Publishing as Self-Education*

## GERRY GREGORY

**During the past two decades,** there has been in England a vigorous growth of community publishing. "Writers' workshops," "people's history groups," and so on have sprung up to stimulate and publish the work of local and predominantly working-class people; and groups set up for quite other community purposes have turned to publishing reminiscences, autobiographies, stories, poems, and so on.

In what follows we hear to begin with, and as a way into discovering the variety of community publishing, four working-class voices from a single project. Next, I sketch briefly the when, where, why, what, and how of community-publishing initiatives, before coming to "who"—the main focus. This chapter is chiefly concerned with the impact on participants of their participation in community-publishing ventures. In exploring the individual and collective experiences of participants, there emerges the portrayal of impressive forms of collective self-education whose successes are potentially of interest to educators generally.

### THE RANGE OF COMMUNITY PUBLISHING

Joe Louis was going to defend his world title and there was a lot of talk and interest in the fight. Mr Jessop's response to this international event was to stuff a Harding Bag with grass and hang it with a piece of string from the clothes line. Stripped to the waist and in his pit pants: originally a pair of his wife's bloomers with the elastic taken out of the legs—all the miners wore these down the pit—he thumped away at the bag. When he hit it a little bit too hard it would swing over and over the line and then he would stop, light a cigarette and wait until Mrs Jessop unravelled it for him. He was a funny man, Mr Jessop. He once tried to ride a pig. (Haythorne, 1981, p. 14)

Aye lad—a thowt a knew yer—an a nivver thow'd 'ad see
The day when tha'd go thro' them gates—and turn thi back on me.

The lines an' lines o' bobbies—tried ter keep us all i' place
But as the bus rushed by us all—a recognised yer face.

Ave worked wi' you for all these years—a thowt you were mi mate
Ave watched yer back while workin'—now a watch it thro' the gate.

Wi've shared us jobs, wi've shared us snap, wi've shared us soap i't bath
But ther'll bi no more sharin in the bitter aftermath. (Gittins, 1985, p. 44)

We didn't have a Sunday dinner for years after my dad died but my mother used
to slam the oven door so the neighbours'd think she was cooking. (Pensioner,
in Adam, 1987, p. 27)

All my life in Jamaica people is telling me, Come to England. Come to Mother
Country, it flow with milk and honey. Van come round with a film show in it:
Come to England. Come to Mother Country, which flow with milk and
honey. . . . in the end, I decide it best that I just go and see for myself. . . .

when I get here. . . . I telling you this: if there was a bridge across the sea long
as from here to Hell, I would have walk it. (Williams & Brown, 1987, pp. 33,
39, 41)

There is much obvious diversity in these fragments: prose/poetry,
speech/writing, light/serious, here-and-now/there-and-then, female/male,
Black/White, single author/coauthors, standard language/nonstandard language—and so on. There is also much less obvious diversity, especially in
respect of the processes of their production.

Evelyn Haythorne, miner's daughter and miner's wife, had turned up for
an evening class titled "Call That a Play? I Could Do Better Myself," and
whose theme was World War II. The convener, Brian Lewis, had said: "Tell
a story."

She told a story . . . and I said to her: "OK, that's bloody marvellous. Why don't
you write it down?" . . . She'd obviously got a real flair for language. She said
she couldn't. So I said: "What do you mean? Haven't you got time?"
"Yes, but I can't. I can't write." I said: "What you mean is you can't bloody
spell. And you probably can't punctuate." I said: "I'm fantastic at them. So *I'll*
do that, *you* do the writing."
A couple of weeks later, almost as a thowaway line, I said: "Did you write
anything?"

She said: "Yes." She gave me a plastic bag which was filled with pieces of paper. It looked as if it was any pieces she could get her hands on. What she had presented me with was 17,000 words of a manuscript.[1]

Early in the Miners' Strike of 1984-1985, Jean Gittins, daughter of a miner, mother of miners, helped to form North Yorkshire Women Against Pit Closures. A colleague said: " 'Barnsley Women Against Pit Closures' have brought a book out . . . Why don't you write us something?' So I thought, right I will." When their book came out, all proceeds went to the National Union of Mineworkers Solidarity Fund.

The Sunday lunch story, along with hundreds of others, was told to a team of community history workers who invited residents to come forward with writing and photographs and who sat in public libraries, a disabled miners' center, an Age Concern bus, to listen to anyone who wanted to talk about their experiences during 1930 to 1945.

> A book like this enables us to put many people into print. It also gives an impression, not just of one life, but of a community's life. (Adam, 1987, Introduction)

Of his collaboration with his friend and neighbor, Alfred Williams, Ray Brown has written:

> For the last few years we have exchanged views on many topics. In the summer of 1986 we began this book together. We have talked and tape recorded, read and re-read, drafted and re-drafted. Neither one of us could have written the book without the other. (Williams & Brown, 1987, Introduction)

Ray has added:

> I said to Alfred: "We'll either get it published or we'll do it ourselves, and your kids will have it for ever."

Alfred has made ironically clear the lack-of-schooling reasons for his needing Ray's help in telling his story:

> So it flogging at home and flogging at school. I look at this and I think I have to be at home, but I don't have to be at school. I decide I might as well make do with home flogging. (Williams & Brown, 1987, p. 23)

A different selection of fragments would have illustrated still greater diversity, especially diversity of *context* in a broad sense. Staying within England, the selection might have been widened from Yorkshire to include examples from, for example, Brighton, Bristol, Liverpool, London, Manchester, Newcastle upon Tyne, Nottingham, Wimborne. Different generative processes might have been represented:

> *Bristol as We Remember It* . . . emerged from the taped meetings we held in Barton Hill. The series began with a boat trip from the city docks through the Feeder Canal which flanks the estate. On this trip, the passengers took over the commentary, matching memories and stories to the places we passed. (Federation of Worker Writers and Community Publishers [FWWCP], 1978, p. 33)

Again, and of special importance here, there might have been examples of work arising from writers' "workshops" (e.g., in Hackney[2] or in Scotland Road, Liverpool[3]) or perhaps of collectively written material, such as QueenSpark's *Who Was Harry Cowley?*—a quest through many interviews for the identity of a former Brighton chimney sweep and tireless champion of the homeless, the unemployed, market traders, and pensioners.

If there is much variety in the publications and projects mentioned so far, they nevertheless also have much in common. All are by working-class people and deal with working-class experience; all involve autobiography; all involve "first-time-published" writers; none was produced with thought of personal financial profit; all appear within "community publications."

## Starting Points

Community publications have a variety of starting points. Pensioner participants in group reminiscence discussions at East Bowling, Bradford, decided to "make a book of it"; one book led to another—and to much more.[4] Publications frequently contain invitations for readers to make *their* voices heard;[5] and there are widely dispersed cases of one book triggering another.[6] It is not uncommon for people in a community to attempt, in book form, to recover a past of which newcomers or the young might otherwise remain unaware;[7] it is rarer for young people to reflect on their communities now.[8]

## Origins and Context

As the above implies, community-published projects are diverse as to origins. Some groups arose from Workers Educational Association classes;[9] others from adult literacy projects;[10] yet others from initiatives to provide bookshops for huge, urban and chiefly working-class populations hitherto lacking them.[11] Some publishing initiatives grew out of community action. For example, QueenSpark (Brighton) came into being as a "campaign to stop Brighton Council turning . . . The Royal Spa into a casino, and to get a nursery school, day nursery and park center instead" (FWWCP, 1978, pp. 150-157). Moves to resist the proposed changes (how things are) turned people's attention to the past (how things were) and led to the taping, writing, and publication of reminiscences. Scotland Road grew out of a tenants' campaign and rent strike whose effectiveness depended on the ability of working-class residents to start to write and "publish" letters, handbills, newsletters, and the like.

Elsewhere (Gregory, 1984), I have attempted to delineate the origins of community publishing and to portray cognate developments and the wider context in which they took root. Such a story incorporates Chris Searle's publication in 1971 of London schoolchildren's poetry and the resultant furor; the development of "History Workshop" ("a coalition of full- and part-time historians" committed to the democratization of historical practice; Samuel, 1980); the growth of oral history; and the new availability of simple and relatively cheap means of printing and publishing. The background to all this is characterized by a broad movement in the wider society away from passive consumption of meanings made and imposed by others and toward decentralism, "desubordination" (Miliband, 1978), and collective self-help. This movement, it must immediately be said, is counterpointed by contrasting centralist tendencies, individualist versions of self-help, "authoritarian populism," and so on.

## Products and Processes

Within community-publishing groups, there are varying and shifting emphases with respect to products and processes. Some groups welcome writing from "out there" in the local community with a view to possible publication;[12] others make the "workshop" central, sometimes stressing participatory processes before products to the point where print publishing is rare. Some groups regard pub readings and other performances as their main modes of publication while others combine a wide range of activities. Yorkshire Art Circus has developed a unique blend of books, linked picture exhibitions, and play performances.[13] Distribution of printed products is many faceted. Conventional systems are beyond the means of community-publishing groups, individually and collectively. Instead, publications are encountered typically in radical/alternative bookshops, at conferences and other gatherings, and in announcements and catalogues distributed by a variety of means, including inclusion in the "mailshots" of sympathetic agencies. As a matter of policy, QueenSpark sell their publications door to door in the East Brighton community where the project is rooted.

## Content and Forms

The large perennial themes of literature appear abundantly in community publications: birth, childhood, adolescence, work, love, marriage, war, bereavement, and so on. Certain matter and themes predominate: working-class home life and conditions; the solidarity and the claustrophobia of community relationships; streetwise childhood, and a schooling "nasty, brutish and short"; relationships with authorities; the experience of women and of minorities—or of both combined:

> One girl is born here . . . in most cases parents expect her like a girl born in Karachi or Bombay—instead of an apple, expecting a Mango. (Manju, in Centerprise, 1984)

Prose reminiscence/autobiography and poetry are overwhelmingly the dominant forms of community writing/publication. In addition, some groups have produced calendars (local pictures plus captions); others, sets of (radical/alternative) postcards; others again, cassettes-plus-printed-text packages.

## Aims

It is clear from the foregoing that community-publishing groups differ as to formal orientation, constituency, and ways of working. One group will produce chiefly poetry (sometimes a reflection of the interest of an influential member at the group's formation); another, autobiography; a third, people's history; another, Black writing; another, feminist writing; and so on. Within groups, emphases and relationships are constantly shifting. For some, the full range of group activity is important; for others, the group is merely a means of publication. As to explicit aims, there is both common ground and diversity. A widely proclaimed purpose is to redress a class/historical imbalance of access to writing and print:[14] to encourage "ordinary" people to present themselves rather than being represented and misrepresented.[15] A commonly held conviction is caught in the logo of Yorkshire Art Circus: "Everyone has a story to tell. We find ways of helping them tell it."

There is a widespread preference for publishing accounts of experience that readers are likely to recognize, and to identify with, as typical and in some sense representative. Publishing as offering a model of publishing possibilities and encouraging emulation has become a stable—perhaps secondary—explicit aim of some groups.[16] Some groups avow the aim of promoting writing as an intrinsically valuable activity.[17]

## PEOPLE AND PROCESSES IN COMMUNITY PUBLISHING

Among community-published writers, there is considerable variety: of educational experience (from graduates to adult literacy students); of age and experience (from those born in the nineteenth century to those still at school); of geographical origin, culture, and ethnicity. Preponderant are working-class women and men. They range from "first-time" writers to those who are already able to write but who are developing a new sense of the uses and potential of writing. All but a handful are, through involvement in community-publishing activity, "first-time-published" writers.

At the heart of community-publishing experience lie two related kinds of activity: one common and universal, the other less so. The first is writing in its inevitably solitary mode: the familiar individual struggle to make meaning on paper or screen. The second is collaborative. Examples are the critical discussion of writers' drafts in "workshop" settings and the processes of producing text by means of taping and transcribing conversation and negotiating approved versions and uses. The collaborative nature of community publishing, on the one hand, makes support available to otherwise isolated writers and, on the other, establishes the possibility of "writing" for those who are "nonwriters" (in a number of senses).

Clustered round this core are myriad publication-related activities. In individual homes, reclaimed huts, community centers, and assorted upper rooms above bookshops and advice centers; in quiet, northern postindustrial mining townships and in East London's noisy Whitechapel Road; to the sound of buffeting sea winds or reggae from the converted cinema down the street—publications are decided upon; text is chosen and edited; and work is undertaken on cost, format, layout, printing processes, print runs, publicity, launch parties, distribution, sales.

Around such work are other activities, "home and away." "At home"—if the group is one of the thirty or so belonging to the Federation of Worker Writers and Community Publishers (FWWCP)—there may be correspondence to be addressed: perhaps the draft agenda of a forthcoming AGM/ Conference to consider, including a proposal that the group should offer a "workshop." Further work may be needed on a group development plan to support a confident application to a Regional Arts Association (RAA) or—an optimistic one—to the Arts Council of Great Britain (ACGB). The latest FWWCP Executive minutes may have come in, stimulating discussion of whether an application for membership by a predominantly middle-class, feminist, socialist group should be supported or debate on appropriate FWWCP approaches to writing with racist/sexist connotations yet working-class authorship. Discussion may range from participation in a campaign to resist a local school closure, local authority spending cuts, and increased evening class fees to preparing for readings and staffing an FWWCP bookstall at a forthcoming local conference.

"Away" are public performances—in community centers, pubs, schools, workers' clubs, and street festivals—or attending conferences, the FWWCP AGM, "History Workshop," weekend or day schools, and so on.

## OUTCOMES OF COMMUNITY-PUBLISHING ACTIVITY

### "Experience" into "Knowledge"

Community publications make more widely available for readers the individual and collective experience of chiefly working-class writers/informants. This is typically explored in private conversation only and so tends to remain visible and unrecognized.[18] Thus the sense of what count as "legitimate" subject matters for publication is enlarged. For writers, this is interwoven with both an enhanced sense of personal and class collective worth and, arising from experience of a publishing process that bypasses the editors and other "gatekeepers" associated with "mainstream" publishing, a broadened, demystified, less reverent view of publication.

The materializing of "experience" into inspectable "knowledge" promotes for writers both "focal" awareness of and a critical perspective on their individual and collective experience, challenging the disposition merely to undergo it.[19] Arising from the writing/publishing process, there is often a palpable excitement of insight, realization, and fresh understanding.

Julia Benson Young (Yorkshire Art Circus) provides an example. From reflecting, in the process of writing autobiographically, on her late father's life, she achieves fresh insight:

> It's strange, but now, twenty years on, I have a little understanding of what he was going through. He saw his lot as a lifetime of being misunderstood, of never being able to prove your worth, of having people around you who keep pulling you back. He died in loneliness years before he stopped breathing because his family didn't have the intelligence to understand. I feel like that. In that sense he lives through me. (Young, 1984, p. 14)

Of the discovery of processing experience in poetry, the same writer comments:

> I don't know why I started to take poetry seriously. One day it seemed to be there, something like a voice in your head. From then on I began to see things differently. It was as if I'd opened my eyes for the first time. (Young, 1984, p. 20)

Ron Barnes (Centerpiece, Hackney) reflects on his motivation to write *A Licence to Live:*

> I realized there was something wrong with life—or with me. I tried to find out by writing.[20]

On the outcome, he comments:

> For years I'd had the feeling of confusion: that nothing had been planned, that life had just gone on. And by writing that it give me some sort of perspective: you could see back as clear as you'd ever see back.

and in a poem:

> And so a different mind,
> Nothing sudden or spectacular,
> But smoothly it moves like a tide,
> And leaving with each sweep upon the beach,
> Pebbles. Clear. Smooth. Precious.
> No longer out of reach. (Hackney Writers' Workshop, 1978, p. 6)

In group discussion, a member of the East Bowling (Bradford) History Workshop hints at a process through which experience has become contextualized and reordered, perhaps—given 1930s/1980s parallels—for new kinds of *use*:

> *Now* they (our family experiences during the Depression) have come into perspective . . . *then* it was a piece of useless information—didn't mean a thing; *now* I've got it into perspective.[21]

Jean Gittins (North Yorkshire Women Against Pit Closures) refers to new understandings of herself derived from the writing process. In the struggle to formulate these, she wins a further understanding—a generalization about her writing experience:

> I have learned about myself since I've been writing. . . . People say, well didn't you know that? I could have told you that. And I hadn't realized: I hadn't noticed in me characteristics that I would have noticed if it was somebody else. Obviously you don't, do you: you're inside yourself, you aren't standing outside yourself seeing. That's it: when you write it's like standing outside, looking at yourself. When you read your work: Oh, did I write that? It's like looking at yourself.

The ordering, reordering, and articulation of "experience" into "knowledge" can occur equally in the tape-transcription/writing partnership processes by which many community publications have been generated.

Toby (Bristol Broadsides), out of the process of producing his autobiography, moves toward an understanding of what determined his lifelong experience as tramp and social outsider, and inductively to the general truth it exemplifies:

> As a young man on the road people said: "Why don't you get married? Why haven't you?" Now I couldn't have given them the answers then; but I think I

can now. It's psychological: from a boy to a man I was tied, which was unnatural. [As the eldest son of a poor widower who had become paralyzed, Toby was kept home from school to attend, precociously, to his father's every need.] And when I think of marriage that's another tie—perhaps not so bad as the other form—but I've got an idea that's why I've never, ever—because it's another tie. . . . If you've got a young mind, a growing child, what's put in that mind is *there,* isn't it. . . . It won't change, not in basic things.[22]

Reflecting on a session of intense introspection and analysis (lasting far into the night and accidentally untaped) undergone by Alfred Williams in developing the concluding passages of his autobiography (shown in one of the introductory quotations), and on Alfred's reaction the next evening to Ray's attempt to capture in writing what had been said and meant, Ray Brown reports:

He is not a touchy bloke, Alfred, but he put his arm on my shoulder and said: "My God, you've got it. You've got what I'm trying to think". . . . It was very moving because it is like a shell cracking open after seventy years and all of the strangeness of another world outside it.

There is, of course, a substantial academic "literature" exploring the effects on cultures and individuals of the repertoire addition involved in moving into writing and print. This body of work is both recent (chiefly 1970s and 1980s) and disparate (including contributions from, for example, linguists, literary theorists, educators, and anthropologists). It features claims about the nature of the writing process—such as entailing feats of "decentration" (Moffett, 1968, after Piaget) and depending on and promoting the ability to cater to the needs of absent readers to produce "autonomous" text; as admitting of highly detailed planning of text; as producing outcomes of thinking for unhurried scrutiny; as accompanying and promoting the development of potent cultural achievements such as categorical, analytic, context-independent, abstract thought (Ong, 1982); as facilitating a growth of reflexivity and inwardness (Oxenham, 1970). Further and strong claims are that writing "is . . . a different form of language in its own right which can lead to different ways of thinking" (Perera, 1986, p. 107) and that it "enables one to understand one's emotions and the emotions of others" (Wilkinson, 1986, p. 3). However, Scribner and Cole (in Whiteman, 1981), from their work among the Vai people of northwest Liberia, have argued against a "monolithic model of what writing is and what it leads to"; Brian Street (1984, 1985) has stressed the importance of understanding the logic of oralities and scrutinizing claims for the superiorities of particular (e.g., academic) versions of literacy; and David Olson (1980, p. 188) has cautioned against treating written language and literacy as "homogeneous."

Taken as a whole, this literature is longer on logic and theory than on evidence. Also, it has been relatively rare for professional writers to introspect their writing processes in print. Donald Murray (1982) is one exception; novelist Stan Barstow (1986, pp. 4-5) is another:

> When you are at work with the pen in your hand . . . you are activating a part of your mind which you normally use only spasmodically. It is the part of your mind in which memory lies, and all the meaningful connections which will form the patterns of your fictions. And inspiration is most likely to visit you when you are hard at work.[23]

The growing body of testimony from community-published writers, sampled above (see also Shrapnel Gardener, 1985), informs the inquiry into how writing impinges on individual writers. It appears to offer evidence supporting some of the claims made—including some of those in the academic literature cited above. However, it is clearly difficult to separate the act of writing from that of the unhabitually systematic reflectiveness that typically attends it. That is to say, the systematic reflection and ordering are necessary to effective writing, whereas writing is not necessary to systematic reflection and ordering.

Roger Mills (Tower Hamlets Arts Project) has stressed precisely the connectedness for him of these related experiences:

> I always think I've got quite a disorganized head. I don't focus on any one thing particularly long, and perhaps don't go a long way down the road of anything. Writing is a great focus, really: it gives you the ability to keep on a train of thought, almost to solve problems. . . . It helps encapsulate ideas, really. It's quite a tight discipline, isn't it. You've got to get down your thoughts on a subject—or on how you see a whole sequence of events happening. It helps me focus on all sorts of things.[24]

## Understanding Writing

Community-published writers have, through their new experiences, achieved insights into the nature and potential of writing. This is especially marked, of course, in the case of those working within adult literacy projects. For some, old assumptions are overturned—about, for example, revision:

Then I think "No, that's not right" so I change it and I think of something else and add it on. People write on a piece of paper and then read it back to themselves—go over the spelling and go over the punctuation. Then you've got a piece that's readable. *I've discovered that this is normal practice; I've always thought that it was just a bad habit of mine to go over re-correct and scrub out.* (italics added)

Also challenged are assumptions about spelling (sometimes promoted by teachers' emphases on this aspect of writing). In their place have developed understandings of its proper place—at the "proofreading" stage—and of the disabling consequence for writers and writing of worry about imperfect command of the system:[25]

I went round a word like enormous. I would write big. As soon as I stopped bothering I were off. (Write First Time, 1978, p. 61)

It was late at night when I realized I should have left a note for the milkman for two loaves for the children's dinners the next day at school. The trouble was I could not spell loaves, and my husband was asleep. After four attempts it went as follows. "Milkman. Can you leave me a cut loaf. Thank you. PS Make that two" (Morley & Worpole, 1982, p. 78)

Fresh characterizations of writing are developed:

It's very hard to have *that conversation with yourself,* which is what you have to do if you are writing alone. (Write First Time, 1978, p. 53)

New understandings about style and register are also developed:

A lot of people lose what they want to say—they learn to write in a certain way and then lose what they are saying. When we were doing "Write First Time", there was this country lad talking about when he was a young lad and he set fire to a barn and he said "and then we hoofed it!" But when he wrote it down he said "We ran away", and it lost the feeling completely. It was nothing. But when it was in dialect, it was very entertaining. But if he was writing for a job and he said "We hoofed it", he wouldn't get the job. (Write First Time, 1978, pp. 70-71)

But when you go for a job it's different, you put on a tie, so you write in a different style. (Write First Time, 1978, p. 70)

New realizations are gained about the communicative potential of writing:

You can send writing all over the place. If it's spoken only one person hears it at a time, if it's written lots of people hear it. (Write First Time, 1978, p. 60)

## "Primary Literacy"/"Secondary Literacy"

J. S. Bruner (in Wilkinson, 1986, pp. 3-4) has stressed the importance of *using* writing as opposed to merely possessing the capacity to write. Such use makes us "profoundly different in mental powers" and "moves language towards 'context-free elaboration' ".[26] While the great majority of community-published writers were literate to start with, for most, the full range of writerly potential had remained latent. Writing had been marginal in their lives—used perhaps for shopping lists, bureaucratic forms, letters, notes on the doorstep for an extra pint of milk. Commercially produced devices had removed the need for even this writing.[27] These writers had immense power available, but in cold storage: In Wilkinson's terms, they *possessed* vast potential but put it to little active *use*. Put differently, they were arrested in one part of the constellation of writing experience: frozen into a sort of restricted, "survival," *primary literacy*.

The "after" picture is different. For many, there has been palpable growth as writers; and new *experiences* of the writing process have conferred fresh insights—new *knowledge*—of both that process and the nature and potential power of *writing itself*.

Early on, Roger Mills came to appreciate the heuristic function of writing: "In writing I can formulate my ideas and even find out answers to things I didn't know before" (Hackney Writers' Workshop, 1977, p. 60). Joe Smythe (Commonword, Manchester) has referred to the potential of writing for enlarging consciousness: "If I didn't write I don't think I'd have a view of the world nor the end of our street."[28] And Evelyn Haythorne has referred to a fresh sense of the importance of particularity and accuracy in writing: "Writing . . . has taught me to be more observant." A strengthened sense of audience—of the needs and possible prejudices of unknown readers—has reinforced the importance of taking pains over surface as well as other features of her writing: "I have learned . . . how to constantly use my dictionary. To check the written word again and again."

What has been entered into is a sort of *secondary literacy:* a range of writing habits, practices, and attitudes that embody an enhanced realization of writerly potential. This label refers to genuinely interactive writing for a range of readerships in a variety of forms and for a variety of purposes:

writing that, through the multiple drafting processes that attend preparation for publication, and with increasing precision, approximates ever more closely "what is meant" (Olson, in de Castell, 1986, p. 157). In addition, moves into secondary literacy imply further sorts of development. These include a heightened metalinguistic awareness—here, centrally about the nature of writing—and new realization of the cultural-political significance of writing as well as of print and publishing and their developing technologies. They also involve uses of writing for communicating with the self. There is opportunity here to refer only to some of these gains.

## Gains: Personal and Collective

Several writers, in reflecting on their writing, have stressed personal benefits in terms of feeling. Jennifer Wallace (Hackney Women Writers):

> Sometimes I wrote to relieve boredom, having been unemployed for years and sometimes because it helped to sort things out. (Hackney Women Writers, 1984, p. 143)

Bill (Write First Time), in a formulation akin to Suzanne Langer's (1953) theory of literature as giving form to feeling, remarks:

> Why I write is to put my feelings on paper, to put what I feel down. I feel as if it helps to discover myself. (Write First Time, 1978, p. 143)

Toby (Bristol Broadsides), reflecting on the production of his autobiography, comments:

> Strange to say, but since the publication of that . . . I've sort of gone ahead more. A wonderful feeling. I've reached what I call clarity of mind.

Jean Gittins:

> Some people have to have alcohol, some people have to have another cigarette: I find that I am happier—this sounds totally crude—but it's like being consti-pated if you like. If I don't write it down when it comes into my head to write down I can't concentrate on anything else and nothing else comes. The more I let it flow the more comes: not always what I expected and not always what I want. . . . And sometimes there's nobody there to listen.

## "Therapy"

Fred Williams (Hackney) portrayed the release aspects of writing in his poem "Liberty Pen" performed at a miners' benefit event (August 1984), and Joe Smythe has referred, neatly, to his sometimes use of writing poetry as a "getaway vehicle."[29] Several community-published writers have referred explicitly to the therapeutic function of their writing activity:

If I was full of worry I would sit and write it all down as a sort of therapy

I would say that writing now has enormous importance in my life. It provides a centre when I don't know where I am, a therapy for banishing the blues and a feeling of satisfaction from the sheer physical act of writing that I don't get from anything else

To me writing can work as therapy. Where some people can bare their soul to another person I can't, but by writing down how I feel enables me to put my thoughts and feelings in the right order.

Clearly, the practice of using writing *privately* in an attempt to sort things out, solve problems, unburden oneself, and thus feel better, must be widespread. However, that community-*published* writing should be classified as "therapy"—and, therefore, patronized and dismissed—has always been vigorously resisted by community-publishing groups. Perhaps three points need to be made.

First, there seems little doubt that there is therapeutic *intention* on the part of the organizers of some projects outside the field under consideration but not entirely remote from it[30] and therapeutic *outcome* for participants in many writing projects. Second, much turns on distinguishing between acknowledging the by-product outcomes for writers, on the one hand, and giving appropriately serious attention, on the other, to texts in the context of the processes and social formations that produce them. Olive Rogers is surely right to point out (in an FWWCP internal report, 1982) the danger of failure to make that distinction: "Once we are seen as therapy, we do I feel lose credibility as serious writers."

Third, some attention needs to be given to the ambiguities in the term *therapy* and distinction made between soothing/healing and private/public therapeutic outcomes for writers. As is shown below, there have been outcomes of restored vigor and confidence—both personal and collective: that is, in class, in language and cultural experience, and in the possibilities of claiming more equal access to writing and publishing.

## "Nostalgia"

Dismissal as "therapy" has been paralleled by dismissal of reminiscence activity as "nostalgia." As well as unaffectionate accounts of grim conditions and experiences, there has been, in the work of some groups, fond recall of warm relationships and joy snatched against odds, some reconstruction of the "good old bad old days," airings of the "sociological myths" (Laslett, 1980) of organic community and extended family, and so on.[31] Such material has sometimes been marginalized as "nostalgia" and its publication characterized as quietistic in tendency. The charge is usually made in ignorance of important contextual information. The developmental trajectory of one group illustrates the importance of appreciating this. East Bowling (Bradford) has been described as

> an area which had once been a proud and busy industrial community, with a real village life of shops and pubs and local characters . . . now a back-water, tucked away between a six-lane highway, a now virtually unused park and the uncrossable ring road. It was an area with no recognition and no center.

Building on an unemployed man's interest in local history, the East Bowling History Workshop came into being. Led by community educator Lydia Merrill,

> one of the prime objectives would be a social get-together and an opportunity for people to look back on their lives and re-evaluate them, sharing experiences and developing an historical perspective and analysis. I hoped to help people to formulate, even formalize, their own history— what eventually happened was this and far more than this. (FWWCP, unpublished conference material, 1980)

"What happened" included a process leading to publications (East Bowling History Workshop, 1980, 1981, 1983), the formation of a group (with constitution and officers), negotiations for funding, and so on. Of most significance here, group members reflecting on their collective *past* provided a context for the analysis of *present* circumstances and proposed *future* developments. The outcomes were impressive: a group member, during a visit from "an official body" was reported as describing the workshop as "giving life back to our village";[32] group members became the prime movers in developing a community association, in opposing a local redevelopment plan (a campaign involving the preparation and distribution of leaflets, including their translation into Hindi and Urdu), and in founding and producing a community newspaper.

In this as in other cases, it is clear that proper evaluation of texts and of reminiscence/writing/publishing activity depends on an understanding of contexts of process and production and, in particular, of the relationship of writing and publishing to other forms of community *action*.

## Confidence

Growth of confidence through writing, publishing, and attendant activities is a constant theme among community-published writers reflecting on their recent experiences:

> It has also bolstered up my confidence a little and I find I can talk to people better, where at one time if someone spoke better English than me . . . I was very conscious of my Yorkshire accent.[33]

Ron Barnes (Hackney) speaks of a newfound confidence, for example, in confronting housing officials:

> It was because I'd become aware of the unfairness. . . . At one time I wouldn't say boo to a mouse . . . I had the courage, I suppose, to stand up and say well no, this is it. I'm not standing for it.

Ray Brown reports an outcome for Alfred Williams of the book they produced:

> Alfred has said that friends of his from the allotments have come and said "we can hear your voice." And that gives him a great deal of satisfaction. And he now actually speaks much more clearly than he did—and again it's something to do with being big inside his skin, I think. He's more significant to himself than he was, and so he projects himself more than he did.

East End (of London) pensioner Gladys McGee, who joined Basement Writers (Stepney) after becoming a widow in 1973, who has published much poetry (print and cassette), has won a street poet award at Covent Garden (*Time Out* July 22-29, 1987, p. 122) and is the subject of a film, ended her volume *Shoutin' and Bawlin'* (1982, Tower Hamlets Arts Project) this way:

> Please read my poetry
> Don't let me write in vain,
> Because it is only in the last few years
> I found I had a brain.

Awareness of effects on others of writing/publishing activity is often involved in the realization of confidence. Looking back with newly achieved confidence and insight, Kevin (Write First Time) comments:

> Most working people . . . feel they are not important. . . . If all the people realized the ability they really have inside, really respected themselves the way they should and were proud of themselves the way they could be, then there would be all sorts of problems for the people who run our society.

This is borne out by Jimmy McGovern (Liverpool). After weeks of getting nowhere with the Department of Health and Social Security:

> I went home and I wrote this lovely letter, at length you know, something like a sixteen-page letter, protesting about the way I'd been treated over a certain case. . . . Anyway, lo and behold this chap writes back who was the kingpin of the dole and gives me a private interview apologizing for the way I'd been treated. . . . I think they must have said to themselves . . . this person can sit down and write a letter, he can cause a spot of bother.[34]

## Costs

Against the array of benefits for participants in community-publishing activity there are, of course, as there have typically been for working-class writers in the past,[35] costs to be reckoned. These costs have been of two broad kinds: the first related to the *what* of written/published material, the second to the *fact* of writing/publishing.

All published writers risk incurring the first kind of cost: ". . . the persons who writes stands up to be shot" (Barzun, in Whiteman, 1981, p. 70). Roger Mills has described just such vulnerability:

> If you've written something it becomes public property, really. If I write, if I state some opinion . . . then you've got the right to come up to me and say, "What's this you say here? I think you're totally wrong." You've laid yourself open far more than if you'd just said it in a pub. If you've said it in print it is open for anyone to come up to you and say "Justify this!"

Risks and costs may well in various ways be increased in the case of first-time-writer autobiographers. Doris White has described the "bad part" of writing/publishing her exuberant book (about her life, including work in the London Midland and Scottish Railway Works, at Wolverton, Bedfordshire, during World War II), referring to letters in the press by local residents stating I had something wrong. One stating that I was laughing and drinking while our boys were being killed, another that I knew nothing of Auschwitz etc. That was really hurtful.

The reactions of a writer's family may be unpredictable. Recalling responses to *A Licence to Live* (1974), Ron Barnes has reported:

> Distant relatives who I had not seen for years phoned to congratulate me. They felt sure I was on my way to fame and fortune. "We hope so, especially the fortune bit."

However, his second book—in which he moves out from autobiography to include stories of the wider family—produced a different reaction:

> *Coronation Cups and Jam Jars* (1976) . . . unfortunately had quite an adverse effect on some of my relatives. I had gone a bit too far, relating to things that were an embarrassment to the family. I had spoken about things that should never have been mentioned, in or outside the family. "In print as well, what a disgrace."

The *fact* of writing/publishing at all has entailed a scale of costs for writers to set against the "benefits" sketched above. Evelyn Haythorne:

> When I tried to write at home the family used to laugh at me. My scribbling as it was known by them was a family joke.

Jean Gittins:

> When people come and say to me, "Oh, you're the poet" I could curl up and die. . . . In our community . . . if you talked with one word where everybody else would use four or five—"Oh, oh, listen at her!" So you'd got to be very careful. . . . it was a situation where if you were going to be accepted you didn't have to be different. . . . Even with my Mother: she'd talk about "getting ideas above your station." I've sat down sometimes and wanted to write about something and she'd say: "Oh, you'll finish up in a garret with a candle. That wont earn your living. Why don't you get interested in something that'll—look at Clarice: she's doing shorthand and typing." . . . It was always a bit of an embarrassment, really. It was like having freckles.

Another community-published writer has reported:

I used to read passages to my husband at the beginning, but he seldom if ever reads books and after a while showed a great deal of resentment if not hostility to my writing. . . . As to other people's reactions, they varied between "Isn't that interesting, I'd love to read some of it," to "I'd love to write too but I haven't the time" to "It's all right for some but I have to *work* for a living!" I have learned to anticipate people's reactions over the years and mainly keep the fact of my writing to myself—like a secret vice.

Finally, Julia Benson Young has reported a spectrum of reactions, from the painful to the hilarious:

Many of my so-called friends also abandoned me at this point. . . . The family stopped indulging what they called "my little hobby" and got down to the serious business of ignoring me. . . . The family couldn't see what . . . writing poems had to do with being a wife and mother. . . . They told me quite clearly that if I went [to a week's residential course at Northern College] they would wash their hands of me. The year I went on that course no one sent me a birthday card or Christmas present. . . .

It was at this time that I collided with Mrs Brittan as she came out of Rossington Co-op and got another perspective on poetry. "Hello love," she said. She speaks with a really loud voice. "Your Val's been telling me you're writing poetry." Then, bending closer, "Eh lass, you want to be careful, they reckon those poets are sex mad and too much of the other sends you barmy. They all end up in the nut house. You know they bloody do, mark my words." . . .

He [a man who had attended her poetry reading] had bought a copy of the anthology . . . I was intrigued when he said he would like to discuss my work further with me, so could he take me home. . . . On the way home we talked about the book and poetry in general but, on stopping the car a few doors from my house, he turned, gave me a straight look, and said, "Can I screw you? I've never had it with a poet before." Bloody hell, I thought, but since it had been a sophisticated evening I kept my cool and said, "And what makes you think you can have it with one now?" "This". He read with difficulty. Attlee Avenue isn't well lit.

"Women are liberated.
Can I make love to you?
Women are liberated
Let me make love to you." (Young, 1984, pp. 23, 24, 27-28)

## COMMUNITY PUBLISHING AND
## COLLECTIVE SELF-EDUCATION

The range of outcomes, pleasurable and painful, inscribed in the testimony sampled above suggests a striking *educational* dimension to participation in the processes of community publishing. Fresh insights into and estimations of self and others; gains of self-esteem and confidence; enlargement of experience and interests,[36] including, often, the reading habit; "getting ideas" above what had come to be settled for as one's "station"; new awarenesses, for example, about language, writing, and publishing; recognizing and coping with the difficulties, disorientations, and alienations concomitant with all this; reassessing, adapting, "assimilating, and accommodating"—such are the traits of that educational dimension.

Ron Barnes's assessments, while acknowledging both profit and loss yet confirming a balance of advantage, have related his community-publishing experience specifically to formal education experience in an interesting way:

> Centerprise brought out in me, in one year, what 9 years of schooling failed to even notice. (*Hackney Gazette,* February 4, 1975)

> I've learnt a lot . . . from the people at Centerprise. They've had a lot of problems with me and I've had a lot of problems. . . . It's given me a lot of problems as well as a lot of advantages. But I'd rather be as I am through that than ever go back to what I was before.

Indeed, the palpable *educational* success of the community-writing/publishing projects under consideration must be set in the context of participants' previous educational experiences. Many have referred to their schooling in terms of failure and disaffection. Evelyn Haythorne:

> I was pretty decent at writing at school but wasn't encouraged at all by the teachers.

Joe Smythe:

> I had no interest in writing at school and less interest in school itself.

Ron Barnes, again:

> I don't think they really told you anything. You give them the book—all the books go in—they corrected your spelling, give you two out of ten, which I

usually got for writing, put on "Untidy work" or something like that. They never really got the child and really showed it.[37]

Schooling may have acted as often to control literacy as to expand it, and, for many participants in community writing and publishing activity, literacy had at school been taught as a technology detached from experience. Disillusioned with its meager contribution to their lives, they had staged a tactical withdrawal from it.[38]

By contrast, in the by-product educational achievements of community-publishing projects, a cluster of educational principles have been vindicated. These include starting from the known and familiar (actual needs, interests, experiences, subject matter, and an actual, envisioned readership); the importance of learning *contexts;* and the learning potency of participation in whole literary-production processes and of bringing *joint attention* to bear on experience and the testing of existing "knowledge"—developing new knowledge in so doing. Also highlighted have been the possibilities of writing as a social activity as well as the importance of dismantling such barriers between "teacher" and "taught" as are dysfunctional and of eschewing dependence on authorities (and an associated general dependence) in favor of collective autonomy and models of partnership to which participants contribute according to ability.

The writers studied have become committed to writing as a "form of life"—and, in many cases, have become different kinds of *readers*—precisely because the tendencies inherent in their formal education have been reversed. The close relationship to the rest of their lives of what they have written and published is self-evident; the skills and "knowledge" developed are "really useful";[39] and their uses of literacy impressively extended. Associated with all this is a developing and palpable sense of control and power—both personal and, more distinctively, collective—and a developing sense of *community* and, in some cases, of *class.* Indeed, the experience of community-publishing projects that has given rise to these developments may be characterized precisely along these axes: as both "community and class educational."

## Community Education

Community education is among the most potentially fertile notions on the current educational "agenda." Some local education authorities have taken on the notion as a principle of provision; agencies (funded and voluntary) exist for its promotion; a burgeoning multistranded "literature" is in formation, for example, one strand starting from the now well-established idea of the "community school," another focusing primarily on adult education provision in a community context. The relationship of community education to, for example, community organization, development, and action is debated. A spectrum of meanings is emerging from, at one end, the integrated use of resources allocated to different sectors for the provision of educational and related experiences, as well as the flexible timetabling of professionals, to a root-and-branch characterization of an education "of, by, with, about, and for the community," at the other. Formidable obstacles are immediately seen in respect to any reconciliation of the latter program with the constraints of a state provision characterized by cultural hegemony, increasing centralism, and accountability to remote agencies or to clients cast as consumers rather than of immediate communities—tendencies that have found their most extreme expression this century in the provisions of the Education Reform Act (1988).[40] Probing the notion itself entails confronting the possibility that stress on (local) community may mean narrowness of vision, limited investigation (such as of the factors that condition learners' circumstances), "imprisonment" in a locality, and parochialism.[41]

It is, therefore, unsurprising that, alongside some exciting innovatory ventures[42] in which "stronger" definitions have begun to be realized in curricular practice and patterns of learning and teaching, some (perhaps many) provided schools bearing the "community" label have advanced little beyond making the school hall available for wedding receptions.

The writing and publishing ventures under consideration, while, of course, entertaining other than educational purposes, seem nevertheless prototypically "community educational." For example, as we have seen, the experience formulated and explored is immediate and rooted in the known community (in contrast, say, to the traditional subject matter of "history"). It is interesting that "oral history" activity and "writers' workshops" often crop up as examples of good, innovative *community education* practice.[43] The community "educates itself": At one time, Centerprise (Hackney) ran an Illich-type "learning exchange." Writing/publishing often arise out of community action or give rise to it, as we have seen. *Community* comes, in these processes, to imply "the sharing of interests as well as of geography" (Selby, in Thompson, 1980, p. 65): that is, people brought into communication. Such processes enact the principle of participants "alternat(ing) between the roles of student, teacher and person" (Fletcher in Thompson, 1980, p. 67). Tellingly, the identity of communication process with community process was spelled out a quarter of a century ago by Raymond Williams:

Since our way of seeing things is literally our way of living, the process of communication is in fact the process of community: the sharing of common meanings, and thence common activities and purposes; the offering, reception and comparison of new meanings, leading to the tensions and achievements of growth and change. (Williams, in Kelly, 1984, p. 50)

## Working-Class Education

The educational *processes* as well as the products of community-publishing projects are for the majority of participants class confirming and class specific. They involve exploring, from experience, what it is to be part of a social formation that is shedding settled identities and, in response to the undermining of employment and security, undergoing radical transformation. Viewed thus, these processes constitute what Weber called an "arousing pedagogy" and correspond to Paolo Freire's notion of exploring one's "thematic universe" as the first stage in "a critical process" (in Lovett et al., 1983, p. 31). Participants, in Freire's terms, are freed to "speak their own word"; and, in contrast to the tendency of formal schooling and the rhetoric of training schemes, *social rather than personal inadequacy* is taken as starting point. The "pedagogy" (which in education is never a secondary matter; the "how" of learning being always part of the "what") lays stress on the informal, collaborative, democratic—a collectivity relating to the traditionally distinctive working-class characteristic of "solidarity." The "skills" are practical and the understanding developed bears relation to the Chartist notion of "spearhead knowledge" (Johnson, in Clarke et al., 1979, p. 86; Lovett, 1988, p. 153). Again, the processes under study accord with Gramsci's principle that working-class people should submit their thought to the discipline of the written word—on the grounds that only through mastery of print might their thinking gain the precision necessary to engage in debate with intellectuals (Gramsci, 1971, p. 29). This enables those to become *producers* of print who have hitherto been, asymmetrically, *consumers* only—thus moving them toward a balanced literacy—fitting Freire's model in which literacy is seen as a basis of a "pedagogy of the oppressed." The *products,* which in their particularity signal an attack on any tendency to view working-class people as masses,[44] bid to become important resources of a "working-class curriculum" and—as has been shown to happen in the case of Black reflections on Black experience (Grambs, in Entwistle, 1978, p. 191)—to rebuild confidence among working-class learners in what E. P. Thompson has called "the agency of working-class people."

In their educational aspects, working-class writing and community-publishing processes are suggestive of practices that signal ways *forward* toward an indigenous and derived rather than an imposed working-class education that starts from and builds on an understanding of the realities of working-class experience. They also direct our attention *back;* for, viewed as collective working-class self-education, they suggest strong correspondences with an early tradition of working-class self-education whose existence has begun to be uncovered and importance made clear.[45]

## CONCLUSION

Community writing/publishing activity, viewed as collective self-education, has begun to realize in practice what teachers have regularly been exhorted to arrange, for example:

paying attention to the speech/writing relationship, language variety/standardization and differential cultural usage;[46]

affording interactive contexts for writing (like those of speech) and plentiful opportunity for "conferencing" (Soter, 1987) about what is written;

starting (for example, in autobiographical publication) with "near" writing for a "near" readership and, in many instances, moving from the "dialogic" (taped interview/transcript) to the "monologic" (solitary writing) (Moffett, 1968);

keeping in focus actual experience and concerns—"action knowledge" rather than "school knowledge" (Barnes, 1976);

promoting collaboration in the writing process (Graves, 1984; Smith, 1988, pp. 64 ff.); and

enacting "relevant," meaningful writing rather than the inert velleities of trivial curricula (Medway, 1986, p. 3; 1988, pp. 26-35) that are recalled with such distaste by so many "first-time" or "second-chance" writers.

Self-education approaches, like all others, clearly raise difficulties. Gramsci stressed the limitations in terms of the breadth and rigor of knowledge based purely on personal experience and was concerned about the need to make the transition from "common sense" to "good sense." It is clear that, in the case of a group of working-class—or, indeed, of any other—students, collective self-education will lead only so far. It is also clear that sustained, systematic, rigorous *study* is required, for example, of interpersonal communication and of personal and collective circumstances and the forces shaping them. Moves into writing/print within participation in collaborative processes constitute crucial learning experiences. Viewed in the context of education, however, they are but necessary early moves. For all this, the striking success, as collective self-education, of community writing/publishing projects, inscribed in the accounts of their participants, bids for recognition in any analysis and rethinking of the processes of popular education. Regarding writing development, specifically, this is decisively about "use"—with people coming to find writing important, sometimes vital, to the business of their social living.

## NOTES

1. This was taken from an interview in 1982 (see Gregory, 1986, pp. 381, 414). Unless otherwise indicated, the writers' testimony cited in this chapter is drawn from conversations, interviews, and correspondence conducted—or from individual/group recordings made at my request—between 1978 and 1988.

2. See for example, Hackney Writers' Workshop (1977, 1978, 1979), *Hackney Writers' Workshop* 1, 2, 3.

3. See items in FWWCP (1978) and Scotland Road Writers' Workshop (n.d.).

4. The trajectory of the East Bowling (Bradford) History Workshop has been from a starting point of reflecting on the past to a sharpened perception of objectionable developments in the present. This has led to the foundation of a community newspaper and to this theme beginning to play an organizing, focusing role in the entire project. Such contextual information illustrates the need to understand the contexts and complexities of "community-publishing" activity and the relationship of writing and publishing to community action. It also cautions against reading and assessing texts without reference to their contexts of production, distribution, and use and against the overhasty dismissal of reminiscence as nostalgia, "false consciousness," and so on.

5. "We know that other Somali women have different experiences. We ask these women, who have so much history, to write their knowledge down, for themselves, for their children and for their people" (Adan, 1987, p. 65).

6. Centerprise (Hackney), QueenSpark (Brighton), and Yorkshire Art Circus provide examples.

7. See, for example, the People's Press of Milton Keynes section of FWWCP (1978, p. 136); Centerprise (1979; piecing together the story of a community located in a cluster of East London streets demolished in 1970 to make way for tower blocks); and projects in East Brighton and (in progress) at Meanwood, Leeds, Yorkshire.

8. See, for example, Strong Words (1978, pp. 10-12).

9. Examples include Hartcliffe (Bristol) WEA, People's Autobiography of Hackney, and Tottenham Writers' Workshop.

10. Examples include Gatehouse (Manchester), Peckham Publishing Project, and Write First Time (Bedford)—a British newspaper produced by basic education students.

11. Centerprise (Hackney) and The Bookplace (Peckham) are examples.

12. A typical pattern is for groups to become overwhelmed by the number of publishable manuscripts submitted. To deal with this, advice on self-publishing (sometimes collected into

booklets) is developed (such as with Centerprise, Peckham Publishing Project, QueenSpark, Yorkshire Act Circus). QueenSpark have, in addition, worked on a nonthreatening, constructive, "people's criticism service" (QueenSpark Development Programme 1984-1987 Brighton; 1984, Section 13.)

13. Evelyn Haythorne's first book (see above) doubled as exhibition catalogue to an accompanying exhibition of pictures. Work is in progress to produce a dramatized version (for community centers, welfare centers, pubs, and so on) of Williams and Brown's *To Live It Is to Know It* (see above).

14. "Our aim is to give local people the chance of putting their words and writing into print" (Bristol Broadsides, 1979, cover; see also Strong Words, 1977, p. 94).

15. "Why let other people speak for you?" (Commonword, 1977, p. 112). Of his coming to write, Bill Naughton (1988, p. 34) observes: "Almost every portrayal of working-class life and people that I read was a travesty."

16. For example, Peckham Publishing Project; Trinity Arts, Birmingham; In the Making, Wolverton, Buckinghamshire.

17. The Liverpool 8 group is an example: "Our common interest is in the craft of writing . . . to encourage ordinary men and women to express their talent through writing" (*19 FROM 8*, n.d., p. 1).

18. "Hidden from history," in Sheila Rowbotham's formulation. Ken Worpole (1977, p. 10) has suggested that "working class life should not just be reflected upon in the pub and the front room, but should be published in the long-lasting form of books, as a permanent record and as a means of maintaining an active local class-consciousness." Tillie Olsen (1980, p. 10) has referred to "the silence of centuries as to how life was, is, for most of humanity."

19. On "focal" and "subsidiary" awareness, see Polanyi (1959).

20. Ron Barnes was brought up in straitened circumstances, suffering considerable ill health. After minimal schooling, he went from job to job before trying the "taxi knowledge" (learning the streets of London, with bicycle and A-Z, in preparation for a stringent oral examination with a taxi license at stake). *A Licence to Live* (1974) brought him considerable attention and some modest ACGB support for the writing of *Coronation Cups and Jam Jars (1976)*. He has published poetry as a member of Hackney Writers' Workshop and is a prolific painter (of scenes of East London working-class life).

21. Compare Bill Naughton's (1988, p. 32) reflection on starting to write in his thirties (in the 1940s): "Often it seemed that one had to write about a happening in detail to spot what it meant and what forces were at work to cause it."

22. After his mother died (in 1918), Toby (aged 11) began to look after his paralyzed father, missing most of his schooling in the process. When his father finally went into a nursing home, Toby (now 24) was alone and homeless. He became a tramp. After eight years (1938)—including a spell in Canada stowing away on freight cars just as he had stowed away to get there—Toby came off the road and settled in Bristol. Settling down meant living in Leigh Woods in a hut built of bits of timber and so on brought down by the river, sharing the woods with other tramps, and reading. Toby stayed there 29 years, until the press and TV took an interest: "I would still be in the woods but my hut was set fire to by hooligans" (Bristol Broadsides, 1979, p. 24). He now lives in a caravan that goes with his night watchman job. Toby's tape/transcript autobiography (above) attracted a good deal of attention (local press, radio, and the like).

23. *The Paris Review* Interviews (Series 1-6, involving some 75 writers and published by Penguin Books) contain other insights.

24. Roger Mills (b. 1954) went to a Clapton (East London) comprehensive school, then to a succession of jobs as "paste-up man" in various advertising studios. Seeing the work of Ron

Barnes and Vivian Usherwood in the Centerprise bookshop emboldened him to take in the writing he had been doing. He joined Basement Writers, Stepney, and later Hackney Writers' Workshop. In 1978, *A Comprehensive Education* was published; later he became a paid worker in Tower Hamlets Arts Project (THAP). In 1983, he became FWWCP Literature Development Worker for the South of England (while FWWCP funds lasted). He has written and published short stories and also has completed a novel as well as a commissioned play about the Seige of Sidney Street.

25. Leslie Wilson's *Dobroyed* (1981) is especially interesting with regard to spelling and punctuation. This story of a year in Dobroyed Castle Approved School near Todmorden is (to quote the blurb) "the result of years of struggle by the author to put down as honestly and accurately as possible his experience there and to overcome his lack of conventional spelling and grammar. . . . Weeks and months were spent painstakingly writing down, rewriting and copying from exercise book diaries. . . . The finished work has been re-written four times." The Commonword team record: "There was a lot of debate about turning all of Les's book into standard English. The problem is that while there are occasional difficulties for the reader in Les's original, Les's unique vision would be lost if his language was taken away from him." Hence the standard conventions of punctuation and spelling have been deliberately ignored. A result of this is that, while meaning is scarcely ever at risk, the book demands considerably closer attention than most comparable autobiographies. The effect seems to be twofold: to give confidence that "messages" may well be of interest despite problems with the surface features of the "medium" (counterbalancing the usual tendency for the latter to be invoked to dismiss the former), and, at the same time, the difficulties experienced point to the value of working at the conventions. Meanwhile, the tidying up of some of his "miscues" ("Rochstale," "cellisiter," "comforsation") would count as a loss—as would any ironing out of his highly distinctive idiolect: "The actule city of Todmorden may well of skiped and just jump for joy of freedom exitemants" (on his release from Dobroyed).

26. John Wilson (in de Castell et al., 1986, p. 28) has also questioned the value of "the mere *ability* to read and write . . . if that ability is never or rarely used . . . if any motivation or desire to read and write is wholly lacking." In the same volume, Harvey Graff (p. 65) quotes M. M. Lewis: "The only literacy that matters is the literacy that is in use. Potential literacy is empty, a void."

27. Examples are "Two pints, please" arrow indicators for the milk deliverer, standard shopping lists with boxes to tick, greetings cards with standard texts requiring only signatures and perhaps a few kisses.

28. Joe Smythe is a Manchester railway guard (after years of unsettled employment). An "omnivorous" reader from the start, he got interested in poetry after being given a volume of Shakespeare. Contact with the Commonword (Manchester) group led to remarkable developments: In 1979, two volumes of poetry were published (*Come and Get Me* and *Viva Whatsisname*). In the same year, he conceived the idea of publishing a further volume in 1980 to mark the 150th anniversary of the Liverpool-Manchester Railway. He approached the NUR, who promptly agreed and gave him three months sabbatical to get on with the project. Working the "night shift" while his family were asleep upstairs, Joe met the deadline with *The People's Road*. (Compare Bill Naughton, 1988, p. 5, "I read of a working-man who had passed an examination by going to bed after work and getting up at midnight and studying, and I decided to try it for writing.") Joe Smythe writes prolifically—including in moments snatched in sidings between journeys. (Compare such earlier working-class writers as Samuel Bamford, B. L. Coombes, Roger Dataller, and, famously, Alfred Williams, the "hammerman" who worked in Swindon Railway Works with his daily stint of Greek verbs chalked up before him.) Joe has

published poems in several magazines, including often in *Voices;* he is especially interested in industrial poetry and working-class history.

29. See also Jim Allen (1986, inside front cover): "Grandad had a bird in a cage—he himself was also in a cage as most of us are. But unlike the bird we can escape by reading and writing."

30. Some conference titles give a sense of such projects: "The Therapeutic Uses of Reminiscence" (Exploring Living Memory) and "Life Histories and Ageing" (British Society of Gerontology/Oral History Society).

31. However, the general "nostalgia" critique seems often to be based on unfamiliarity with whole group processes as well as on limited samples and sampling of texts. It tends to ignore, for example, evidence of strategies designed precisely to probe people's sense of "the past/present relation": "One subject in particular had come up repeatedly: the impression that violent crime today was far worse than in the past. To an elderly person, the media coverage of street crime and violence generally seems a daily and brutal contrast to childhood memories of peaceful neighbourhood life. We . . . wanted to challenge statements such as 'Youths never attacked old ladies in our day', and got copies of one or two local press reports from the 30s to extend the discussion" (Lee Centre, n.d., p. 17).

32. Report from the FWWCP AGM/Conference "workshop" (April 1980). See also reference to action undertaken by literacy students when faced with proposals for the abolition of the Adult Literacy Service in Leicestershire (Clare, 1985, p. 47).

33. Note also the growth of confidence inscribed in Norma Dolby's diary (1987). Again, note the poignant story of Gladys Allsop "burst[ing] into print at 79" after writing "little more than notes to the milkman since leaving school" and days before her death following a fall (*The Guardian,* March 17, 1987, p. 11).

34. See also Jeffrey and Maginn (1979), where the transforming effect of coming to write in a context of urgent purpose is clear in the case of Jimmy (pp. 10-11) and Mike (pp. 28-29).

35. John Clare (1792-1864): "I live here . . . like a lost man in fact like one whom the rest seems careless of having anything to do with—they hardly dare talk in my company for fear I should mention them in my writings & I find more pleasure in wandering the fields then in mixing among my silent neighbours" (Letter to John Taylor, February 8, 1822, in Tibble & Tibble, 1951, p. 132; note the correspondence with the experience of Susan Price, in Morley & Worpole, 1982, p. 58).

B. L. Coombes (1893-1974): "The village disliked but faintly revered 'that writer chap', pardoning Coombes his non-attendance at pub and Chapel and the ritual Sunday promenade" (Philip Norman, *The Times,* December 29, 1979).

Willy Goldman (1940s East End Jewish working-class writer): "My brothers, who are in the clothing trade, unfortunately still have to do a great deal of work from time to time. But they claim, proudly, that I, who am a 'writer', have brought the family tradition of loafing to its logical conclusion ("A Saint in the Making," quoted in Worpole, 1983, p. 109).

Bill Naughton (1910-): "Anyone hoping to write a story would have been regarded as odd, not all there" (Naughton, 1988, p. 4). Later (pp. 84-85), he refers to "people who didn't do real work—and real work was something that brought the sweat out . . . were all in some way estranged from our people and their feelings."

36. "While doing the book we have got interested in things that we thought could never be for us. We started going to meetings such as to set up evening classes with the Workers Educational Association, to Wakefield Community Arts Panel to apply for a grant, to Normanton to meet a group of miners wives who were thinking of doing something similar to us" (Ledger, Watkin, & Wall, 1986, p. 23).

37. Note the tendency among teachers still to dwell on the surface, "secretarial" aspects of pupils' writing remarked on in the HMI surveys of secondary schools published in 1979 and 1988.

38. Compare examples of similar withdrawal from literacy drawn from both cargo cults (New Guinea and Melanesia) and from "an all-black working-class community in the Southeastern United States" supplied by Shirley Brice Heath (in de Castell et al., 1986, pp. 18, 22). Heath observes (p. 24), pertinent to the developments under discussion here, "learners frequently possess and display in out of school contexts skills relevant to using literacy that are not effectively exploited in school learning environments." Jeffcoate ("Class of 87," in *The Times Educational Supplement,* July 31, 1987, p. 17) refers to school pupils' "inability or reluctance . . . to write anything longer than a single paragraph"; and Czerniewska, Director of the SCDC National Writing Project ("Write on Time," *The Times Educational Supplement,* October 18, 1985, p. 20), remarks that "children don't expect to write much after they leave school."

39. See Johnson (in Clarke et al., 1979; Lovett, 1988). Heath (in de Castell et al., 1986, pp. 22-23) comments: "The extent to which physiologically normal individuals learn to read and write depends greatly on the role literacy plays in their families, communities, and jobs."

40. The Education Reform Act (ERA) of 1988, among many other measures, imposed on 5-16 education a 10-subject "National Curriculum" in terms of "attainment targets," "programmes of study," and pupil testing at ages 7, 11, 14, and 16—all to be defined in detail in statutory orders by the Secretary of State for Education and Science. The Act requires the publication of overall school scores and the introduction of local financial management and "open enrollment"—intensifying school-school competition in the education marketplace. According to one estimate, the Act gave the secretary of state 182 new powers; certainly, it altered radically the distribution of power between the traditional partners in education: central government, local government, and schools.

41. For example, see Merson (in Golby et al., 1975) and Entwistle (1978, pp. 88 ff.). For a fuller critical discussion of community education ventures, see Cowburn (1986).

42. For example, Lee Centre (n.d.).

43. For example, Lovett et al. (1983, p. 39).

44. See Williams (1958). Ron Barnes's (1974, pp. 85-86, 1976, p. 66) distinction between the "rough" and "posh" ends of his street and his family (and, in a sense, of himself) is part of a project against seeing the working class as amorphous. See also Willmott (1979) for similar distinctions: such as between parents who kept their children in and those who let them play where and with whom they liked.

45. Harrison (1961, 1984), Simon (1965), Kelly (1970), Johnson (1979), and Watson (1989) have done important work in recovering and celebrating a distinct, minority tradition of education both of and *by* the working-class: of self-help initiatives of a formidably energetic, serious, committed kind—whose impetus was sometimes the suspicion with which working-class people viewed various sorts of educational *provision* (Webb, 1955, p. 18) and sometimes linked with political activism and sometimes not. Included in this outgrowth of working-class self-education are the corresponding societies of the 1790s: the "dame" schools ("truly indigenous institution[s] for educational self-help of the working-class"; Harrison, 1984, p. 288), whose numbers were hidden by the way "state-istics" were produced (Yeo, 1986, p. 309); the prodigious and often solitary activities of extraordinary individuals; remarkable hall-building initiatives; "communal reading and discussion groups [and] facilities for newspapers in pub, coffee house and reading room"; the educational activities of friendly societies, cooperative societies, and trade unions; and, especially close to community-publishing groups in many respects, informal, spontaneous, mutual improvement societies.

46. "I used to admire people who said, 'There are two points. . . .' But they really meant 'on the on hand this, on the other hand that.' It's a process you have to go through. The respect falls away. You realize you're not inferior" (contributor at FWWCP AGM and Conference, 1981).

## REFERENCES

Adam, R. (Ed.). (1987). *When poverty knocks on the door loves goes out of the window.* Castleford: Yorkshire Art Circus.

Adan, S. et al. (1987). *Daqan miyi iyo magaalo* [Our strength comes with us: Somali women's voices]. London: Somali Women's Association.

Allen, J. (1986). *So you may know.* London: Peckham Bookplace.

Barnes, D. (1976). *From communication to curriculum.* Harmondsworth: Penguin.

Barnes, R. (1974). *A licence to live.* London: Centerprise.

Barnes, R. (1976). *Coronation cups and jam jars.* London: Centerprise.

Barstow, S. (1986, December). Working-class artistry: Stan Barstow searches for his soul and finds his voice. *Writers' Monthly,* pp. 4-5.

Bristol Broadsides. (1979). *Toby.* Bristol: Author.

Centerprise. (1979). *The island.* Hackney: Author.

Centerprise. (1984). *Breaking the silence: Writing by Asian women.* Hackney: Author.

Clare, M. (1985). *The adult literacy campaign: Politics and practices.* Birmingham: University of Birmingham, Centre for Contemporary Cultural Studies.

Clarke, J. et al. (Eds.). (1979). *Working class culture: Studies in history and theory.* London: Hutchinson (in association with the University of Birmingham, Centre for Contemporary Cultural Studies).

Commonword. (1977). *Coming up.* Manchester: Author.

Cowburn, W. (1986). *Class ideology and community education.* London: Croom Helm.

de Castell, S., Luke, A., & Egan, K. (1986). *Literacy, society, and schooling: A reader.* Cambridge: Cambridge University Press.

Dolby, N. (1987). *An account of the Great Miner's Strike.* London: Verso.

East Bowling History Workshop. (1979). *Bowling tidings.* Bradford: Author.

East Bowling History Workshop. (1980). *East Bowling reflections.* Bradford: Author.

East Bowling History Workshop. (1981). *East Bowling schools.* Bradford: Author.

East Bowling History Workshop. (1983). *Do you remember? Further reflections.* Bradford: Author.

Emig, J. (1983). *The web of meaning: Essays on writing, teaching, learning, and thinking.* Upper Montclair, NJ: Boynton/Cook.

Entwistle, H. (1978). *Class, culture and education.* London: Methuen.

Federation of Worker Writers and Community Publishers (FWWCP). (1978). *Writing.* London: Author.

Fletcher, C. (1980). The theory of community education and its relation to adult education. In J. L. Thompson (Ed.), *Adult education for a change.* London: Hutchinson.

Gittins, J. (1985). *Strike 84-85.* Leeds: North Yorkshire Women Against Pit Closures.

Gittins, J. (1986). *Striking stuff.* Bradford: "1 in 12" (Publications) Collective.

Golby, M. et al. (Eds.). (1975). *Curriculum design.* London: Croom Helm.

Grambs, J. D. (1965). The self-concept: Basis for re-education of Negro youth. In Lincoln Filene Center for Citizenship and Public Affairs, *Negro self concept*. New York: McGraw-Hill.

Gramsci, A. (1971). *Selections from the prison notebooks of Antonio Gramsci* (Q. Hoare & G. N. Smith, Eds.). London: Lawrence & Wishart.

Graves, D. (1984). *A researcher learns to write*. London: Heinemann.

Gregory, G. T. (1984). Community-published working class writing in context. In M. Meek & J. Miller (Eds.), *Changing English: Essays for Harold Rosen* (pp. 220-236). London: Heinemann.

Gregory, G. T. (1986). *Working-class writing, publishing and education: An investigation of three "moments."* Unpublished doctoral dissertation, University of London.

Hackney Writers' Workshop. (1977, 1978, 1979). *Hackney Writers' Workshop 1, 2, 3*. Hackney: Author.

Hackney Women Writers. (1984). *Hackney women writers*. Hackney: Author.

Harrison, J. F. C. (1961). *Learning and living: 1791-1960*. London: RKP.

Harrison, J. F. C. (1984). *The common people*. London: Fontana.

Haythorne, E. (1981). *On earth to make the numbers up*. Pontefract: Yorkshire Art Circus.

Hendrix, R. (1981). The status and politics of writing instruction. In M. F. Whiteman (Ed.), *Writing: The nature, development and teaching of written communication: Vol. 1. Variation in writing: Functional and linguistic cultural differences*. Hillsdale, NJ: Lawrence Erlbaum.

Jeffrey, J., & Maginn, C. (1979). *Who needs literacy provision?* London: Macmillan.

Johnson, R. (1979). "Really useful knowledge": Radical education and working-class culture, 1790-1848. In J. Clarke et al. (Eds.), *Working class culture*. London: Hutchinson.

Johnson, R. (1988). "Really Useful Knowledge" 1790-1850. In T. Lovett (Ed.), *Radical approaches to adult education: A reader*. London: Routledge.

Kelly, O. (1984). *Community, art and the state: Storming the citadels*. London: Comedia.

Kelly, T. (1970). *A history of adult education in Great Britain from the Middle Ages to the twentieth century* (2nd ed.). Liverpool: Liverpool University Press.

Langer, S. K. (1953). *Feeling and form*. New York: Scribner.

Laslett, P. (1980). Educating our elders. *New Society, 13*, 560-561.

Ledger, J., Watkin, P., & Wall, J. (1986). *Livin' in t' pit yard*. Huddersfield: Activan and Woolley Colliery Writers and Photographers.

Lee Centre. (n.d.). *Something to say*. London: Author.

Liverpool 8 WW. (n.d.). *19 from 8*. Liverpool. L8 WW.

Lovett, T. (Ed.). (1988). *Radical approaches to adult education: A reader*. London: Routledge.

Lovett, T. et al. (1983). *Adult education and community action*. London: Croom Helm.

McGee, G. (1982). *Shoutin' and bawlin'*. London: Tower Hamlets Arts Project.

Medway, P. (1986). What gets written about. In A. Wilkinson (Ed.), *The writing of writing*. Milton Keynes: Open University Press.

Medway, P. (1988). The student's world and the world of English. *English in Education, 22*(2), 26-35.

Merson, M., & Campbell, R. (1975). Community education: Instruction for inequality. In M. Golby et al. (Eds.), *Curriculum design*. London: Croom Helm.

Miliband, R. (1978). A state of de-subordination. *British Journal of Sociology, 29*(4), 399-409.

Mills, R. (1978). *A comprehensive education*. London: Centerprise.

Moffett, J. (1968). *Teaching the universe of discourse*. New York: Houghton Mifflin.

Morley, D., & Worpole, K. (1982). *The republic of letters*. London: Comedia.

Murray, D. M. (1982). *Learning by teaching: Selected articles on writing and teaching*. Portsmouth: Boynton/Cook.

Naughton, B. (1988). *On the pig's back*. Oxford: Oxford University Press.

Olsen, T. (1980). *Silences*. London: Virago.

Olson, D. (Ed.). (1980). *Social foundations of language and thought: Essays in honour of J. S. Bruner*. New York: Norton.

Ong, W. (1982). *Orality and literacy: The technologizing of the word*. London: Methuen.

Oxenham, J. (1970). *Literacy: Writing, reading and social organisation*. London: RKP.

Perera, K. (1986). Grammatical differentiation between speech and writing in children aged 8 to 12. In A. Wilkinson (Ed.), *The writing of writing*. Milton Keynes: Open University Press.

Polanyi, M. (1959). *The study of man*. London: RKP.

QueenSpark. (1984). *Who was Harry Cowley?* Brighton: Author.

Samuel, R. (1980, February 15). *Truth is partisan*. New Statesman.

Scotland Road Writers' Workshop. (n.d.). *Scottie old and new*. Liverpool: SRWW.

Shrapnel Gardeners. (1985). *Conversations with strangers*. London: Write First Time.

Simon, B. (1965). *The two nations and the educational structure 1780-1870*. London: Lawrence & Wishart.

Smith, F. (1988). *Joining the literacy club: Further essays into education*. London: Heinemann.

Smythe, J. (1979a). *Come and get me*. Manchester: Commonword.

Smythe, J. (1979b). *Viva whatsisname*. Manchester: Commonword.

Smythe, J. (1980). *The people's road*. Manchester: NUR.

Soter, A. O. (1987). Recent research on writing: Implications for writing across the curriculum. *Journal of Curriculum Studies, 19*(5), 425-438.

Street, B. V. (1984). *Literacy in theory and practice*. Cambridge: Cambridge University Press.

Street, B. V. (1985). Literacy: "Autonomous" v "ideological" model. *Viewpoints: A Series of Occasional Papers on Basic Education, 4*(10).

Strong Words. (1977). *Hello, are you working?* Whitley Bay: Author.

Strong Words. (1978). *Missile Village*. Whitley Bay: Author.

Thompson, J. L. (Ed.). (1980). *Adult education for a change*. London: Hutchinson.

Tibble, J. W., & Tibble, A. (1951). *The letters of John Clare*. London: RKP.

Watson, M. I. (1989). Mutual improvement societies in nineteenth-century Lancashire. *Journal of Educational Administration and History, 21* (2), 8-17.

Webb, R. K. (1955). *The British working class reader*. London: Allen & Unwin.

White, D. (1981). *D for Doris, V for Victory*. Milton Keynes: Oakleaf.

Whiteman, M. F. (Ed.). (1981). *Writing: The nature, development and teaching of written communication: Vol. 1. Variation in writing: Functional and linguistic cultural differences*. Hillsdale, NJ: Lawrence Erlbaum.

Wilkinson, A. (Ed.). (1986). *The writing of writing*. Milton Keynes: Open University Press.

Williams, A., & Brown, R. (1987). *To live it is to know it*. Castleford: Yorkshire Art Circus.

Williams, R. (1958). *Culture and society*. London: Chatto & Windus.

Wilson, L. (1981). *Dobroyed*. Manchester: Commonword.

Willmott, P. (1979). *Growing up in a London village*. London: P. Owen.

Worpole, K. (1977). *Local publishing and local culture*. Hackney: Centerprise.

Worpole, K. (1983). *Dockers and detectives*. London: Verso.

Write First Time. (1978). *Write first time*. Bedford: WFT.

Yeo, S. (1986). Whose story? An argument from within current historical practice in Britain. *Journal of Contemporary History, 21*(2), 295-320.

Young, J. (1984). *Getting ideas*. Pontefract: Yorkshire Art Circus.

# 7

# *The Schooling of Literacy*

## JOANNA C. STREET
## BRIAN V. STREET

**The meanings and uses** of literacy are deeply embedded in community values and practices, yet they tend to be associated in many accounts simply with schooling and pedagogy. Recent approaches to literacy, however, have come to focus upon the varied social and cultural meanings of the concept and its role in power relations in contemporary society (Besnier, 1989; Bledsoe & Robey, 1986; Cook-Gumperz, 1986; Fingeret, 1983; Finnegan, 1988; Heath, 1985; Tannen, 1985; Varenne & McDermott, 1983). Literacy is not a given, a simple set of technical skills necessary for a range of educational competencies, as much of the earlier literature would suggest. Literacy practices are neither neutral nor simply a matter of educational concern: They are varied and contentious and imbued with ideology. There are different literacies related to different social and cultural contexts rather than a single Literacy that is the same everywhere (Street, 1985, in press-a). This raises the question of how it is that one particular variety has come to be taken as the only literacy. Among all of the different literacies practiced in the community, the home, and the workplace, how is it that the variety associated with schooling has come to be the defining type, not only to set the standard for other varieties but to marginalize them, to rule them off the agenda of literacy debate? Nonschool literacies have come to be seen as inferior attempts at the real thing, to be compensated for by enhanced schooling.

We are interested in exploring the ways in which, both at home and at school, dominant conceptions of literacy are constructed and reproduced in such a way as to marginalize alternatives and, we would suggest, to control key aspects of language and thought. We hypothesize that the mechanism through which meanings and uses of "literacy" take on this role is the "pedogogization" of literacy. By this we mean that literacy has become associated with educational notions of Teaching and Learning and with what teachers and pupils do in schools, at the expense of the many other uses and meanings of literacy evident from the comparative ethnographic literature. We use *pedagogy* not in the narrow sense of specific skills and tricks of the trade used by teachers but in the broader sense of institutionalized processes of teaching and learning, usually associated with the school but increasingly identified in home practices associated with reading and writing. Whether we are observing parent-child interactions, the development of educational toys and "software" in the home, or the procedures associated with classroom learning, *pedagogy* in this sense has taken on the character of an ideological force controlling social relations in general and conceptions of reading and writing in particular.

The chapter is organized around a number of key theoretical concepts, informed by some illustrative data from fieldwork undertaken in the United States during 1988. We begin with an analysis of what we mean by the "pedagogization" of literacy, highlighting the cultural specificity of this form with reference to comparative material from social situations in which literacy is not associated with schooling or pedagogy. We then briefly describe the school and community from which we draw some illustrative data; we consider in this context some of the processes of pedagogization, such as the objectification of language, metalinguistic usages, space labeling, and classroom procedure. After having suggested some of the ways of studying *how* the schooling of literacy is effected, we conclude with some suggestions as to *why* this form of literacy has acquired such importance in contemporary society, focusing on the relationship between literacy, ideology, and nationalism. Finally, we draw some conclusions regarding possible directions for future research. The chapter as a whole is informed by an "ideological" model of literacy. It eschews the notion of a great divide between literacy and orality; and it develops earlier critiques of the "autonomous" model of literacy, with specific reference to its role in contemporary schooling (Street, 1985).

## LITERACY WITHOUT SCHOOLING

We begin by establishing what is meant by the notion of different "literacies" and of conceptualizing literacy outside schooling and pedagogy. Literacy is so embedded within these institutions in contemporary society that it is sometimes difficult for us to disengage and recognize that, for most of history and in great sections of contemporary society, literacy practices remain embedded in other social institutions. While Ogbu's definition of *literacy* as "synonymous with academic performance," "the ability to read and write and compute in the form taught and expected in formal education" (Ogbu, 1990), would probably receive general agreement in contemporary society, it is put into perspective by a recent account by Reid (1988, p. 218) of literacy in pre-sixteenth-century South East Asia:

> The old Indonesian ka-ga-nga alphabet . . . was taught in no school and had no value either vocationally or in reading any established or secular literature. The explanation for its persistence was the local custom of *manjan*, a courting game whereby young men and women would gather in the evenings and the youths would fling suggestive quatrains written in the old script to the young women they fancied.

Many cultures in this region adopted writing systems originally introduced from India, and "women took up writing as actively as men, to use in exchanging notes and recording debts and other female matters which were in the domestic domain" (Reid, 1988, p. 218). With the arrival of Islam and Christianity in the sixteenth century, however, "a more restricted, male-based literacy drove out the old script" and a pattern emerged that is common in the contemporary world as Western influence spreads: "a curious paradox that the growth of written culture probably reduced the number of people who could write by associating writing with the sacral and the solemn" and with male uses of literacy. The widespread use of literacy by women, in noneducational contexts prior to the introduction of Western schooled literacy, is becoming attested for a range of times and places: Yin-yee ko (1989), for instance, describes how, in seventeenth-century China, educated middle-class women wrote poetry as a means of constructing a private female culture against the homogenizing male character of late Imperial Chinese culture. Mickulecky (1985, p. 2) records the uses of literacy by women from the rising gentry in fifteenth-century England to write letters "concerned with business affairs of the family, personal intrigues, duty and death." The accounts of literacy in contemporary Lancaster, England, in this volume show women using "community" literacy in mediating with outside agencies such as social services (Barton and Padmore, this volume). Rockhill describes how Hispanic women's uses of literacy to manage the home in Los Angeles were invisible to a community that identified literacy with male employment and schoolings: These "illiterate" women had then to attend classes to acquire "proper" literacy, that is, the reading and writing skills and conventions associated with schooling that can be tested through the TABE and other formal mechanisms (Rockhill, 1987). The invisibility of women's literacy (along with much of their social activity) is a product not only of patriarchal society but also of dominant definitions and concepts of literacy.

Similarly, the literacies of non-European peoples have been ignored by developers bringing Western institutions and schooling to different parts of the world. Only recently has it been recognized that many writing systems have been developed outside of the Western context, the best known being those of the Vai (Scribner & Cole, 1981) and Mende (Bledsoe & Robey, 1986) in West Africa and of the Apache and Cherokee among native North Americans (Harbsmeier, 1989). More significant for the current argument has been the variety of "literacies" that are being documented by ethnographers, in which a script brought by outsiders such as missionaries or teachers has been "taken hold of" by local people (Kulick & Stroud, 1991) and adapted to indigenous meanings and uses. In the village in New Guinea that Kulick and Stroud studied, missionary literacy was incorporated into local conventions of language use rather than being used for the purposes intended by teachers. Skills developed in speech making, involving the avoidance of self-assertion or of putting others down, were also prominent in the ways that letters came to be written. As literacy is added to the rich communicative repertoire that already exists in the receiving societies, they adapt and amend it to local meanings, concepts of identity, and epistemologies: as Kulick and Stroud express it, the question is not what "impact" literacy has on people but how people affect literacy. Besnier's (1989) account of how the people of the Pacific atoll of Nukulaelae took hold of missionary literacy, shows how, whereas, in New Guinea, literacy was absorbed into preexisting communicative conventions, here it was used to add a genre to the repertoire. In speech, it was conventionally improper to express affect, while the new literacy gave scope for its full expression, particularly in letters. This suggests a further challenge to dominant assumptions about literacy in which speech is usually associated with self-expression, feeling, and subjectivity while writing is conventionally associated with detachment, objectivity, and "scientific" discourse (Tannen, 1985). The Nukulaelae material, along with that from many other parts of the world, brings home how far the associations commonly made with literacy are in fact cultural conventions rather than products of the medium itself. The uses of literacy by women; its association with informal, nonreligious, and nonbureaucratic practices; its affective and expressive functions; and the incorporation of oral conventions into written usage—all are features of literacy practice that have tended to be marginalized or destroyed by modern, Western literacy with its emphasis on formal, male, and schooled aspects of communication. Much, then, of what goes with schooled literacy turns out to be the product of Western assumptions about schooling, power, and knowledge rather than being necessarily intrinsic to literacy itself. The role played by developmental perspectives in schooling, for instance, means that the acquisition of literacy becomes isomorphic with the child's development of specific social identities and positions: Their power in society becomes associated with the kind and level of literacy they have acquired.

These examples of the relationship of variations in literacy to relative power and knowledge are not confined to the "Third World" or to technologically simpler societies: Recent ethnographies of literacy in the United States provide similar evidence of the rich varieties of literacy outside of school and formal learning processes and their significance for people's identities and positions in society. Weinstein-Shr (1991), for instance, compares Hmong refugees in Philadelphia in terms of their literacy practices and discovers two quite different sets of meanings and uses. One man, Chou Chang, learned standard schooled literacy in an evening class and used this to be a "gatekeeper" for his community, mediating with agencies such as social services. Pao Youa, however, dropped out of the literacy class and appeared to "fail" in dominant terms. However, Weinstein-Shr came across him some time later in a position of considerable authority that was largely legitimated through his uses of literacy: He kept scrapbooks of cuttings and pictures from newspapers, magazines, and letters that mentioned the Hmong and that represented an authoritative "history" of his people in recent circumstances. Members of the community would go to him as to a man of knowledge, and he would call upon the corpus of written material he had collected to discuss and determine key issues of community identity. The literacy with which he was dealing had nothing to do with formal schooling or pedagogy, and indeed it is likely that he could not formally decode the phonemic signs in all of the materials with which he was surrounded; but his literacy played a significant role in local politics and identity and in establishing his authority in the community (see also Camitta, in press; Shuman, 1983).

Similarly, Fishman's account in this volume of Amish literacy demonstrates the close association of literacy practices with identity, authority, and concepts of knowledge that are not necessarily those of schooled literacy. When she arrived in the community, she asked the girls of the family she was staying with to keep "dialogue journals" as a way of observing their literacy practices and establishing communication with them. But they refused, and it later became obvious that their conceptions of literacy were at variance with those that underlie the use of such journals. Amish communicative conventions require an "other-centeredness" that involves downplaying the self and focusing on the community. As in the New Guinea case, self-assertiveness was considered improper, and this became reflected in written conventions as these were added to the communicative repertoire: For the Amish girls to write of their own experience and feelings would be wrong—a challenge to Amish conceptions of identity and knowledge. The conventions associated with current writing practices and pedagogy in American schooling are not simply matters of technique and of neutral learning skills but may be associated with deep levels of cultural meaning and belief: Other literacies exist alongside the dominant, school-oriented versions.

Also in the United States, Arlene Fingeret has shown how the kind of community literacies described above and elsewhere in this volume may mean that literacy and other skills become reciprocal parts of an exchange process, thus obviating the need for each individual to develop each skill to a high degree. A person without highly developed literacy skills may get done all of the literacy tasks required of him or her in modern urban America by passing the tasks of filling out forms, writing letters, and the like on to another member of the community in exchange for, say, skills at mending car engines or managing transport arrangements. Within such community networks, there is no more stigma attached to lacking reading and writing skills than there is to lacking the skills of the motor mechanic (Fingeret, 1983). Similar findings occur in work from Mexico (King, 1991), the United Kingdom (Street, 1988), Somalia (Lewis, 1986), and many other parts of the world.

Literacy, then, need not be associated with schooling or with pedagogy: Ogbu's definition with which we began is inappropriate if we are to understand the full and rich meanings of literacy practices in contemporary society. Research needs, instead, to begin from a more comparative, more ethnographically based conception of literacy as the *social* practices of reading and writing and to eschew value judgments about the relative superiority of schooled literacy over other literacies.

## LITERACY IN THE COMMUNITY AND
## IN THE SCHOOL

While mainly concerned with exploring these issues at a theoretical level, we suggest how they might be developed empirically by reference to a small, pilot research project we conducted on home and school literacy practices in a community in the United States (a full research program is planned for the future). Just as we wish to eschew culturally biased judgment of different literacies in different communities, so we wish to avoid making judgments on schooled literacy. We are not concerned with evaluating the practices we describe below but with analyzing them ethnographically as social phenomena. The peculiar practices associated with literacy in schools and, increasingly, in the home and community in much of late-twentieth-century American society represent a fascinating and important addition to the complex and varied repertoire of literacy practices across both time and space that ethnographers and historians are now beginning to reveal. Why and how this particular version of literacy practices is reproduced and sustained in contemporary society is a theoretical and ethnographic question—crucially bound up with issues of power in the wider society—rather than a matter of educational evaluation. While Cook-Gumperz (1986), Soltow and Stevens (1981), and Howard (this volume) have amply documented the historical processes by which "schooled" literacy has become the dominant mode over the last century, the comparative questions their work poses have less often been applied to the current situation itself and to the reproduction of that dominance. It is within this framework that we developed a small pilot project to attempt to work out how such research might be framed and conducted. The material presented here is not sufficiently full or detailed to merit the term *ethnography,* rather, we see it as contributing toward future research of an ethnographic kind in this area.

The school on which we focused was set in an upper-middle-class suburb of a major American city that suffered from gross poverty, social inequality, and inner-city decline. Many of those who lived in this suburb had fled there to avoid these problems. The school was one of the few state schools that enjoyed a high reputation in middle-class and professional circles, and many families made considerable financial efforts to buy themselves into the area. House prices were high, and, in most families, both partners were obliged to work to meet mortgage costs and so on. They would frequently leave for work in the city early in the morning, leaving their children at the day-care center at the school, and returning in the evening to pick the children up from the center, which remained open well after school closing time. The school had classes from first grade through fifth with about 20 pupils per class and two or three classes in each year. We observed and taped classroom practices, in the first and fifth grades, each of us spending three mornings or afternoons in each class. We also taped discussion sessions with each of the teachers in which we asked about their conceptions of literacy. Outside of the school, we conducted interviews with half a dozen parents of children who attended the school and the classes we were observing, asked them to keep a "Literacy Diary" by recording literacy events in their homes, and asked some families to tape-record the speech around these events. This focus upon literacy in middle-class, suburban homes is an aspect of literacy in the "community" that has not received much research attention. Shirley Brice Heath's *Ways with Words* (1985), for instance, makes reference to it but she does not research it in any detail, appearing to assume that we all know what middle-class life and literacy are like.

We began the project by assuming a distinction between literacy practices in the community and in the school. We wanted to explore the ways in which the particular variety of literacy that we labeled "school literacy" comes to dominate other forms of literacy in contemporary society. Our experience forced us to refine these ideas, particularly those regarding home and school literacies, and to recognize that the extent of similarity between practices of literacy in the community, in the home, and in the school make our earlier dichotomy unhelpful. Underlying literacy in all of these contexts is a common thread, derived from wider cultural and ideological processes. We focus here on one particular aspect of this common thread, the processes of pedagogization.

## PROCESSES OF PEDAGOGIZATION

We found that one way of answering our questions about the pedagogization of literacy was to break it down into a number of specific processes and then to examine these processes in both home and school. In this chapter, we are particularly concerned with the processes that help construct an "autonomous" model of literacy—in which many individuals, often against their own experience, come to conceptualize literacy as a separate, reified set of "neutral" competencies, autonomous of social context—and with the procedures and social roles through which this model of literacy is disseminated and internalized.

The construction and internalization of the autonomous model of literacy is achieved by a number of means, some of which we will briefly attempt to illustrate from our data: the distancing of language from subjects—the ways in which language is treated as though it were a thing, distanced from both teacher and learner and imposing on them external rules and requirements as though they were but passive recipients; "metalinguistic" usages—the ways in which the social processes of reading and writing are referred to and lexicalized within a pedagogic voice as though they were independent and neutral competencies rather than laden with significance for power relations and ideology; "privileging"—the ways in which reading and writing are given status vis-à-vis oral discourse as though the medium were intrinsically superior and, therefore, those who acquired it would also become superior; and "philosophy of language"—the setting of units and boundaries for elements of language use as though they were neutral, thereby disguising the ideological source of what are in fact social constructions, frequently associated with ideas about logic, order, scientific mentality, and so on.

Among the institutional processes that contribute to the construction and internalization of the pedagogic voice in school, we focus on "space labeling" and "procedures." The institutionalization of a particular model of literacy operates not only through particular forms of speech and texts but in the physical and institutional space that is separated from "everyday" space for purposes of teaching and learning and that derives from wider social and ideological constructions of the social and built world. "Procedures" represent the way in which rules for the engagement of participants as teachers and learners are continuously asserted and reinforced within practices supposedly to do simply with using and talking about literacy: While apparently simply giving instructions about handling a text, for instance, teachers and parents are also embedding relations of hierarchy, authority, and control.

A "mix" of oral and literate media, sometimes referred to as an "oral-literate" continuum, is to be observed in all of these processes: Participants employ both oral and literate discursive strategies as they interact, in both home and school. But this interactive aspect of literacy and orality tends, within actual practice, to be disguised behind prescriptions and linguistic conventions that represent the linguistic modes as entirely separate, as though there were a "great divide" between orality and literacy. This conception of literacy appears to be one of the major means whereby an autonomous model of literacy is internalized and disseminated in contemporary society. It is a conception endemic to pedagogized literacy.

## OBJECTIFYING LANGUAGE

Much classroom discourse turns upon explicit attention to language and what it means for children. The contemporary literature on learning to read places great emphasis on the achievement of metalinguistic awareness and frequently presumes that the development of this highly valued ability is associated with the acquisition of literacy (Bruner, 1985; Teale & Sulzby, 1987; Wells, 1985; Wertsch, 1981). Self-awareness about language and the development of specific terms for describing it are seen as part of cognitive development, leading to critical thought, detachment, and objectivity, and it is taken as self-evident that the writing down of language facilitates these processes (Olson, Hildyard, & Torrance, 1985). Given the powerful pressure in favor of this model of language within teacher training institutions in both the United Kingdom and the United States, it is not surprising to find it underpinning much classroom practice. However, while recognizing the significance of metalinguistic awareness, we would reject the claim that it is peculiarly associated with literacy and also question the tendency to focus on certain syntactical and formal features of language at the expense of other aspects as though language awareness were a matter of specific grammatical terminology.

## OBJECTIFYING LANGUAGE AT SCHOOL

In the classroom we observed, teachers appeared to treat language as though it were something outside both the students and themselves, as though it had autonomous, nonsocial qualities that imposed themselves upon its users. The language of instruction presupposed and helped to construct distance between children and their language. Writing is one way of creating that distance—putting it on the blackboard serves as one technique for enabling children to see and objectify that process of learning. Once the language is on the board, on the worksheet, in the book, and so on, it becomes a separate problem for the teacher and children to work on together. In the sessions we observed, the teacher made an effort to get the children to identify with her as she worked out a problem in grammar or expression, as though they were commonly struggling against an outside authority to which they were both subject. The aim was to get children to follow her own work processes and mimic them. There was little discussion of the meaning of language, of alterative interpretations of texts, or of how the teacher arrived at her sense of what they meant. This was so even after library reading: Views might be elicited before reading but responses were not called for afterward. Similarly, book reports, in which students were asked to read a book and then present orally a structured report on it to the whole class, took on a ritualized and nonsemantic character in which the aim appeared to be to develop schooled language rather than to actually discuss the books. In contexts such as these, it would seem, the final object is to achieve mastery and authority over the text, whose meanings are not negotiable. The book reports are modeled on written language, as conceived within this subculture: planning, the use of topic sentences and paragraphing, and explicitness are carried over from how written language has been learned into spoken language. The school presentation of the text is, then, unproblematized regarding its meaning and content, focusing on form. Technical problems are set, to do with grammar and syntax, and solutions once given are assimilated to a general list of rules and prescriptions about the nature of language itself.

There were a number of ways in which this process operated collectively, so that the whole class was constructing a collective voice in ways that excluded exploration of the meanings of what was being uttered: the pledge of allegiance in which teacher and students chanted formulaic phrases together, certain question-and-answer sessions, some circle games. Similarly, diagnostic and evaluative tests were used as a way to create distance between the children and their own perception of their knowledge. The teacher identified with them and helped them through the process. This identification exacerbates the notion of the objective, neutral status of the text and reduces the role of speaker/reader to passive recipient rather than active negotiator of meaning. While the aims of language learning were spelled out in school documents as being based upon "communication," the practice was frequently concerned with learning formalized uses of language and subjecting oral to written conventions.

## OBJECTIFYING LANGUAGE AT HOME

We observed similar processes in the children's homes, although they did not necessarily carry over directly from school as we at first imagined. Parents in middle-class homes are indeed frequently concerned about structuring learning for their children in the ways legitimized by the school (see Brooks, 1989). Similarly, from our observations, it appeared that attention to children's school exercises played a dominant part in everyday life: book reports, in particular, could take over the weekend as parents helped their child to spot "topic sentences," develop links, and work up endings for their presentation to the class on Monday morning. Project work could take the whole family to the local library, which would be filled with teams of family researchers scanning encyclopedias and the nonfiction section for accounts of shells, electricity, fish, and so on. Acquisition of proper literacy was perceived as a "problem" to be solved, a task to be accomplished: Rules were set from outside and the child and parent were collaborators in responding to this hegemony. Tests were as much part of home practice as school.

From these practices, it at first appeared that home was simply dominated by school and that this would explain the pedagogization of literacy there. But the extent of the internalization of the pedagogic voice for literacy acquisition and dissemination suggests it is part of wider social and cultural currents. It is produced and reinforced through newspaper discussions on literacy, labeling on educational toys, political debates, and parental discourses. In our interviews with parents of the children whose classes we observed, we found an ambivalence toward the school as an institution but a ready adoption of the pedagogized view of literacy that we identified there. These parents did not always see the school as the source of value and legitimacy in this area; they were developing their pedagogic voice from other sources too.

A number of parents had formed a Parent's Information Committee (PIC) to put pressure on the school where they thought it was failing to develop the appropriate model of literacy. At these meetings, it appeared that parents, not teachers, were the guardians of proper literacy. An example of this activity was parents pressuring school to adopt "Writing Process" approaches, and the PIC supported and lobbied for developments already taking place in the school district that involved in-service days on these ways of teaching literacy. Our findings suggest that the shift was not as radical as they believed because the same pedagogy underlay the focus on writing as process rather than as product. As Rudy (1989) demonstrated through research on Collaborative Learning of Writing in secondary classrooms in a nearby city, new approaches are frequently assimilated to traditional assumptions and ways of relating to students. We are not concerned here with evaluating these different approaches—collaborative, process-oriented writing instruction and traditional product-oriented writing instruction—but with demonstrating how both may be subsumed under the more general principle of the pedagogization of literacy. The reason the change from one to another is not always as significant as exponents of the different approaches would hope may be that they both persist in reducing reading and writing to particular social practices associated with "learning," thereby missing the range of literacy practices associated with nonschooled purposes and concepts. In the classrooms we studied, the methods of teaching and learning associated with product-oriented teaching did not alter much as process approaches were introduced: Literacy was still "out there," an objective content to be taught through authority structures whereby pupils learned the proper roles and identities they were to carry into the wider world. Nonpedagogic literacies did not—indeed could not—figure in this process: The parents in the PIC were not trying to introduce alternative literacies to the school but simply to keep the teachers up to scratch in their pedagogic activities.

Similarly, in their own homes, the parents were claiming authority to direct their children's learning and thereby challenging the sole dominance of the school while at the same time marginalizing the alternative literacies that children may have encountered in the context of home, peer group, and community in favor of a "schooled" literacy. Homes were full of toys, games, and videos that were explicitly directed toward school achievement and readiness, but the definition of that achievement became as much the property of the parent as the teacher. The labels in which these toys and the like were packaged and the accompanying leaflets used academic language, frequently derived from psychological literature, to legitimize and reinforce their educational value, and some of this language had crept in to parents' discussions around literacy. It was within this discourse that they strove to keep the teachers up to scratch. Similarly, the project work on weekends was not simply subservient to school demands but used the school to create and reinforce home demands: Children were learning to participate in the achievement culture that their parents saw as essential if they were to reproduce the parents' life-style and avoid the horrors of poverty of which the nearby city provided such stark evidence.

A perception of literacy as the major source of Western supremacy, scientific achievement and so on lay behind the willingness to engage in specific literacy tasks. An "autonomous" model of literacy was thus crucial to the commitment parents showed, which they also expected of their children. Home interest in the use of tests, concern with formal features of literacy and language, the treatment of language as an external force with rules and requirements to be learned, and the intertwining of conventions associated with literacy and the management of texts with assertions of authority and control, including the organization of other people's time and space—all of these features of home literacy practice indeed complement the uses of literacy apparent in the children's school. The source, however, may not be the school itself but derived from larger cultural and ideological currents that influence both home and school. Just as in the Amish example (Fishman, this volume), it may be more fruitful to focus on continuities between home culture and school culture rather than on the discontinuities with which much of the research has been concerned. To do so, we argue, requires us to theorize literacy practices differently—to develop not only ethnographies of home and school but also ethnographies of literacy, of the kind being attempted in this volume.

## SPACE LABELING

In popular discourse, *the school* refers perhaps to the people who run or attend it, perhaps to the building in which it is situated that symbolizes its presence. But the school as an institution finds its main form of expression through a particular form of language, in evidence not only in the speech of teachers and the text of the written materials but in the classroom, on the walls, and in the stream of bureaucratic paperwork through which it constantly signifies and reproduces itself. The language of the teacher and of the text positions the subject (whether student or researcher), pins them to their seats, locates them in a socially and authoritatively constructed space. How this space is constructed is crucial to our understanding of the particular linguistic and literacy processes with which this chapter is concerned.

The main building of the school we were investigating is large and square and breathes public importance. It is part of a whole genre of public architecture representing the state. Above the doorway in large letters, embedded in the wall, as part of the permanent structure, are the words X Elementary School. Inside the school, space is designated by authority and authority is expressed in signs: Rooms are numbered and labeled, they have designated functions that are likewise labeled. The first notice one sees as one enters the building is "All visitors must report to the office." When one enters the building, one is situating oneself physically inside a particular universe of signs. Within a classroom, the pictures and notices on the walls continue this process of situating the individual within a sign system. This is particularly evident in the first grade classroom. The children sit at the center of a system of codes through which their experience is to be transformed. It is as though the walls themselves were a filtering screen through which the world outside the school is transformed and translated into various discrete sets of analytic concepts: lists of numbers, the letters of the alphabet, shapes and colours, lists of measurements—all the devices by which the experience of the senses can be filtered and then transformed into discrete social and analytic concepts, tabulated, and measured. The five senses themselves dangle on separate little labels from a mobile. Time is filtered through a grid of days of the week, seasons, birthday charts, and clock faces. The birthday chart situates the child herself within this catalogue of time, just as she is situated within space. The classroom's four walls are labeled "south," "east," "north," and "west," right and left hang on the wall—the room is framed as a signifying space with the child at the center, making sense of things. These spatial categories only make sense when oriented to the child at the center of the classroom, and they indicate in a very powerful way the contract between the individual and the institution that underpins the ideology of language within the school. This process of writing down and labeling experiences incorporates them into a visual system that is external to the child. The organization of the visual environment itself helps to construct and provide a model of the child's relationship to language and to the written word. The walls of the classroom become the walls of the world. The maps of the United States and the world on the wall at the front of the classroom indicate the system of signs through which that world may be attained.

## PROCEDURES

Procedures for organizing classroom time, work practices, and literacy materials dominate the classroom and form a major part of the pedagogic voice. One teacher told her students explicitly that they had to speak differently in class: "Now you are in school, use your inside school voice." Thereby school is separated from other times and places, and familiar everyday processes of speaking, reading, and writing are given a distinct character and a special authority. A session is divided into phases by means of linguistic markers that have illocutionary force in actually constructing the separate times and spaces (but compare with Collins, in press). The teacher continually interrupts students' work with statements about where the class are in her time frame and what to do next: "Journals now: write how the group work went"; "close your scripts up, all the pages inside. You're going to be putting them inside"; "the first thing you're going to do when everyone gets back is go over the homework so this would be a marvellous time to get it finished"; "get out last night's reading assignment"; "break now, have a snack now." "Now we're running overtime. Quick, reading groups. Get your maths papers out." "We'll finish now. A new book on Monday." These interjections are not simply practical features of classroom activity, although they do have specific surface functions in organizing the day where only one teacher takes a class right through. They also, however, help to define what literacy is: They define the organization of texts, papers, and reading and writing materials as the organization of cultural time and space. While they appear to be teaching strategies, they in fact set the boundaries of literacy itself and assert its place within a culturally defined authority structure. The teacher has the authority to bound time and space for the students, and this authority reinforces her control over the definition and bounding of linguistic practices: Literacy is placed in relation both to oral discourse and to specific material practices with which it becomes entwined and defined.

In the same voice as she marks phases of time during the day, the teacher sets out procedures for this material practice of literacy: "When you've finished, put all the papers in the folder I gave you. You're going to be responsible for finding all the things when we're going through it. That's why you have the folder"; "If you want to write the sentences on lined paper, then take some from your book." "Turn over on the back of the paper." The ending of a session is defined by a combination of linguistic markers and literacy practices: "Put your scripts in a folder. You may fold it in half once to get it in."

Oral procedures for finding their way around a written text also combine teacher authority over texts with a "mix" of oral and written conventions that is not explicitly addressed. It is as though the words were not being spoken but assimilated to the written form:

TEACHER: "Top of page 62. What does C's mother do about that? . . . Let's look at page 66 now. I'm sorry, page 64. Read to me the third sentence. That's the third sentence not the third line. How can you find a paragraph? It starts in."
STUDENT: "It starts with a capital letter."
TEACHER: "Yes, but it also starts in." . . . "Can you tell me the last word of the sentence? What was that word? Page 59 now. So D. was going home . . . what was the friend's name? . . . the last two lines tell you. Page 60 now. Read what Steve says . . . Bob says that."

Much of this discourse depends upon shared assumptions about the visual perception of a text, its layout and organization—a paragraph "starts in," page numbers mark the physical boundaries of written material, "sentences" are visual presences whose opening and closing words can be easily identified (unlike in much oral discourse). The oral representation of the materiality of the written medium becomes a means of organizing actual social relations in the classroom.

Another teacher, getting students to read the parts in a television script, similarly combines oral and written strategies in asserting her authority to determine who has the right to speak at different defined points and where they are in the text:

TEACHER:    "Page 5, first column, down near the bottom . . . we'll switch reader when
we get to that spot. Narrator for 1, 2 and 3. For 4, 5 and 6 Sarah. M for all those
sections David. That should take care of everything up to the end of 6. If you
get stuck on a word don't worry about it, everyone can see it and knows it. Try
to pronounce it. . . . Wait, remember to read that dark print stuff first, where is
it happening now, the dark print tells you that. We'll finish at the end of 7. I'm
going to do 7. I know I said we'd finish at 6, but we're going to do to the end
of 7."

The visual and linguistic markers for moving around a text dominate the
discourse and establish the teacher's authority over the direction readers will
take. The text becomes a concrete set of signs on a pathway and students are
busy looking for cues to their own involvement and for ending. It is interesting that there is much scope here for the teacher to address metalinguistic
features of oral/literate interaction (Fairclough, 1989; and to decode the
significance of different print faces and so on) but these are not the kinds of
metalinguistic issues with which the pedagogic voice is concerned. Rather,
it develops procedural skills in moving around texts, asserts who has authority over the text, and reinforces the pressure on students to see written
language as something separate and detached.

## HOMOGENIZATION OR VARIATION?

There is not space here to extend the analysis in this degree of detail of
literacy practices in the home, although our experience was that there were
many similarities, particularly in the link between literacy and linguistic
practices, on the one hand, and the organization of time and space, on the
other. A key question for future research in both contexts is how the assertion
of authority and the allocation of participants to specific roles and relationships are inscribed within particular literacy events and practices. At first,
this may lead us to conclude that the conception of literacy associated with
schooling and pedagogy, in particular the emphasis on Teaching and Learning, is transforming the rich variety of literacy practices evident in community literacies into a single, homogenized practice. Mothers and children in
the home adopt the roles of teachers and learners; a toy is treated not as a
source of "play," to be used according to the cultural conventions associated

with leisure, relaxation, childhood, and so on, but instead is located within a framework of teaching and learning, scaffolding the child to future academic achievement; reading a story aloud is transformed by the pedagogic voice from a context of narrative, character, and morality to a pre/scribed role for the listening child in the achievement of school "readiness."

However, as ethnographies of literacy in the community proliferate, a more complex picture may emerge, and we expect to find forms of resistance and alternative literacies alongside "schooled" literacy. Moreover, it is already apparent that the process of pedagogization of literacy does not derive solely from schools, although its institutional and historical roots are clearly found there, as Cook-Gumperz (1986) and Soltow and Stevens (1981) have demonstrated. It is not simply a matter of how school imposes its version of literacy on the outside world—as we originally imagined and as a rich educational literature has presumed. Rather, the question to be explored is how and why this version of literacy is constructed, assimilated, and internalized in many different contexts, including the school itself. We have tried to suggest ways in which the question of *how* this process is effected may be answered. We conclude with some suggestions as to *why* the process is so important in contemporary American society.

## THEORETICAL CONSIDERATIONS:
## LITERACY, IDEOLOGY, AND NATIONALISM

The new ethnographies of literacy tell us that people can lead full lives without the kinds of literacy assumed in educational and other circles. The reconceptualization of literacy suggested there involves moving away from the dominant view of literacy as having distinctive "autonomous" characteristics associated intrinsically with schooling and pedagogy. It also entails a shift away from the characterization of the literate person as intrinsically civilized, detached, logical, and so on in contrast with "illiterates" or those who communicate mainly through oral channels. If the qualities of logic, detachment, abstraction conventionally associated with the acquisition of literacy turn out to be available in oral discourse, as Finnegan (1988) and others have amply demonstrated, or rather in some mix of channels that does not require the conventions and rules usually associated with literacy-in-itself, as we have been suggesting here, then literacy loses some of the status and mystification that currently underpin the investment of vast resources in both teaching and measuring it.

How, then, can we explain the almost obsessive attention to literacy in American society, and why is literacy assumed to be "functionally necessary" there? One possible answer, suggested by our analysis here of the pedagogization of literacy, is that the language of "function" disguises and effectively naturalizes the ideological role of literacy in contemporary society. The pedagogized literacy that we have been discussing becomes, then, an organizing concept around which ideas of social identity and value are defined; what kinds of collective identity we subscribe to, what kind of nation we want to belong to, are encapsulated within apparently disinterested accounts of the function, purpose, and educational necessity of this kind of literacy. Literacy, in this sense, becomes a symbolic key to many of the society's gravest problems: Issues of ethnic identity, conflict, achievement (or underachievement) can be diverted into accounts of how literacy acquisition can be improved and the distribution of literacy enhanced; issues of poverty and unemployment can be turned into questions about why individuals failed to learn literacy at school, or continue to refuse remedial attention as adults, thus diverting blame from institutions to individuals, from power structures to personal morality; issues concerning the effectiveness and achievement of American society as a whole, in comparison with others such as Japan that are seen to be "overtaking," succeeding where America fails, are located within a framework of educational debate about reading and writing, again diverting attention away from the institutional explanations for budget deficits, space program failures, and productivity declines. All of these issues become focused within a single, overdetermined sign—that of literacy. The signification of literacy has, then, to be decoded not simply in terms of a discourse around education—school quality, teacher performance, testing and evaluation, approaches to writing instruction, and the like—but in terms of discourses of nationalism. It is around the concept of nation and national identity that the social issues currently diverted into the literacy debate essentially focus. To understand the uses and meanings of literacy, then, we need to analyze their relationship to contemporary nationalism.

Indeed, much of the debate about literacy "standards," currently highlighted in the work of Hirsch (1987, 1988) and Bloom (1986) in the United States, does make explicit as well as implicit reference to nationalism. Hirsch, for instance, bases his concept of "cultural literacy" upon the idea of "a shared national standard." He likens the hard-won uniformity in economic laws and interstate commerce to the "literacy uniformity" that is crucial to the formation and underpinning of the nation: "The two kinds of uniformity are closely allied" (Hirsch, 1988).

Similarly, Ernest Gellner's (1983) account of the growth of the nation-state in the modern world rests upon the privileging of a particular literacy, that purveyed in specific educational institutions:

> Modern industry requires a mobile, literate, technologically equipped population and the modern state is the only agency capable of providing such a work force through its support for a mass, public, compulsory and standardized education system. Modern societies require cultural homogeneity to function. (in Smith, 1986, p. 10)

Which culture is to provide the model for such homogeneity and which cultures are to be marginalized within this hegemony is not spelled out: "It is a question simply of function rather than of power struggles between competing cultures. The question of which literacy is to provide the standard and which literacies are to be marginalized is similarly disguised beneath the discourse of technological need and institutional necessity. And yet, behind their appeal to apparently neutral forces, Gellner and Hirsch make it quite clear that they have in mind a specific culture and a specific literacy—that of their own subculture. The assumed agreement about what constitutes literacy serves to naturalize their own ideological position: It appears not as an argument in favor of their own preferred kind of literacy and culture but a given fact of modern life, a necessity by which we are all driven. To question their claims would be to undermine the success and achievements of the nation, to challenge its very identity. Within this discourse, an appeal for cultural plurality and literacy variety appears to be a recipe for chaos.

Why this is the case and how these particular views of literacy assert and reproduce their hegemony are the central questions that we hope this chapter has raised, if not resolved. We would like to encourage research into literacy and its relationship with nationalism and with culture that starts not from the premises assumed by Hirsch, Gellner, and much of the educational literature but from a more culturally sensitive and politically conscious perspective.

It is, then, within an ideological model of literacy that such research needs to be framed. This model of literacy is situated within the larger ideology of language, of which distinctions between writing, reading, and oral events are only subcategories themselves separated out and defined within the ideology. We do not mean an "ideology" of language in the weak sense of referring to "ideas about" language, although these are obviously significant, but in a stronger sense that encompasses the relationship between the individual and the social institution and the mediation of the relationship through sign systems. When we participate in the language of an institution, whether as speakers, listeners, writers, or readers, we become positioned by that language; in that moment of assent, myriad relationships of power, authority, status are implied and reaffirmed. At the heart of this language in contemporary society, there is a relentless commitment to instruction. It is this that frames and constructs what we refer to as the "pedagogization" of literacy.

## CONCLUSION

We have suggested that research in this area should not focus on the school in isolation but on the conceptualization of literacy in the "community." In rethinking concepts of literacy associated with pedagogization, particularly focused around the language of literacy, procedures for its dissemination, and the construction of an autonomous model of literacy, we have come to recognize how they derive not so much from the school itself as from wider cultural and ideological patterns. Within school, the association of literacy acquisition with the child's development of specific social identities and positions; the privileging of written over oral language; the interpretation of "metalinguistic" awareness in terms of specific literacy practices and grammatical terminology; and the neutralizing and objectification of language that disguises its social and ideological character—all must be understood as essentially *social* processes: They contribute to the construction of a particular kind of citizen, a particular kind of identity, and a particular concept of the nation. The community in its wider sense, including the "nation" itself, participates in these ideological constructions through processes that are equally represented as politically neutral, simply educational matters. Parents, whether helping their children with school tasks or challenging school control of literacy through local lobbies, reinforce the association of literacy with learning and pedagogy; the construction and filling of the home space with literacy materials are associated with specific theories of learning; the kinds of literacy children might be acquiring from peer groups and the community are marginalized against the standard of schooled literacy. This reinforcement of schooled literacy in the community contributes, alongside that of the school itself, to the construction of identity and personhood in the modern nation-state. The home and community practices feed back in turn into school practice, helping to assert and refashion there too the pedagogization of literacy. These, then, are the characteristic social processes and values through which literacy is construed and disseminated in mainstream America today, very different processes and values than those evident from the ethnographies of literacy currently emerging from research in the Third World, in the history of America, and in sections of contemporary American society itself. If we wish to understand the nature and meanings of literacy in our lives, then, we need more research that focuses on literacy in the community—in its broadest sense—and on the ideological rather than the educational implications of the communicative practices in which it is embedded.

## REFERENCES

Besnier, N. (1989). The encoding of affect in Nukulaelae letters. *Text, 9,* 69-92.

Bledsoe, C., & Robey, K. (1986). Arabic literacy and secrecy among the Mende of Sierra Leone. *Man, 21,* 202-226.

Bloom, A. (1987). *The closing of the American mind.* New York: Simon & Schuster.

Bloom, D. (1986). On the nature of events, classrooms, classroom literacy and procedural display: An interactive sociolinguistic perspective. Unpublished manuscript.

Brooks, A. A. (1989, January). Too much, too soon: With so much emphasis on structured learning, preschoolers are in danger of forgetting how to invent their own games—or even how to play. *Parenting,* pp. 74-92.

Bruner, J. (1985). Narrative and paradigmatic modes of thought. In E. Eisner (Ed.), *Learning and teaching the ways of knowing.* Chicago: University of Chicago Press.

Camitta, M. (in press). Vernacular writing: Varieties of literacy among Philadelphia high school students. In B. Street (Ed.), *Cross-cultural approaches to literacy.* Cambridge: Cambridge University Press.

Clanchy, M. (1979). *From memory to written record: England 1066-1307.* London: Edward Arnold.

Collins, J. (in press). The troubled text history and language in basic writing programs. In A. Luke & P. Freebody (Eds.), *Knowledge, culture and power: Literacy in international perspective.* London: Falmer.

Cook-Gumperz, J. (1986). *The social construction of literacy.* Cambridge: Cambridge University Press.

Department of Education and Science (DES). (1988). *English for ages 5 to 11* (The Cox report). London: Her Majesty's Stationery Office.

Fairclough, N. (1985). Critical and descriptive goals in discourse analysis. *Journal of Pragmatics 9,* 739-763.

Fairclough, N. (1989). *Language and power.* London: Longman.

Fingeret, A. (1983). Social network: A new perspective in independence and illiterate adults. *Adult Education Quarterly, 33*(3), 133-134.

Finnegan, R. (1988). *Literacy and orality.* Oxford: Basil Blackwell.

Fishman, J. (1986). Nationality-nationalism and nation-nationism. In J. Fishman, C. Ferguson, & J. Das Gupta (Eds.), *Language problems of developing nations.* New York: John Wiley.

Gellner, E. (1983). *Nations and nationalism.* London: Basil Blackwell.

Goody, J. (1986). *The logic of writing and the organization of society*. Cambridge: Cambridge University Press.

Graff, H. (1979). *The literacy myth: Literacy and social structure in the 19th century city*. New York: Academic Press.

Harbsmeier, M. (1989). Inventions of writing. In K. Schousboe & M. Larsen (Eds.), *Literacy and society*. Copenhagen: Center for Research in the Humanities.

Heath, S. B. (1985). *Ways with words*. Cambridge: Cambridge University Press.

Hill, C., & Parry, K. (1988). The test at the gate. Occasional Paper. New York: Columbia University.

Hirsch, E. D. (1987). *Cultural literacy: What every American needs to know*. Boston: Houghton Mifflin.

Hirsch, E. D., Jr. (1988, January). Cultural literacy: Let's get specific. [Special issue]. *NEA Today*.

Holland, D., & Street, B. (in press). Literacy, testing and *Nationalism*. Occasional Paper. New York: Columbia University.

Ivanič, R., & Barton, D. (1989). The role of language study in adult literacy. In J. McCaffery & B. Street (Eds.), *Literacy research in the UK*. Lancaster: RaPAL.

King, L. (1991). Roots of identity: Language and literacy in Mexico. In B. Street (Ed.), *Cross-cultural approaches to literacy*. Cambridge: Cambridge University Press.

Kulick, D., & Stroud, C. (1991). Conceptions and uses of literacy in a Papua New Guinea village. In B. Street (Ed.), *Cross-cultural approaches to literacy*. Cambridge: Cambridge University Press.

Lankshear, C., & Lawler, M. (1987). *Literacy, schooling and revolution*. London: Falmer.

Lewis, I. (1986). Literacy and cultural identity in the Horn of Africa: The Somali case. In G. Baumann (Ed.), *The written word*. Oxford: Clarendon.

Maclaren, P. (1986). *Schooling as a ritual performance*. London: RKP.

Maybin, J. (1988). *Peer group language in the classroom*. Unpublished master's thesis, University of Sussex.

McCaffery, J., & Street, B. (1988). *Literacy research in the UK: Adult and school perspectives*. Lancaster: RaPAL.

Mickulecky, B. (1985). *The Paston letters: An example of literacy in the 15th century*. Unpublished manuscript.

National Academy of Education, (1985). *Becoming a nation of readers*. Washington, DC: NIE.

Ogbu, J. (1990). Cultural mode, identity and literacy. In J. W. Stigler (Ed.), *Cultural psychology*. Cambridge: Cambridge University Press.

Olson, D., Hildyard, A., & Torrance, N. (1985). *Literacy, language and learning*. Cambridge: Cambridge University Press.

Ong, W. (1982). *Orality and literacy*. London: Methuen.

Reid, A. (1988). *South East Asia in the age of commerce: 1450-1680: Vol. 1. The lands below the winds*. New Haven, CT: Yale University Press.

Rockhill, K. (1987). Gender, language and the politics of literacy. *British Journal of the Sociology of Language*, 8(2), 153-167.

Rudy, M. (1989). *The dynamics of collaborative learning of writing (CLW) in secondary classrooms: Control or cooperation?* Unpublished doctoral dissertation, University of Pennsylvania. (UMI Dissertation Information Services)

Scribner, S., & Cole, M. (1981). *The psychology of literacy*. Cambridge, MA: Harvard University Press.

Shuman, A. (1983). *Story-telling rights.* Cambridge: Cambridge University Press.

Smith, A. (1986). *The ethnic origins of nations.* London: Basil Blackwell.

Soltow, L., & Stevens, E. (1981). *The rise of literacy and the common school: A socioeconomic analysis to 1870.* Chicago: University of Chicago Press.

Street, B. (1985). *Literacy in theory and practice.* Cambridge: Cambridge University Press.

Street, B. (1988). Literacy practices and literacy myths. In R. Saljo (Ed.), *The written word: Vol. 23. Studies in literate thought and action.* Berlin: Springer-Verlag.

Street, B. (Ed.). (in press-a). *Cross-cultural approaches to literacy.* Cambridge: Cambridge University Press.

Street, B. (in press-b). *Literacy, power and ideology.*

Street, B., & Besnier, N. (in press). Writing and the consequences of literacy. In T. Ingold (Ed.), *The encyclopedia of anthropology.* London: RKP.

Tannen, D. (1982). *Spoken and written language: Exploring orality and literacy.* Norwood, NJ: Ablex.

Tannen, D. (1985). Relative focus on involvement in oral and written discourse. In D. Olson et al. (Eds.), *Literacy, language and learning.* Cambridge: Cambridge University Press.

Teale, W., & Sulzby, E. (1987). Literacy acquisition in early childhood: The roles of access and mediation in storybook reading. In D. Wagner (Ed.), *The future of literacy in a changing world.* New York: Pergamon.

Varenne, H. & McDermott, R. (1983). Why Sheila can read: Structure and indeterminacy in the structure of familial literacy. In B. Schieffelin & P. Gilmore (Eds.), *Ethnographic perspective in the acquisition of literacy.* Norwood, NJ: Ablex.

Weinstein-Shr, G. (1991). Literacy and social process: A community in transition. In B. Street (Ed.), *Cross-cultural approaches to literacy.* Cambridge: Cambridge University Press.

Wells, G. (1985). Preschool literacy-related activities and success in school. In D. Olson et al (Eds.), *Literacy, language and learning: The nature and consequences of reading and writing.* Cambridge: Cambridge University Press.

Wertsch, J. V. (Ed.). (1981). *The concept of activity in Soviet psychology.* White Plains, NY: Sharpe.

Yin-yee Ko, D. (1989). *Toward a social history of women in seventeenth century China.* Unpublished doctoral dissertation, Stanford University.

# 8

# *Learning to Write as an Adult*

## SUE GARDENER

**Adults "learn to write"** in all sorts of different ways and settings and for all sorts of different reasons. Talking to friends about this piece of work while I have been drafting it, I've been offered the experience of relearning essay writing for an in-service training course, writing poetry after years of writing to make reports or raise money, and changing from working on text as a printer to being again a composer and producer of text. But those people have in common a reasonably successful completion of their initial education, so that whatever difficulties and struggles they have had since are built on a foundation of recognizable competences. Most of us find that those competences are acquired with remarkably little explicitness or direct teaching, so that, if we develop a professional concern later with helping others acquire or recover them, we have to conduct an analysis that we may never have confronted before. But the range of learning I want to address here is that covered by adults whose writing competences may never have reached what would be expected of someone completing secondary education.

This is indeed a range, and a wide one. Adults who come to classes identified as part of adult literacy or basic education will themselves vary, from having little more than a signature to different degrees of fluency damaged by mechanical difficulty with transcription, usually spelling, but also possibly punctuation and other aspects of presentation. Adults who come to other classes in the broad range now described in the United Kingdom as "return to learning" will overlap with this group and will also include people whose difficulties are principally with the formats and procedures appropriate to formal study. (These courses offer a general education, not shadowing school curriculum but possibly leading to reentry into higher education as a mature student.)

The chapter that follows is based on conversations with people from both groups. I have chosen to see what can be drawn from the evidence of learners' reflections on and understanding of their own learning and not their written productions. It would be valuable to study changes in writing over time and to see how the descriptive and analytical categories available to us fit with what adults produce. But what I have chosen to set out instead is what they think they are doing and how they are able to process and make use of the activities we propose for them and the discourse we offer them. So I shall be drawing on the responses to questions about learning activities, about change, about the value of audiences and readerships, and of taking writing through to the point where it has a broader readership. I will be looking incidentally at the categories of writing that people do (and the categories they recognize) and at their understanding of relationships between talking and writing. I read what they said in the context of my own explorations of what the scholarly norms are in the field of writing and writing development, which has increasingly turned into an argument with emphases and absences. I will set out a little more about the contexts for the two sets of conversations and, in doing that, hope to show what my problematic is and how it developed.

## THE "CONVERSATIONS WITH STRANGERS" GROUP

The first set of conversations was part of my work from 1981 to 1984 as a "writing development worker" for a voluntary group called Write First Time. This group published, with subsidy from the British Adult Literacy and Basic Skills Unit, a paper containing mainly the writing and transcribed speech of adult literacy students. It was designed both as a reading resource and to indicate a place for writing as part of literacy learning and, in particular, writing of an expressive or argumentative kind rather than that of the functional curriculum. Functional literacy for adults in industrial societies, most of whom will not be doing or expecting to do jobs that require much paperwork, is liable to offer a very limited repertoire, most of it not involving the production of much continuous text. This became an issue in curriculum development, because the pressure of time and the urgency of learning could be offered as reasons for not doing anything that didn't have a practical return. However, work based on what could loosely be called *creative* writing—another term we were led to contest—did take hold in many teaching centers, and there were plenty of takers for the offer of editing and producing an issue of *Write First Time* in association with members of the national editorial group.

The writing development worker post was created because we realized that we had only a slight contact with learners and teachers, and they might welcome more support in developing this aspect of the literacy curriculum.

The bulk of the work I did in this job was advisory and developmental work by invitation in different parts of the country for one or two terms. But the practical involvement, and the chance to concentrate on this one aspect of the work as against the many-sided commitment of a tutor/organizer, also stimulated an interest in the theory, worked out or not, that underlay this particular kind of practice. I began to read more and to find out that, while there were illuminations to be had from many different disciplines in which issues of writing, language, and culture had been addressed, none of them shared all the concerns of teachers and learners engaged in this particular work. In particular, those writers, principally educationists, who had addressed issues of learning to write most thoroughly had all based their work on the writing development of children during the years of schooling. This was not surprising, but it left us with problems. In particular, models of writing development all seemed to have as a necessary accompaniment models of general cognitive, emotional, and social development, because they followed the years of childhood and adolescence. How could I apply them to the developmental procedures of adults learning? I could not assume that the *immaturity* of their writing, to adopt a term I have to see as a metaphor, corresponded to other kinds of immaturity: I had to detach the lack of this particular skill (or these skills) from notions about deepening understanding of and versatility in the adaptations of spoken language to different social situations and from progressions toward the capacity to abstract and reason. Or did I? Wasn't it after all the ruling assumption that those not so far educated were, with exceptions that could be described in casualty terms, less educable? That they did not reason on paper because they could not reason well at all, or, in some versions, that they could think less well because they were deprived of the cognitive advantages of working through writing? From comparing models, I had moved into a mine field of social, linguistic, class, and cultural issues.

I am not offering in this chapter to resolve them, rather to indicate in more detail what it is that remains to be worked through. The material I will use comes from one of the methods I found to clarify what our teaching procedures were and should be. I asked, through our network of teachers and organizers, to meet adult learners who would identify themselves as having made progress in writing, so that I could conduct extended interviews with them to find out what they meant by *progress* and how it had happened. Seven of the interviews used here—semistructured, tape-recorded interviews of an hour or more—were done in this way. Others were done later and with a different interview frame, as part of the research that went into *Conversations with Strangers* (Gardener, 1985a). This was the end report of the Writing

Development Project; it was presented as a pack of "ideas about writing for adult students," not classroom worksheets but a resource pack for learners and tutors together. Further material is derived from *Opening Time,* a teaching pack produced by Gatehouse Books (Frost & Hoy, 1986).

## THE "RETURN TO LEARNING" GROUP

When the Writing Development Project finished, I was looking for support to research adult writing development further. This was unsuccessful, except that the Inner London Education Authority's Inspectorate (ILEA) funded me part-time for six months to produce *The Development of Written Language Within Adult Fresh Start and Return to Learning Programmes* (Gardener, 1985b). This took me into the further end of the range of competences and difficulties described above. I worked through classroom observation and tapes of classroom sessions and through group and individual interviews about learning: Material from these sources will be referred to as well. Because many of the learners in these groups intended to go on to more formal study, issues relating to a shift from "writing from experience" to writing an essay came to the fore and brought with them questions about the cultural familiarity and boundaries of the formats of academic study and their claims to greater objectivity. The other issue that surfaced during the study, and that some of the interview material concentrates on, was the relationship between language awareness and language performance. Did learners need a model, for example, a sociolinguistic model, of different uses of speech and writing in order to manipulate and produce language in appropriate forms? Did they need to situate themselves in relation to normative judgments of language use and its presumed power to indicate thinking capacity, if they were themselves to claim the right to classify and analyze? Again, questions too large to deal with in a small-scale study, but they bore down on all the local observations.

I am spending as much time as this on context not only to let the reader know the nature and limitations of the study that led to the speculations that follow but also to make the point that what is known is what someone with the power to fund research needs and wants to know. The learning processes of the years of compulsory schooling are well studied; if adults return to the formal system as mature students in higher education, their learning and in particular their struggles with appropriate written composition may again receive research attention. In between, we are dealing with marginal educational provision, part-time unfunded study by working-class adults, and, not surprising, a history of very little research. I am glad to contribute to this volume if it raises the profile of what we as teachers and curriculum planners need to know. The final piece of context, and a further hook into fields of relevant study by others that I have not adequately explored, is a reminder of the linguistic and cultural pluralism of the United Kingdom in its postimperial phase. As well as the dialect diversity of White British people, the interviewees represent speakers of non-U.K. dialects of English, speakers of other languages now resident in the United Kingdom, and childhood learners of English from homes where little or no English was spoken. So their desire to write in English spans the "first-language/second-language" divide.

## HOW WE WORKED AS TEACHERS

The working assumptions that underlay our educational practice, and that set up the starting point for my first interviews, went something like this. Adults need to write as well as read because they will not be fully literate if they can only see themselves as consumers of text produced by others. An appropriate process is one that takes their capacity to produce spoken language as a starting point. This should create confidence in an ability to generate meaning and communicate effectively. With this understanding, it should be easier to put in place and, therefore, overcome the difficulties of transcription, because they will be seen as secondary to the difficulties and achievements of composition. The distinction between composition and transcription, between the struggles of making up text to represent what you want to say, and the struggles of setting it down in readable and acceptable form, is in itself something that needs to be learned. Most adult learners expect writing to be commented on only for purposes of correction, usually of spelling and punctuation. They, therefore, need to be offered learning situations in which the reception of, and response to, what they want to say is at least as important as correction; and they need to experience their writing as a real communication entering into real social exchanges. It will probably be appropriate for early pieces of writing to be based on personal experience and close to spoken language forms: The particular demands of written language will emerge with increasing skill. The reader will be able to see that this model was not uninfluenced, whether we knew it or not, by some school-based models and approaches, such as those of the Britton/Institute of Education school in London and the Graves and National Writing Project work in the United States. I do not want to subject our assumptions either to explanation or to critique at this stage but to move straight to the confirmations and challenges that were offered by the learners whose reflections on their learning I invited.

## TWO AGENDAS?

When I asked these learners to tell me what activities they had done as part of their learning, the answers were not always either clear or detailed. There was no chance, for example, to compile a popularity score for various methods of teaching spelling. All of them reported being able to spot errors better, and being more willing to risk errors, and identified both of these as important gains. But what also became clear is that talking at this level was not where the real matter lay. Some said that, when they came back to classes, this was what they expected to be doing; although the terminology of transcription and composition was not known or used, they would to start with identifying the difficulties of writing as lying in aspects of transcription. And all of them speak strongly about the frustration and sense of misrepresentation that lies in trimming and distorting what you write to fit what you can spell: This in itself is a major discouragement from writing. But all of them had clearly moved on to other agendas: The second agenda is the one about meanings and communication. For Brian, it was a shift of which he was well aware:

SG:    Did you ever think as well as spelling it's the business of getting your ideas sorted, or—you hadn't got that far.

Brian:    It just never entered my mind.

SG:    Would you say that now?

Brian:    And I would say only in the last couple of months I realized that you got to be able to put it sort of down in English to be understood. I can put it down and explain myself, people would know it, but it ain't what you call like English, you know what I mean?

This isn't just about a shift to working on composition, it's a note that was struck by several people in different ways and ties in to a different concern. Are some of the difficulties of composition associated with a belief that you do not have the appropriate language resources with which to compose? If so, are they inappropriate because they are a subordinate English, or because speech is qualitatively different from writing, or both? We'll explore this further later. For now I want to return to the change in agendas.

For almost all the people I spoke to, the shift was associated with something that had to be called a *key experience,* which was usually a key piece of writing—its composition and its reception. An extended account of this experience is Linda's, quoted at length in *Conversations with Strangers* (Gardener, 1985a, section A13, p. 3) under the title "How Strong I Felt." It was a moment with two kinds of power: putting down an account of past difficulty in reading and writing and how it had been overcome and then immediately offering it to an audience by reading it aloud to a tutor and a group:

> Now it's the first time I'd ever read anything out to anybody what I'd actually wrote. And when I finished actually writing it, 'course you proof-read it; and it was the first time I'd actually put it down on paper, what it felt like; and when I got to the bottom, finished, I cried myself. Because it's . . . I only realized how strong I felt about illiteracy when I wrote that.

I will return later to the suggestion here about writing as discovery; there is a lot to say about these learners' changing concepts of how their thoughts and meanings exist before writing.

My focus here is the nature of the experience that is the subject for this key piece of writing. The need to write about past learning difficulties, to go beyond past failure or review it, or break away from self-blame is fairly common, but so are other autobiographical themes. For Brian, it was an account of a difficult childhood; for Bessie, the narrative of her journey to Australia with her husband shortly after her marriage, which her tutor identified as part of her mourning after her husband's death; for Isaac, it was living with a stepparent, being separated from other children by not going to school, and hard work from an early age. For Tina, born in southern Italy and living in Halifax, it was the need to make sense, for her immediate family, of a life in two places, neither half understandable to those with whom she shared the other half. She has written about her early life and her move to Halifax in English for her children and grandchildren and now wants to write it in Italian for her nephews and nieces there. For John Glynn, there is more than one key piece, but the first one he talked about had classic subject matter—school—and an additional element: the control that could be taken by writing in a different way.

I was so hung up about school, I felt it was all my fault. . . . So I couldn't just write, "this was bad about school," I had to write it in an obscure way, by making characters: like if somebody had a bad temper, you made him into a real ogre. . . . So you wrote about the people you didn't like and hated, and you put a lot of hate into it, without actually naming names or—if anybody read it, even if I read it now, I wouldn't be able to recognize it. It was a way of getting rid of a lot of hassle and aggro. And it was like breaking down a barrier. Since then, that helped us relax.

The reception of these pieces is also central to their value, though sometimes the key experience of being received well comes with a different piece of work. Linda's had immediate validation from the group and the tutor to whom she read it. Brian got his feedback and encouragement from the tutor and is deeply ambivalent about the work ever going to other readers. Bessie's autobiographical piece is for her, but it has been transformed into something she can keep: "I've got it in writing now." Her other motive for writing is to keep in touch with her son, who is in the navy. Tina's grandchildren are the prime audience, but, like several of the others, she has also had the experience of revising her work for printing in a magazine. She, like others—Isaac, Felicity, John, Graham, and Linda in this group—has had work published beyond the local circuit of fellow students. The frequency with which this is reported no doubt reflects the professional network I was using to contact these students, but their account of the value of a readership still stands. Felicity wrote a piece about unemployment (because of her feelings about what her husband was going through), and it was accepted by *Write First Time:* I asked her if this had been important.

Felicity:   My goodness, yes, I can't tell anybody what a feeling that was, when it came through the post. . . .
Ann:   We heard somebody say it on the radio as well. . . .
Felicity:   . . . he just read parts of it out, he was using it more as a reference to somebody who knows what it's like to be unemployed. . . . I was quite proud of that.

Isaac produced one version of his life story by dictating it to a tutor; some years after this was published, he began to work over it again, this time writing it himself. His responsive audience was fellow students first of all, and then strangers, and they spurred him on to write again:

For the amount of encouragement I get, and the amount of praise I get for the first one, I try to make this one more better yet.

## THE PUBLIC REALM

The point doesn't need laboring—there is obvious stimulus in going beyond being read for the purposes of practicing and being corrected and in going beyond hearing your own voice. But the self as reader doesn't go off the map, and these writers maintain a strong sense that writing is a statement from self and of self, sometimes to the exclusion of concern for a readership. The other extreme is that, once the writing is seen to enter a public realm, that realm is limitless, for better and for worse. The good part of it is that you can "tell the world." Tina writes about her wartime experiences and matches it up with what she has heard from a fellow student who fought in Italy:

> . . . and he write—during the war when he were in Italy, that time when I were there, and he say he were happy every day when he was there.
>
> SG:    So you were putting it into—and it brings out someone else's experience, yes?
>
> Tina:    Yes, I put it over to some people—or maybe, it could stop the world another war, you know. . . . I don't know, it's hard, it's very hard to put into everybody mind, like.

Ellen, too, wants to tell the world:

> The lot of them, you know what I mean? Something that's really important to me. Whatever I wrote down I would not want to keep it myself. I'd want to show everybody, you know, just—because I think it's important this way because the people that was afraid to come to these classes, they wouldn't be any more if they knew just how a person felt.

Her context shifts between the whole world and the world of those like herself; and neither she nor Tina has yet the experience to know how segmented the apparently universal readership out there can be or how much silence can follow the exposure of publication. "The world" isn't standing out there shoulder to shoulder in the public square, and most authors hear very little from their readers. But there is something powerful here about the sense that writing is a means to fuller and wider human communication, which is one thing that the isolation of limited literacy has prevented.

The converse of this is that you risk total exposure; and because the nature of writing is seen so clearly as being a projection of bits of your self, what you risk exposing is also yourself. The expression and validation of self is a motive for some writers and an important touchstone of progress—how genuinely is the self, the meaning or the feeling, coming out? But because control is still incomplete, censorship and reticences and a sense of danger still hang around writing. To explore first the understanding of writing as registering identity: Tina's account of why she wanted to find a teacher to show her how to write English touches on needing to explain to her grand-children why she spoke English differently, and needing to escape the humiliation of dependency on others to fill out forms, and settles firmly on "telling my grandchildren my branches and my roots."

Having access to direct expression is one of the great gains of losing the fear of misspelling:

SG:      You can write things the way you think them. Anything you want to say.
Isaac:   I say it. Any word I buck 'pon and I don't know it, I ask her [his wife].
SG:      But you don't change the word, or change the meaning?
Isaac:   No.

Ellen wants to record her life, and its understandings and feelings, and to be more than she has seemed to be:

... to really write what I want to write down, I mean—my friends and my relations, I mean they've known me, part of my life, and they've never known that I've been able to ... well, they have known that I've not been able to read and write, but to me just, you know, I'd be really pleased to think that I'd wrote it.

Writing is magic. It is the registration of the invisible, neglected, and unimaginably rich consciousness. As such, it has to be *you:* Linda said, "If I had changed it, it wouldn't have been me." The strongest advocate of this line was Jay, also quoted at length in *Conversations with Strangers* (Gardener, 1985a):

... it doesn't really matter to anybody else whether it looks a mess or what you write is a mess, and I'm just coming to the strong conclusion, if I do it and I think it's fine, fantastic, it's great for me. . . . you can have millions of ideas I should imagine, pouring around inside there, and it might be an idea to just write what comes out and then sort it out.

For other people, the richness of the lava flow inside only registers how obstructed is the process of getting it out: The ideal may be unobstructed passage, but the reality is otherwise, and learners have to explore to know whether this is to be put down to their shortage of skill—do skilled writers experience less obstruction?—or whether it is in the nature of the writing process itself, in the fit and lack of fit between thoughts and feelings and words and writing. "Sometimes I had a word in my mouth but just can't find the form to put it down" (Isaac). This is not, I think, a comment about spelling. "I have a lot in my mind but it won't all come out. . . . I want to write and many time I write it two, three time over again while it is sunken in my head" (Tina). Words have a physical presence for these writers. They come up to you (or don't), they sink in your head or stick in your mouth, you have to get over them or round them, the "big words" stand in your way.

Both in spite of and because of the imperfection of what is registered, you may need to put limits on what gets put down in writing. Recording of any kind produces evidence: I've hardly ever used a tape recorder with a group without someone saying, "taken down and used in evidence." Evidence is used by others, for reasons that are not yours and probably against you. It's a factor in the most practical tasks. This is Graham:

> You get to think, what the heck do you put on a form? Am I spelling it right, am I doing it right, sort of thing, am I putting it right? How should I present myself?

Bessie dealt with the sense of exposure by censoring herself: It's all right to write one's own life story

> 'cause nobody else is involved in it though, are they really? . . . 'cause if you write about everyday things, you've got to bring somebody else into it—well, you don't really want that, do you?

And she could only consider sending some writing in for a college magazine on the grounds that "they won't know it's me anyway."

Brian says he always "clamped up" when tutors suggested he write about himself, and, although he has now done so, we got into a long and tortuous negotiation about what he is putting in and leaving out, and why, and, in particular, whether it will ever go to other readers.

> Brian:  I don't really want anyone to see it, haven't even shown my kids yet.
>
> SG:  Do you see why I asked that though, because in a way, the way you're describing it, you're sorting out which bits go on paper, which bits don't, and it's as if putting it on paper is a bit making it public even now.

Brian:     Yes. . . . I've got a thing about putting things down on paper and how I've
           writ that I don't know.

SG:        But you've been working at it quite hard, it sounds as if it must be quite
           important in a way. I mean it's not the sort of job you go on with if you think
           it's a real pain. . . . Who does it matter to, if it's depressing or of it's brightened
           up, if no one's going to read it?

Brian:     As you say there, right, now at this moment in time I don't expect anyone
           to read it, you know what I mean, but at the same time, in case it does happen,
           I don't want to make it too depressing. . . . I think if the names were changed,
           and it was—possibly out the eastern area, yes. No, I don't know. I think if the
           names were changed, yes, I think I would go along with it.


## TELLING AND WRITING


Any writing, then is different from telling, and the difference is at least
partly independent of audience. For some of the people I spoke to, there was
no problem about expression in speech. This is Linda:

> Well, you're always able to speak, so you've no problems like that. When it
> comes to writing you do have problems. You're always able to speak so you just
> accept the fact. When you come to writing you know that you can't write, so it
> is—it is a bit of a barrier.

Many of these learners have tried and have benefited from the approach
through spoken language, used for dictation to a tutor, taped as a resource for
writing, or as a preliminary warmup discussion with a tutor or in a group
preliminary to writing. But their experience of this method takes them into
reflection on the difference between talk and writing as much as into
recognition of connections. Ellen was, at the time of the interview, still
dependent on this method to get her thoughts down: "I tell her what to put
and she writes it down."
But there are limitations:

> . . . well, if I wrote it myself, I think I would put more feeling into it, how I
> wanted to write it, but to ask someone to write it, you don't seem to have that—I
> think you're a bit afraid to put too much feeling into it, maybe. . . . If you were
> writing something yourself, you would start from the beginning.

Writing in class, through a scribe who also has other people to teach, is fragmentary as well as interposing another channel, to revert to the metaphor of flow. Isaac has an unusual basis for making this comparison, in that he has reworked, in his own writing, material that first came out by the language experience method—spoken language elicted and written down by a tutor to provide a practice text—and then more systematic dictation. We were dealing with the issue of reticence again when the comparison came up: Hadn't he been doubtful, to start with, whether he would want his children to know about his early life? But he had written about it at greater length in the second version.

Isaac:    It's different. At the time when I did the first book, I didn't wrote it up myself. So how I say it to you, I say it to you differently, but me now wrote it myself, I able to say it different and put it the way I say it.

SG:    Right. . . so—you're more in control?

Isaac:    Correct. Now you see, same thing now, me have a scaredness there, to say it to you that way; but do it on myself now, I have the control myself.

This was developed later:

Some of what I wrote in my own writing now in this book here, I wouldn't able to tell you, and I shy to tell you about it. But now I can do it myself I put it down on the paper. . . . Since I can wrote now, I can able to write anything and understand it, for—you know?—I don't feel ashamed again about it; for you see I understand it clear myself now. . . . You have more trust in yourself to wrote it down than stand up in front of a person and tell them.

It may not be possible to say whether the understanding comes from the change of mode of composition or from spending more time reflecting on the same history. Isaac's comments also emphasize how peculiar and context specific is the role we have become used to, of scribe who is a nonjudging but not neutral medium for the passage of words on to paper.

Speech as a resource for someone who has changed her language is not going to be easy. Tina finds that

I was thinking in English, but I was thinking my own way—like we talk broke English, you know. . . . So it's a lot of thing, it coming easy to me in English, but the majority of them question in my mind, they had to be calculate in Italian and put down in English.

It seems to have been crucial for her capacity to recall and order that she had kept a diary of her experiences as a young woman, although it was now lost. Ranjit, a Return to Learning student, came to London when she was 3, and, when she was asked to map her language use, drew two distinct branches for English (formal and informal) and for Punjabi. The shift has given her a high awareness of different language use; but she still says that "when I'm with my aunties and that, it just comes to me, my language; the flow of language is just . . . can't stop" (ILEA Tape 10).[1] She sees a need to rehearse in speech the language she wants to write:

> I think the more you get used to speaking that way, it'll be more flow when you're writing as well; I think.

> When you don't use these different words often, they won't come to you when you're writing, you just describe them in a different way, describe the subject in a plain way. Because when [tutor] speaks, she always speaks in long words: her writing must be the same. If you compare it—it's habit and the use of it all the time, that comes out. . . . And when they sort of come along together, they just flow out of you, don't they? (ILEA Tape 10)

Other learners emphasize the difference between speech and writing more than the notion of continuous flow. For some of them, like above, and Joan Graham in a taped group discussion in Sheffield, it's that

> I can write better than what I can talk. . . . I can put down on paper my feelings and everything. But not—if I come to anybody then I start thinking, "now am I saying this right? is that the right word to use?

These are people for whom the chance that writing brings to revise and have second thoughts is invaluable. Judith (in the *Return to Learning* study, Gardener, 1985b) struggles toward a clear perception of difference:

> I think talking is you're speaking to someone and you expect a reply. But when you're writing, you're speaking to the paper and it comes back at you. So your words, you're hearing your words or seeing your words as other people—you're finally talking to yourself. (ILEA Tape 20)

Our classroom practice and the provisional model I outlined at the beginning do not only argue that speech is a resource in terms of the individual's assurance of her capacity to produce language. We have also been accustomed to emphasize the value of discussion it the learning group; and this is supported by some learners, particularly in terms of ideas:

Linda:   When you discuss a particular subject you get some ideas from everybody else and then when you go home you can recall them ideas and put them ideas into your own piece of work.

SG:   I think sometimes it's actually even hearing your own ideas; you know, you can say something and you say, "Oh god, I didn't know I thought that."

Linda:   Yes, that's perfectly true, yes.

The idea that you write to discover and recognize your own meanings is also commonplace but not necessarily one shared by inexperienced writers. The model of "language in the head" that has begun to emerge from some of the more romantic utterances of these speakers doesn't necessarily lead to a concept like Britton's "shaping at the point of utterance": It can, in ways that seem unhelpful, lead to a model of preformed thought waiting to be pulled through the barrier. To recognize discovery of meaning in speech may be a help toward recognizing it in the writing process. Isaac made this recognition: "You don't really realize what you done till when it done—you see?"

What do these learners say about the varieties of spoken English that they and others use? We have already heard how Brian associates "proper written English" both with logical and clearly explained content and with correctness of transcription; and there is Tina's description of her "broke English." Apart from possible ambiguities about what "writing my own way" means, only one other of the *Conversations* group comments on the issue and, not surprisingly, it is Isaac. As teachers and editors, we had a history of discussion with him about the representation of his spoken language. It is not a surprise that he is full of contradictions; he chose, after considerable debate, to leave his first book in a form corresponding to the modified Jamaican he uses to speak to us, White teachers. He is capable of being censorious about another Jamaican woman's book on the grounds that "she didn't have much English, don't it? Just like my first one. . . . Just how she speak, just how she wrote it."

He wants to have proper written English in his repertoire. He wants to hang on to turns of phrase that he can see either as personal or as typically Jamaican. He associates his old ways with bad language and a lack of understanding: This passage makes such interesting connections that it needs some length of quotation:

I think reading—reading is a part of your life. Before I can do what I can do today in my life, I think my life was more reckless; when I say reckless, more rougher, didn't have any—no background. Things what I know today, I can able to put them in the right order. I couldn't able to do that two years ago. And I know up to now I can not able to speak properly to anybody, but I think I can able to speak more properly now. . . . I have more confident in myself more to speak. But before, you know what I mean, we used to chop up the Jamaican

language, you know; like, me and the other coloured people round here, we just
chop up the language and carry on: dammit man, fuck—beg your pardon—fuck
it man, raas man, don't bother about that fucking thing man—just carry on that
way. Now we don't speak those things any more, we just try to speak more
English style.

Yes, he knows that English people swear too; yes, he is willing to concede
that there may be learned attitudes that make him cast Jamaican language as
bad and rough: but "you're brought up [to think that] and you just cannot get
it out overnight." Neither straightforward cultural pride nor efficient code
switching are options for everybody.

It is the learners in the *Return to Learning* study, (Gardener, 1985b), the
ones who are considering an educational move that may offer to change their
social situation, who speak more strongly about the judgments attached to
nonstandard speech. This is Raymond, another Jamaican:

What I'm disgusted about is what I call a social snobbery. . . . The minute you
open your mouth you condemn yourself by your accent. People are not interested
in what you have to say. (ILEA Tape 18)

And Daisy, a working-class Londoner in her fifties:

. . . as regards as actual speech is compared with education, you can still speak
rough and ready and everything, but it still doesn't mean to say that you're
senseless. You can still have the brains and you can still do the things as brainy
as someone that speaks with their diction correct and every word pronounced
properly.
SG:     Do you think that other people think that you haven't got so much sense if
        you talk like that?
Daisy:  Oh, yes. Yes. If you don't talk properly then you're ignorant. I think it's a
        kind of first impression, isn't it, before you get any tests to see if you're ignorant
        or not, your actual way you speak—same as I think the way you dress. . . . But
        it bears no relation to the ability of the person. (ILEA Tape 19)

A few years ago, I would have said that these people were displaying the
damage from an old set of prejudices that were changing; now I don't know.
The consequence for the undertaking of higher education is, of course,
considerable: You are being asked to learn the language of a group who have
used exactly that language and its codifications to mark the difference
between your group and their own. Some of the difficulties experienced by

working-class women and men, Black and White, in learning the writing
forms of the academic world, are at least in part resistances.

## MAKING IT BETTER

Revising and improving work is something that many learners have been
unable to do, to propose to themselves, before coming back to study.
Discussions about revising work take us back to the two agendas: Are we
talking about producing a more correct transcription or about making it better,
truer, more communicative, more effective? The transcription issues remain,
and progress in spelling in particular is frustratingly slow. But, whether or
not it is because of the emphasis offered by tutors, what these learners choose
to talk about is the developing capacity to make other kinds of improvements
to a draft. For most of them, the concept of "draft" is itself recently learned,
and it corresponds to a change in the function of the teacher as critical reader.
The old experience shows in the habitual terms for comment and marking:
"pulling it to pieces," "pulling you to bits," "pick holes in it." A more positive
description is of the tutor as editor. Tina speaks for them all when she says,
"I still wish I could do it perfect," but there's a great deal of willingness to
attend to the other agenda and satisfaction in working on other definitions of
making it better.

What is better? There's an area that can be seen as intermediate between
issues of correctness and issues of expression, which includes vocabulary—
"the big words, you know," which some say they can use in speech but not
in writing   and that nebulous entity, grammar. What is Linda saying here?

SG:     Do you think that formal grammar was important to you, I mean when you
        said, you know, learning about the parts of sentences and what's the verb and
        all that, did that matter to you as you were learning?

Linda:  No. No, not at first. The verbs and that didn't. But still, I know about the
        verbs, I know what they are, but it isn't important really. . . . I didn't bother at
        first with things like that, but when I was getting on, I wanted to know more
        and more about the English structure and how to do it proper.

I didn't follow this up then; I wish I had. The *Return to Learning* study
(Gardener, 1985b) brought the same issue up again, because to teach or not
to teach grammar became the subject for some classroom negotiations. I
began to see "grammar" as a code word for "conscious knowledge about how

language works." Few adult students I have spoken to believe that learning grammar will make them write better, though some do; there's a different understanding, and one that takes some discussion, about whether or not they *use* grammar when they produce language for everyday purposes. But this student's statement is, I think, typical and suggestive: "It's only when it's brought to my attention, it bothers me because I'm not clear about it" (ILEA notes, November 21, 1984). Working on writing is liable to bring it to attention. I am not sure that teachers have enough resources to offer to make it clearer.

The major gains in revising and editing procedures lie on the other side of this transitional area, though features of the middle ground may be means for achieving the ends that are identified. The kinds of change people say they want to make in a first draft include

expanding,
emphasizing certain things,
elaborating,
putting different words to it,
making it sound better,
deciding what's important,
putting down what you really want to put down,
getting out what's in your mind,
putting more feeling into it, and
phrasing it differently.

The discovery they have all made—and I think it's arguably the key development and the one that marks these learners in particular as having made progress—is the capacity to review a draft with different eyes. Linda puts it clearly:

Before I thought it was okay, but now I can look at my work, read it and think, it could sound a little bit better if I put that in. It might be just one word, or it might be a complete sentence, or I might have to start all over again. . . . I think it's because I am getting better of reading my own work and pulling it to pieces myself.

It's important to say that this learning is independent of reading skill as such: Ellen relies on work being read back to her and also on comment from others: "Somebody sees it in a different light than you have." For several of these learners, reading aloud or the silent reading that still summons up *sounding* right as a criterion is vital. It is the unconscious knowledge of language that proposes change and improvement. Many comment on the value of a time delay:

> Specially if you leave it for ten or fifteen minutes and go back to it, because if you write it, finish it like at the bottom, then you start reading, you're reading exactly what you've said, full. You're not reading it, you're just memorizing. (Brian)

And John Glynn has a particular note on the value of working alongside a more experienced writer:

> I don't feel afraid to ask stupid questions and look stupid: instead of, "Oh god, they know better than me about that." Not being scared, and accepting that nobody can do anything perfect first time off, and do—like doing a report: offering the first draft out to people to look at and pull apart; and always remember that, one, it's the first draft, two, it's the first time you've done that; and, OK, people say, "You've missed that out"—all right, and accept it.

The points about decentering the self from the writing are familiar from school-based studies of learning, but the important addition to make in this context is that it isn't a question here of moving from egocentricity to awareness of others, and of sociolinguistic expectations *in general*, but of moving in the specific task of writing. People in adult classes have done their growing into plural and socially grounded language uses. There are a few adults in literacy classes (and outside them) who appear not to be able to make shifts from self to others as audience for reasons of personality, but overwhelmingly we are talking about people grasping a skill because they have, for the first time, been taught it and continuously exposed to a practice of exercising it. This is a development we can, at least, facilitate.

Another key area of development that turns out to be relatively independent of decoding and transcribing skills is in the mental grasp of a long piece of work. Isaac talks about his composition process in a way that would have been impossible for him earlier:

> Most of my writing as to there, well I would say three quarters of it, I sit in the car and do it: get in the back seat and sit out there in the late afternoon. And when I was doing it, when I doing a sentence then I don't finish it: I don't say, "Right, full stop there." When I don't remember what to say, I leave that one and go to the other one. And when I remember now what to say, I go back to the first one and I start. . . . The part about my mother-in-law and my father, is a lot I didn't remember, and then I wrote half and I leave it and go back then

and do something else, and then I think about it; then everything just come up into my mind, and I go back for it.

For him, though, this process is premised on being his own transcriber and on the fact that the source is memory. Joe, who contributed to *Opening Time* (Frost & Hoy, 1986) the section called "Tackling a Long Piece of Work," relied on a tape and its transcript and quarried the words he wanted for his redraft out of the transcript. Even with these limitations, he has broken one of the developmental barriers: more than you can write at a sitting. And he writes about it with a grasp of a whole process:

> Now since that first page, I jump from one point to another. I had to go through all the whole book. And if I go back to the second page and there's something on the second page that would suit a point in the first page, it clicked in my head that I could put it in there better. It clicks in my mind even days after. I mean I don't do it all in one day. So I'd put them all down on bits of paper and go over and over and over them again, see if there was anything there I'd missed. Then I write out the whole page again because I want it right" (Frost & Hoy, 1986, p. 15).

## READING TO WRITING?

It would be reasonable to propose that increasing reading experience, to provide more examples of written language for unconscious analysis and use as models, would be a central source of development. Here the interviews are contradictory, and, if any such process is going on, it lies below awareness for many learners.

Ellen was able to say that one of her problems in writing letters was that "you don't know how letters are supposed to be." She and others found that reading some of the literature, now quite substantial, of other "ordinary lives" encouraged them to put their own down on paper. But others will say that there is no connection, that they are unaware of learning anything from what they read about how to write. If this is true, it's surely a major gap in our teaching process. There are writers who, with or without direct connections being made, do bring their critical reading into the writing frame. Brian was very critical of another student-written story.

Brian:    I thought, well it's a student, and I said, it's the sort of thing I would write ... not explaining myself which is not proper English, what I'm saying earlier. You know, it's down there, it's good enough, you know, bit of weight off my mind.

SG:      ... You've said two things and I want to know if you think they're the same
         as each other or not. You said he didn't explain himself properly, and it wasn't
         proper English. Is that the same thing or is that two things wrong with it?

Brian:   It wasn't proper written English. He wrote it how he talks and thinks, but
         he didn't go into greater detail why the chef was on strike, know what I mean?
         'Cause he was saying about some of the women was £5 a week worse off, you
         know, and he wasn't saying if the chef was worse off.

It's an open question how Brian would apply this to his own work; and it may
not be helpful in terms of process that he specifically refused to separate
issues of content and clarity of ideas from the notion of "proper written
English," which he later explains as

> ... like when you have English exams in school, things like that, I mean proper
> grammar, that's what I mean. Anything which is written down and understand-
> able is English, to me anyway, but as for like question marks, brackets, speech,
> that all ... you know what I mean.

Students learning to adapt their writing to formal educational uses face a
particular problem of how their reading experience can help them, particularly because there is likely to be little in that reading experience that offers
them models for the short discursive essay. During the *Return to Learning*
study (Gardener, 1985b), I also began to speculate that there is a gap in the
model of learning that tutors bring to this transition—or perhaps a gap
between two models. A case in point was a group who were using their time
in the morning to "write from experience" and in the afternoon to study
written language as readers. To summarize a longer discussion, it appears
that, for reasons that will be now be familiar, the morning's discussion was
dominated by the language of self-expression and self-revelation, and the
reception of writing shared in the group (by reading aloud, not by study of a
text) was celebratory. Even the writer who started by asking for help with
features of style and presentation finished by relocating the narrative in his
or her life experience. The language in which a text read in the afternoon was
discussed was simply not continuous with this: None of the comments was
about the personality of the writer or the biographical relevance of her
writing. There was a wider ranging critical vocabulary in operation, and one
able to pay attention to text rather than to the origins of the text, but it wasn't
easy to bring it to bear on the group's own writings (ILEA notes, December
12, 1984).

One of the interviewees who was most willing to deploy notions of style,
and most able to give an account of writing and critical reading that presented

the two activities as interactive, was John Glynn, who has access to a singular set of opportunities in that he has moved from being a student to being a group worker, tutor, editor of student-produced work, and worker in a collective project in which tasks are shared. He is also, you will recall, the writer who chose to manage his unpleasant memories of school by displacing and caricaturing them; so we may have to talk about inclinations to write in varied ways as well as experiences, but the experiences are surely important. The model we started with supposed that kinds and uses of writing would be learned from real communicative situations. It is only to a limited extent that the adult classroom has supplied these. I have no wish to undervalue what has been done, by me and by many others, in providing readerships, live audiences, the discipline of revising for print, feedback from unknown readers, and the validation of silenced lives and ideas through the kinds of publication we have worked on together with learners. But John's many-sided perspective on the writing process depends on further experiences than these and on roles other than that of student within these practices themselves. He started going to classes to support his work for City and Guilds building:

John:     And then summer, when the pressure was off, I used to write things of my own, and I started enjoying it, instead of being terrified. Then I used to experiment with different styles—but they were just for my benefit, not for anybody else's. . . . I still felt that if I'd done it, it's no good. . . .

We used to do our own center magazine. . . . And in a way that was going outside, 'cause I did a lot of linking, practical stuff with that, like drawings, and also like editorials. . . . That was different again for me; and that *was* being assessed, that was going outside—well as far as I was concerned, it was going from my little desk and little book, to being typed, and people saying, "Here—I don't like that." I had to cope with that, which I found difficult. . . .

When I was working at Gatehouse, when we used to do writing workshops, somebody would write something, and I'd see that, and to me, that could be better. I felt I was going back to people and saying, "Look, you can do better than that, I know you can; you probably don't"—and I probably hadn't made the connection with myself. . . .

SG:     So, Gatehouse had come into being, and you got a job with them. Let's just list the things you've had to write since then I mean, obviously, letters, yes?

John:   Yes. Ordinary letters, fund-raising letters, say business letters, like writing to the company to say, "This is what we want in the building." . . . And—funding applications; introductions to books; oh—yesterday a reference for somebody. Reports; and—like when there's other groups like ourselves, and their funding's up for grabs—to justify them, what do you call it?

SG:     What was the most difficult thing to learn about those jobs?

John:   Trying to work out what people wanted. Trying to work out how their minds work, putting it in the right style.

SG:     How do you think you learn? Trial and error, reading other things?

John:   A bit of both. . . . When I did an introduction to a book, I just grabbed as many books with similar types of introduction, read through them, thought, "That was bad—I'm not going to fall into that trap," or, "That was good, I'll try and do something similar to that." Instead of trying to do something totally unique. You can only build on what other people have done, or what you have done in the past. I've just become aware of that.

This is not just someone who has learned to behave as a writer, it is someone who has learned to locate himself among a community of users of writing.

## DISCOURSE AND SITUATION

The use I want to make of this long quotation (above) is to establish two of the conclusions I draw from this survey: They relate to issues of discourse and issues of situation. The interviews themselves represent a rare set of demands on both thinking and language, for it is not very often that people are asked to think and speak in a sustained way about writing. The issue of discourse is not one I have often seen confronted in our curriculum. Language is not necessarily what adults think they are coming to study when they come to learn reading or writing; neither is it what teachers feel they have to know. Many of us are operating with ad hoc terminology ourselves, and we don't often have a clear policy about what we need to use even as labeling, let alone as tools for analysis, in our classes. There are instances of terminology and ways of seeing procedures, and procedures themselves, passing explicitly and directly from tutors to students: "drafting," "proofreading," writing through dictation, taping and transcribing, and some forms of planning are all part of the tutors' discourse and ways of working that learners have acquired. But, overall, it seems to me that we share very little with learners; that if we do have a model underlying what we do, of how meaning is in its prelanguage forms, of how language is generated, how it is extended, how it relates to social context both in speaking and in writing, what we mean by proper English, whether written language is a further dialect or a situational variant of spoken language, what "kinds" of writing are and how and when we construct and use them, how our reading relates to writing—if we as tutors are able to give an account of these things, it appears we do not often do so with our learners. The overall impression from what these learners say, under the pressure of my questioning but also arising out of their interest and pressure to articulate something of importance to them, is that these are new attempts and discoveries. They do not arise out of a discourse current between us.

This would not matter if we were confident that learning to write could be achieved through a set of practices and activities, without the need for reflection. The evidence of these interviews for me is that what I have called the two agendas are embedded in how learners themselves see what they need to learn and what to change, and so that we have to work out of the second agenda—which could be summarized as changing the relationship of the self to writing—as well as the first, which is the long and thankless battle with the difficulties of transcription. If this is so, the reflective process *is* a learning process and needs to be made into curriculum and not just feedback on curriculum.

The self that needs to be resituated is a socially as well as psychologically constructed self. Reentering education as an adult is in itself a situational change that challenges previous situatings; and it brings with it new offers and demands for language use, both spoken and written, that produce change seen by learners as valuable. (Several of this group speak about being more confident in speech as a result of or in association with doing more with writing—or doing more talking in class, perhaps.)

What also has to be said, though, is that educational situations themselves may not be sufficient to produce *decisive* change, in the direction of casting yourself as a continuing learner and user of writing. Several of these writers, in speaking about what I have called their "key piece of writing," say in one form or another, "That's it now: I don't think I'll be doing a lot more." There may be nothing wrong with this, as there is nothing wrong with the fact that not all users of practical reading skills become ambitious readers or readers of habit. But it may also reflect the fact that, apart from education, which they do identify as a change experience, nothing else has changed: The social context of writing for them is the same, and they have made no breakthrough, occupationally or otherwise, that will present them with a continuing and changing set of demands for writing, of different types and for different purposes and readerships.

It may be for the same reason that few of them cite "real-world" functional tasks that they are now able to do better, or, if they do, the tasks are returned to almost as a by-product of the other learning. It does matter that they can write letters without dependence, and make written language operate in the world—to deal with the builder or to get your daughter on the Jimmy Saville show. But you still aren't called on to do very much with your writing. That is why John Glynn's account is so remarkable: The version of literacy education that he encountered did lead him to a situational change, and much of his learning has derived from it. This can't be engineered for all learners, but it should surely inform our curriculum, organization, and procedures.

When I planned this chapter, I expected to be making more reference to the professional and academic discourse about writing and to the points where it fits or doesn't fit my observations and conclusions. It seems I shall have to leave this to another occasion; but I do want to return to the issue of writing development and cognitive development.

It seems to me that formulations like the following depend too much on the self-reflection of the group who have been fully enfranchised into writing, which is a minority in industrialized society and a tiny minority globally:

> Writing becomes for many people the organizing force in their mental development. . . . Although a powerful generator of thought and knowledge, conversation's outputs are social products, negotiated meanings. We do not truly own our thoughts or experiences until we have negotiated them with ourselves and for this writing is the prime medium (Bereiter & Scardamilia, 1983, p. 31).

I now recontext these ideas in the history that Raymond Williams describes:

> It is only in the last hundred and fifty years, in any culture, that a majority of people have had even minimal access to this technique [writing] which already, over two millennia, had been carrying a major part of human culture. The consequences of this long (and in many places continuing) cultural division have been very great, and the confusion of developments beyond it, in societies at last becoming generally literate, is still very much with us. (Williams, 1981, p. 95)

All the people whose experiences and ideas, "owned" by them or not (though how can we say not?), are the subjects of this chapter, live out this "confusion of developments"; and my case is that, although I have drawn the material from a group that is itself numerically a minority, their experience is more continuous with that of the majority than that registered by Bereiter and Scardamilia. What is exceptional is that they have put themselves in a situation where this experience and their reflections on it will be tested, extended, and made articulate.

## APPENDIX: INTERVIEWEES

*Write First Time* interviews:

(1)  Linda—Bradford, four years' tuition (June 16, 1983)
(2)  Issac Gordon—Jamaica to London, seven years (June 20, 1983)
(3)  Bessie—London to Stevenage, six months (June 28, 1983)
(4)  Felicity—Cambridge, two years (June 29, 1983)
(5)  Tina—South Italy to Halifax, two years (November 7, 1983)
(6)  Ellen—Halifax, one and a half years (November 7, 1983)
(7)  Brian—East London, two years (November 16, 1983)

*Conversations with Strangers* interviews:

(1)  Graham—Bedford (June 13, 1984)
(2)  John Glynn—Manchester (June 18, 1984)
(3)  Jay Lancaster (1983, interview by Roz Ivanič)

## NOTE

1. The ILEA tapes and notes referred to, for the interviewees not described in the Appendix, were used in conducting the Gardener (1985b) *Return to Learning* study.

## REFERENCES

Bereiter, C., & Scardamilia, M. (1983). Does learning to write have to be so difficult? In I. Pringle & J. Yalden (Eds.), *Learning to write: First language/second language*. New York: Longman.
Frost, G., & Hoy, C. (1986). *Opening time*. Manchester: Gatehouse Books.
Gardener, S. S. (1985a). *Conversations with strangers: Ideas about writing for adult students*. London: ALBSU.
Gardener, S. S. (1985b). *The development of written language in adult Fresh Start and Return to Learning programmes*. London: ILEA.
Williams, R. (1981). *Culture*. London: Fontana.

# 9

# *Bringing Community Writing Practices into Education*

## ROZ IVANIČ
## WENDY MOSS

**This book has reexamined** the cultural understanding of literacy as monolithic and autonomous and examined writing practices within community
contexts. One main discovery of people studying writing in the community
is that writing in everyday life is different in many ways from writing in
traditional English classes. They have also contributed to a richer way of
thinking about writing: Writing is a set of practices that include purposes,
procedures, processes, and strategies, ways of learning to write, feelings
about writing, attitudes to writing as well as the physical form the writing
takes. In this chapter, we are interested in how this information about writing
practices in particular communities can be used by educators.

We want to acknowledge from the start that there is no simple clear-cut
distinction between "community" and "school." First, educational institutions are themselves "communities"; and subject areas ("disciplines" in
higher education) are all different from each other. (See Jolliffe, 1988, for
recent studies of academic writing communities.) One important lesson
educators can learn from studies of writing in the community is to recognize
the role of social context in writing —whether that context is everyday life,
work, or the educational community itself. (See Bloome, 1987; Odell, 1985;
Rose, 1988, for further discussion of this point.) In this chapter, however, we
are not using the word *community* to refer to educational domains, as our
purpose is to distinguish these from others. We will concentrate on the way
in which the teaching of writing inside school (or college) can take account
of what has been discovered about writing outside school.

A second complication is that writing can be *imposed* or *self-generated*
both in and out of school. These terms need some explanation. There is some
writing for which the style and range of allowable content is laid down for

us by social institutions ("imposed literacy"), and there is some writing that stems from our own needs, interests, and purposes, in which we are free to adopt our own content and styles ("self-generated literacy"). This distinction can be applied to purposes for writing, meanings expressed in writing, writing conventions, writing processes, and criteria for assessment of writing. In everyday life at home, at work, and in the community, a lot of what people write is self-generated, but most people encounter a lot of imposed writing tasks too, particularly filling out forms. These are usually part of the bureaucracy surrounding employment, health services, taxation, being a consumer, and so on. (This is also mentioned by Barton, Chapter 1, p. 8.) Imposed writing is also very common in education, where teachers tell learner-writers what to write, what about, how to write, and what counts as good writing.

The distinction can become polarized, and indeed has in recent debates about the teaching of writing. (For further discussion, see, for example, Bartholomae, 1985; Delpit, 1986; Martin, 1985/1989). Some educators believe they should focus on imposed writing, trying to equip their learners to hold their own in the system as it is. Others recognize the value of self-generated writing and focus on this exclusively, running the risk of leaving the learners unable to deal with imposed writing when they must.

In this chapter, we will pursue the idea that writing in the community (as defined above and as described in other chapters in this book) can make an important contribution to education. This idea is already taken seriously by many educators. Some focus on bringing the language of the community into learning to write (for example, Heath, 1983; Richmond, 1982; Schwab & Stone, 1987). Others focus on bringing burning social issues from learners' communities into writing lessons (Moll & Diaz, 1987; National Writing Project, 1990).

We are not challenging the general assumption that educational institutions have something to offer. Our question is this: How can educational institutions contribute to, rather than detract from, people's experience of writing and learning to write in the community? This leads to several subsidiary questions. How can education nurture self-generated writing? What should education do about the imposed writing that is such a major part of people's community writing experience? How can education give people access to the statusful writing of school, without it becoming a further imposition? How can educators challenge the dominance of schooled literacy and draw on community-based literary practices? We will suggest that educators can take a "descriptive" or a "critical" view of different types of writing and that the critical view provides a principled way of integrating "self-generated" and "imposed" writing.

In the first section we will compare a descriptive with a critical view of community writing practices. In the second section, we will compare different relationships between education and community. In the third section, we will present three case studies from our own experience in adult basic education, which we hope will also be relevant to people working in compulsory education. In the fourth section we will outline how an understanding of writing in the community can contribute to the teaching of writing and how a critical view of language and literacy can underpin a creative, dynamic pedagogy for all ages.

## DESCRIPTIVE AND CRITICAL VIEWS OF WRITING IN THE COMMUNITY

Here we will explain what we mean by taking a descriptive or a critical view of writing in the community, as we believe a critical view provides a better foundation for educational practice. Halliday (1970) and Hymes (1974) opened linguists' eyes to the fact that language varies according to context. This observation led to the study of different types of language (often called "registers" or "genres") and to the notion that certain types of language are appropriate to certain contexts. These concepts are central to modern linguistics and are also relevant to education: For example, the growing "language awareness" movement in Britain takes this view of language. However, there are two ways of thinking about context, register, and appropriateness: a "descriptive" approach and a "critical" approach.

A "descriptive" view of language represents variety, appropriateness, and register as if they were unquestionable and unchangeable. This suggests that it is somehow natural and proper that these differences exist. The educational interpretation of this model is "normative": that is, people have to accept things as they are and accommodate to the norm. In this view, language development consists of acquiring as many of these registers as possible. Many educators believe that it is somehow right and inevitable that certain types of language have status, doing their best to give all learners access to them. The unfortunate result is that, when some learners do less well than others, it is blamed on them, not on the inflexible values of educational institutions. Failure appears to be the individual's sole responsibility ("not clever enough," "playing up," "a truant," "could try harder"). In this way, literacy is used to select out the dominant groups to access society's rewards under the guise of "equality of opportunity." This overlooks the fact that this endeavor is heavily weighted in favor of some and against others. Those entering the education system from more statusful backgrounds are already grounded in the statusful linguistic forms, and this continuity between school and home enables them to control the writing practices of school more easily.

A descriptive view of the difference between writing in and out of school would be that it is not appropriate to use the writing practices of the local community(ies) in school: The educational context demands specific conventions for writing, specific purposes for writing and types of writing, specific ways of writing, specific ways of learning to write, specific criteria for successful writing (often measured by testing and focusing on easily quantifiable things such as standard spelling and grammatical conventions). These are often very different from the practices of most of the communities using the school. This approach devalues the practices of the community, implying that they are inappropriate where it really matters—in school.

By a "critical" view, we mean a view of language that represents variety, appropriateness, and register as open to question and change. Critical linguists and educators are explicit about the difference in status between different types of language. They question why different practices are considered appropriate in different contexts. They recognize that all language conventions have a history and that particular conventions have become established because they have been used by influential people of various sorts. Critical linguists believe that language is in a constant state of flux: Registers can merge, rules of appropriateness can be challenged and will eventually change. (See, for example, Fairclough, 1989.)

Critical educators start by valuing the language practices of the different communities from which learners come. They recognize that the language and literacy practices of some communities have less status than others and that this is a function of the power and status of particular groups, and the denial of status to others. Where writing is concerned, this means that community writing practices should not be disregarded in school. School practices can and probably should change through contact with the communities from which their learners come. A critical educator would recognize and challenge the fact that community writing practices have less status than those of the school. Heath (1983, p. 369) encourages this approach at the end of *Ways with Words:*

> Unless the boundaries between classrooms and communities can be broken and the flow of cultural patterns between them encouraged the schools will continue to legitimate and reproduce communities who control and limit the potential

progress of other communities and who themselves remain untouched by other values and ways of life.

A critical view of language also takes account of differences in status and access between spoken and written language. Writing is a secondary form: Far fewer people need or acquire more than a few types of writing. Most types of writing have been developed by a relatively small section of the population for their purposes, using their language, and disseminated through means they control. It is far harder to develop these writing practices substantially outside the context in which they originated. Critical educators recognize that the writing practices generally valued in school and employment are not equally accessible to all: They are much easier to acquire by those belonging to some social groups than others. A critical view of literacy recognizes that

> [the hegemonic culture is] the only culture that operates as such through literacy—the very construction of a standard national language belongs to a literate elite. The very process of reading and schooling diffuses it, even unintentionally. (Hobsbawn, 1978, quoted in Graff, 1979, p. 35)

Finally, critical language awareness recognizes the symbolic meaning of the literacy taught in formal schooling and differentiates it from everyday writing. Cook-Gumperz (1986) argues that, since the nineteenth century, literacy has become a school-based rather than a popular skill and a means of measuring and evaluating other skills. The decontextualized styles of schooling have become synonymous with "literacy" that is neutral, standardized, and measurable, in contrast to more pluralistic literacies of early nineteenth-century Britain and the United States.

> Schooled literacy was thus differentiated from everyday uses of literacy. What was learnt through schooled literacy was no longer part of local common culture, so that ordinary people had less control over their own cultural products. (Cook-Gumperz, 1986, p. 31)

This is reflected in what Street and Street in this volume call "the pedagogization of literacy": the way parents are desperate to give their children a head start at school, buying toys and playing games that treat the written word as an object rather than as a tool. The school definition of literacy seeps out into everyday life.

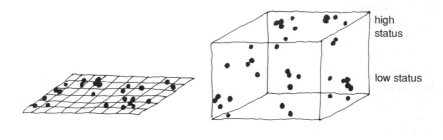

a. A descriptive view                          b. A critical view

**Figure 9.1.** Representations of "Descriptive" and "Critical" Views of Language Varieties

"Schooled literacy" is the means by which people are assessed and gain access to jobs and qualifications. Although everyday writing outside school has the prime function of communicating, people often suffer humiliation—internally or externally imposed—because of writing that may be perfectly good at communicating its message but contains misspellings or punctuation errors. The "B+" mentality lingers on after school among all sections of society. Uncertain spelling, punctuation, and "writing as I speak" are seen as symbols of lack of education and worthlessness. This symbolic meaning of writing, as much as a practical need to write, may be responsible for people coming to adult education groups to improve their writing skills. This distinction between the "meanings" versus the "uses" of literacy is confirmed by Levine's (1986) study of the imbalance between literacy requirements for entry at a Nottingham factory and the actual requirements of the job. Western culture values people who can write above those who can't, whether or not they have any need of writing in their lives. As one ex-student with spelling difficulties put it: "People want to *be able to* write, not necessarily *to* write." Critical educators need to confront this anomaly and not sweep it under the carpet.

The difference between descriptive and critical views of language can be characterized as the difference between a two-dimensional and a three-dimensional model as in Figure 9.1 A descriptive view is a two-dimensional model of language setting out all the different types in fixed positions, with those sharing similar characteristics clustering together, those similar in one respect but not others adjacent, and those that are dissimilar far apart (see Figure 9.1a). The result would be a sort of "rich tapestry of language," with the implication that all types of language are equal. This may be linguistically true, but it is socially naive.

A three-dimensional model would add the dimension of status (see Figure 9.1b). This no longer represents all types of language as equal but explicitly shows how some are highly valued in a culture and others aren't. Where language development is concerned, the more statusful types are more accessible to those who come from more statusful backgrounds. Varieties of language are unfixed, subject to change in their closeness to each other and in their relative status. When this view of language underpins education, it helps teachers and learners understand why language learning is so difficult for some, and it encourages everyone to take action for change.

## COMMUNITY, WRITING, AND EDUCATION

In this section, we will compare writing in four settings, each representing a different relationship between education and community. Where possible, we will draw on examples from earlier chapters in this book and outline the role of writing in each. Table 9.1 suggests some key characteristics of the four settings we are discussing. We have chosen the features listed on the left-hand side of the table to give a broad characterization of writing and to point out contrasts between the settings.

### Writing in Communities

Column 1 represents writing as it is described in many chapters in this book: writing as it is when there is no overt educational intention (although it frequently involves incidental learning for the participants—adults and children). This is writing in Lancaster, in the United Kingdom (Barton & Padmore, Chapter 4 of this volume), writing in the Amish community in Lancaster, Pennsylvania, in the United States (Fishman, Chapter 2), and writing in the Hispanic community in Toronto, Canada (Klassen, Chapter 3).

It is characterized by the fact that it is motivated by people's everyday needs and interests. Some of it is in response to the "imposed" demands of bureaucracy, some for "self-generated" purposes. Writing is embedded in other activities rather than being a separate activity. In other words, people write to get something done that matters in their lives, not just to write well

**TABLE 9.1: Writing in Community and Educational Settings**

|  | 1. Writing in Communities | 2. Writing in Traditional Education | 3. Writing in Self-Education | 4. Writing in Community-Based Education |
|---|---|---|---|---|
| Purposes for writing | both imposed and self-generated | imposed by teacher | self-generated | discussed and self-selected |
| Situation | embedded in daily life | decontextu-alized | created by writers | often simulated |
| Read by | receiver | teacher | group members | teacher and others |
| Writing processes | little drafting; using networks | usually single draft; competitive | often many drafts; sometimes collaborative | discussed and self-selected |
| Criteria for success | whether it achieves its purpose | standardized norms | writers' satisfaction | agreed by learners |
| Educational intention | X | ✓ | ✓ | ✓ |

(though they may wish to do this too). An important aspect of many examples of community writing (see, for example, the chapters by Howard and by Gregory in this book) is that people's own situations and experiences can be expressed and valued—this is writing that is self-generated rather than imposed and addresses issues that concern the writers. People can put literacy to their own cultural uses. Writing is the communication of the known and familiar to real audiences, not "writing for teacher."

The processes of writing may become real and important: drafting, discussion, editing, typing, and presenting. The writing becomes part of a range of broader processes—accessing the right person, reaching the media, telephoning, negotiating with a printer. Writing in the community is collaborative as well as individual. In community action, for example, one or two people may take on the group's writing tasks with advice on what to say from the rest of the group.

Finally, community writing is measured in terms of whether it achieves the purpose for which it was intended. For example, a "bad" letter is one in which it is unclear what the writer wants the reader to do or one that makes the reader angry instead of helpful; a "badly filled in" form gets returned because not all the needed information is on it. Writing in the community is "good" or "bad" according to whether it works, not because a teacher has awarded it a B+ or a D.

These are general observations, but it is important not to overgeneralize about what "community writing" is. A theme of this book has been that there are many different communities and thus many different literacies, though these are not separate literacies. This assumption could have the normative effect of locking people into one set of writing practices or another. In our complicated culture, different literacies overlap. People who appear to belong to one recognizable writing community may in fact have passive knowledge and an understanding of others. Individuals may belong to many writing communities simultaneously: "horizontally," according to, for example, geographical, class, or racial groupings, and "vertically," by social, work, study, and community institutional membership. One individual may, for example, have a child at school, work in a bank, and be a member of a local tenants' association, and variable writing practices will be demanded by each situation. At the same time, she may be writing cards at Christmas, making notes to remember things, and writing letters to family abroad. Some control of these writing styles may have been learned at school—but much she will have learned since leaving school. There is no evidence on how far the decontextualized writing of school is transferable to these other domains. Below we shall consider how far writing in educational settings can reflect the range of possible literacies people may encounter beyond school.

Another important dimension of writing outside educational settings is that, even though Great Britain is a "literate" society, many people have little need to write in their everyday lives. In our experience in community and adult education, many people have written little since leaving school—perhaps a signature on a card, a shopping or task list to aid their own memory, a name and address on a form. People in this group may not have a lot of confidence in their writing skills simply because of lack of use. Writing becomes important only in exceptional circumstances, when dealing with bureaucracy, for example. Within families, there is often someone who is "the writer" who takes on many writing tasks in the public domain. In families where the older generation have come to Britain in adult life, one or more of the children will commonly take on this role. It is clearly possible not to write much and not experience this as a chronic "disability" as some commentators on literacy in industrialized societies seem to think inevitable. Levine (1986) notes the presence of subcultures where there is a systematic avoidance of literacy. He suggests that attachment to "oral values" may reflect a rejection of schooling and its culture and standards (Levine, 1986, p. 191).[1] The significance of this is that "reflecting community in school" is not a straight-forward matter—as, for many children at school, the kind of continuous writing demanded by school will have few echoes at home.

Furthermore, whereas communities practice and identify with alternative registers and varieties of spoken language (despite the dominance of statusful varieties in the public sector), there is little opportunity for communities to develop and practice alternative writing styles and conventions, consonant with their spoken varieties and serving their own purposes. For those adults who do write (still a very small section of these communities), it is very difficult to have their writing disseminated and so to establish a firm base for alternative cultures of writing. This is because publishing is controlled by dominant cultural groups. New writers, therefore, have to use the writing conventions of dominant groups as there are few other models to follow. In this context, a critical approach to the existing conventions, and identifying who has access to them becomes very significant.

In summary, there is a general sense in which writing at school differs from "real-life" writing, but writing outside the education system is full of contra-dictions. It is purposeful but often amounts to responding to purposes imposed by public bureaucracies. The writing practices of various interlock-ing communities are different from most school practices, but they are also different from each other. School criteria for success, such as neat handwrit-ing, correct spelling, and use of Latinate words, are often applied outside school even though they are not really essential to the task. Where members of communities wish to take on "the system," writing can be empowering, yet they often have no way of maintaining their identities as they are sucked into the existing practices. As we understand more about these contradictions, we realize that the writing practices in traditional education are themselves located in their context and their history; different than, but not unquestion-ably superior to, others.

## Writing in Traditional Education

Column 2 caricatures "traditional education," education as it was almost everywhere until about 20 years ago, in which the communities from which learners came were not given a second thought in educational institutions. Above all, purposes for writing were "imposed," not "self-generated." Writing in English classes was for the purpose of learning to write—an end in itself—writing in other classes was for the purpose of showing what you had learned of the subject matter. Writing was an isolated, competitive activity, in which learners produced a text to be read and marked by their teacher. Standardized spelling, punctuation, and grammar were the main criteria for assessment of writing. School writing used the language of dominant cultural groups and was relatively easy for children from those groups to acquire. Because writing is easy to collect and scrutinize, it became the means of "discriminating" between children in examinations. This had the effect of separating out an elite under the guise of "equality of opportunity."

We have used the past tense in the last paragraph optimistically, as we know the climate has changed in many places. There has been a National Writing Project in the United States and in the United Kingdom, both of which have pioneered more enlightened approaches to the teaching of writing, emphasizing purpose, context, and readers. However, examination systems and textbooks seem to maintain philosophies well beyond their time, and it is all too easy for teachers to fall back into this traditional mold. One of our purposes in this chapter is to restate the dangers of educators limiting their sights to the school walls; another is to suggest ways in which writing within the education system can be demystified for those who find it unfamiliar.

## Writing in Self-Education

Column 3 represents writing in the sort of collective self-education documented by Gregory (Chapter 6) and Howard (Chapter 5). Here education emerges from community needs, opening new purposes and opportunities beyond those immediately perceived. Community publishing, as it is described by Gregory, shows the importance of meanings based in community experience: "self-generated"[2] meaning versus "imposed" meaning. Writing of this sort means the writers make meaning and do not reproduce "objective" meaning.

The stimulus for developing in this way often comes from a need to publish, but it can come from other forms of action. Sometimes members of a community invite an educator to help them achieve some practical aim. Adult education outreach workers often actively solicit this sort of relationship. Learning to write doesn't have to happen in educational institutions.

Here the group members determine the purpose for writing. "Collective self-education" creates a range of real writing situations that teachers would have to manufacture. If group members write in response to "imposed" demands, it is by choice. Typically, a lot of their writing is self-generated and cooperative. It is not assessed, unless group members request assessment and establish their own criteria for assessment. It is frequently quite extensive, including the publication of books, because the reason for introducing an educational element is to take group members beyond the demands of their everyday lives.

Self-education is an ideal, and certainly one of the educational implications of this book must be that, wherever possible, writing development should grow out of community activity. However, this can be limited: One of the main reasons people go on to "second-chance" education is that education located in the community often remains low status; it doesn't give people opportunities to develop control of the dominant conventions (Edwards, 1986). It is also impractical on a large scale, particularly with children: Most teachers will find themselves in setting 2, attempting to make it more like setting 4.

## Writing in Community-Based Education

Column 4 represents educational settings where educators are trying to take account of various elements of the practices of the communities from which the learners come. This is common in adult and community education in the United Kingdom, particularly adult basic education, voluntary literacy projects, and women's education in various settings. It is represented in this book by Gardener's chapter and by the examples we offer in the third section below. It is also represented in the United Kingdom and the United States by some of the work of the National Writing Projects.

Typically these settings have most of the following characteristics:

—Educators recognize that writing must be embedded in context and must have a real purpose and real reader(s), though generally they have to create this artificially or use simulated situations.

—They try to take account of community ways of learning, community-based knowledge, and community literacy practices, including the way writing is integrated with other activities. Many adult basic education groups include "language experience writing" stemming from people's own spoken language, allowing people to express the values, culture, and language practices of their own communities in written form.

—They try to develop in their classrooms the processes of writing that have been identified in the community. These include literacy events where different people have different roles and writers don't have to work in isolation.

—They try to downplay formal assessment and encourage learners to state their own criteria for success.

In the rest of this chapter, we will explore further the ways in which education can take account of community practices, examining its possibilities and pitfalls. In other words, we will consider what is involved in attempting to make setting 2 more like setting 4. With the distinction between descriptive and critical views of writing in mind, we will present some examples from secondary and adult education. We will consider to what extent they take into account community literacy practices, how far they incorporate a critical perspective, and ways in which they might develop.

## THE ROLE OF COMMUNITY WRITING PRACTICES IN EDUCATION: SOME EXAMPLES

It is important to anchor the above discussion of writing in different settings with some concrete examples. In this section, we will look at some case studies drawn from research and published textbooks and consider to what extent educational practice in each case incorporates community writing practices and critical language approaches.

### Case Study 1: Comparing Approaches to Writing in Traditional Education and on a Fresh Start for Women Course in Community Education.

This case study looks at one woman's varied experiences of learning to write in different settings. The quotation below is in the words of Marie, a student on a Fresh Start course[3] for women at a North London adult education institute, who was interviewed toward the end of the course, along with seven other women, as part of a research study in 1986 (reported in Moss, 1987). All the women had left school with few or no qualifications, and, since school, most had done a variety of routine, poorly paid jobs, often part-time to fit in with child care, with little opportunity for training. All the women had come to Fresh Start in the hope of eventually finding "new horizons" for themselves. In the interviews, the women were asked to comment on how their experience of learning, and of learning to write, on their Fresh Start course compared with their school experiences. In the (largely unpublished) extract below, Marie comments on her experience at school, in a General Certificate of Education (GCE) "O"-level course she took in her early twenties, and on Fresh Start:

> I think for a lot of the women it was marking that made them nervous [at school]: in school you're marked on mistakes. I started an "O" level English course in Cardiff . . . but had to come up to London before the exam came. After I began [Fresh Start] I went back to my folder. . . . All across it was red ink. But when I actually looked at my essays I found they were very good. It was just that I was looking at the red ink all over them and that's all I thought about.

> On this course [Fresh Start] we've written about *our* experiences: how we felt at school, where we lived when we were young. This is very different from school where the teacher just used to say "I want you to write about a holiday" (we didn't have holidays) or "Write about the river." [At school] you weren't taught *how* to write . . . they didn't say do it in parts, you plan it first. You just had to sit there with a blank sheet of paper and write. Up until I went on the course writing a letter was next to an impossibility for me because . . . panic set in. What am I going write? What do I do that anyone want to hear about? But once you plan it it flows. I've written letters now . . . and I've enjoyed reading them through and thinking, "I wrote that letter and it was no big thing."

In the extract, Marie identifies several problems with traditional approaches to teaching writing and how she felt inferior and excluded by school writing practices. At the same time we can note approaches in the Fresh Start course that enabled Marie to develop confidence in her ability to write and that seem to echo many features of "community writing practices" we have referred to above.

(1) At school, Marie was not able to draw on her own life experiences in her writing —the subjects ("holidays," for example) were alien to her and did not reflect her day-to-day experiences as a working-class Black young woman growing up in an urban environment. They were "imposed," not "self-generated." In contrast, in Fresh Start, it was exactly her lived experience that acted as a basis and starting point for her writing.

(2) "All across it was red ink," Marie comments, and later "I was looking at the red ink . . . and that's all I thought about." We may presume that the "red ink" recorded "errors" in spelling, punctuation, standard English grammar, and syntax. School and GCE English language courses traditionally take

these as the main criteria for writing success. Marking Marie's writing "on her mistakes" undermined her sense of herself as a writer (this had been so for other women too). In Fresh Start, in contrast, the women recorded receiving constructive and positive feedback from their tutors, who treated their writing as communication, not a test of achievement: "[The tutor] gave me confidence because she used to find my writing interesting and I used to be so surprised at first," another woman in the same course commented (Moss, 1987, p. 24).

(3) Marie says, "You weren't taught how to write—you were expected just to know." In traditional schooling, many of the processes of writing—of construction, organization, drafting, editing, and proofreading—were not taught. Those whose cultural background and use of language was consonant with that of the school might successfully and unconsciously acquire the skills of producing decontextualized expository prose. Those whose language backgrounds were not so consonant would clearly find it much harder. These processes were explicitly taught in Fresh Start. One women remembers saying rather bitterly after a study skills session, "Why didn't we do it before? It's so simple. If we'd known that when we were younger we could have done so much" (Moss, 1987, p.24).

(4) In traditional education, writing was an isolated, individual activity—writing "for teacher." In Fresh Start, the women shared their writing with the whole group—they were writing for an "audience," not as a means of assessment. In addition, the tutor encouraged the women to exchange ideas with each other and bring their drafts to her for comment—a process comparable with "networking," which we have identified as a community writing practice.

In this case study we have seen how the traditional writing practices of school excluded Marie from writing. In the next case study, we look at how another area of community education—adult basic education and community publishing—also successfully draws on community writing practices in the teaching of writing.

## Case Study 2: Adult Literacy in Community Based Education.

This is a case study of community-based education that also uses community writing practices as the basis for learning and confirms, as Gregory has explored in Chapter 6 of this book, the educative value of community publishing. At the same time, it demonstrates problems with the rather simplistic view that bringing community writing practices into education means concentrating uncritically on everyday "survival" writing skills—filling out forms, letter writing, and so on—what is generally termed *functional literacy.*

This case study is taken from *Language, Writing and Publishing: Work with Afro-Caribbean Students* (Schwab & Stone, 1987). Julia Clarke is talking about working with Isaac Gordon, the author of "Going Where the Work Is" (published by Centerprise) which is an autobiographical account of Isaac's experiences coming to the United Kingdom from the Caribbean and was written by Isaac dictating the book to his tutor (commonly called the "language experience approach").

> When I started working with Isaac he could still only read his own book with frequent prompting; he could not write a simple letter without help; and apart from writing his name and address he could not handle official forms with any confidence. I wondered whether some of the "more important" work had been neglected while Isaac had been involved in the process of editing and publishing his book. We launched into work on forms, letters, reading electricity bills, strategies for spelling and a whole range of "survival skills." . . . we continued to use the language experience approach until Isaac was able to construct the written words to express his views and feelings by himself. . . .

> During this time I gradually realized how much Isaac had gained from the previous experience of dictating and publishing a book. He was seeing literacy as being about communication with other people, beyond merely responding to demands made by our form-ridden society. In his own assessment of his progress, Isaac does not mention the functional skills which I had seen as "more important" but emphasizes achievements which stem very directly from the publication of "Going where the work is."

Julia cites as examples of these achievements Isaac reading his book at lunches, being asked by a teacher from a Brixton school to speak to the class about growing up in Jamaica, and keeping up correspondence with people who have written to him about his book and finally to old friends in Jamaica, to whom he had previously relied on his wife to write on his behalf. Eventually he wrote another book, this time not using a tutor as a scribe, but by himself.

Community education in the United Kingdom, as in the above example, often draws, in its practice, on the strengths of community publishing and collective self-education referred to by Gregory—providing, for example, oral history, writing workshops, or a base for community publishing itself. This is self-generated writing, genuinely community based, collaborative (people are encouraged to share their ideas and writing with each other), and purposeful—the writing finds audiences through printed texts, exhibitions, and so on. This writing offers a genuine chance for learners to express their own language styles and culture.

At the same time, Julia, the tutor, expresses her concern that Isaac should be learning functional adult literacy, much stressed in the early days of the adult literacy movement in Britain. However, this writing is determined by the public domain and imposes its own language and structure on writers—it doesn't stem from people's own lives and experiences. It is an important part of adult literacy work for most learners—and needs to be contexted in situations and the processes in which it is embedded. *Working Together: An Approach to Functional Literacy* (ALBSU, 1987) provides good examples of how to put this principle into practice. Isaac's story illustrates how oppressive it might be to lock learners solely into this "imposed" form of writing.

Finally, this is an example of educators taking a critical approach to writing. Elsewhere in *Language, Writing and Publishing*, Schwab and Stone (1987) describe how *critical language awareness* was part of the program at Hackney Reading Centre. Isaac fully discussed the meanings of writing in Jamaican English (as in his first book) or in standard British English and the links of these with status and power. He chose to learn and adopt the standard variety in his second novel. Gregory notes that the benefits of community publishing are enormous but that education based on personal experience can only go so far. To access power, those of nondominant cultures need to move beyond the immediate community experience, acquire new and more statusful writing conventions, and adopt a confident, critical stance toward them.

In the final case study, we look at how far the state examination system in the United Kingdom gives scope to the incorporation of community writing practices in "mainstream" education. Marie (case study 1) attended school and her "O"-level course in the 1960s and early 1970s. In our third case study, we move on to consider the writing practices fostered by the new GCSE examination in the late 1980s.

## Case Study 3: Writing for the General Certificate of Secondary Education (GCSE).

In this case study, we look at the new GCSE English language examination recently introduced in the United Kingdom as a state examination for 15-year-olds and over. One reason for focusing on this examination is that, under its old title of General Certificate of Education (GCE) "O" level, it has traditionally been the yardstick of "literacy" in British culture and is an essential qualification for many types of employment and higher education. It is also of interest because, on the surface at least, it offers British educators the opportunity to radically depart from the traditional "O"-level syllabus. We are interested in how far it takes into account community writing practices and fosters critical approaches to writing.

The old GCE "O" level in English language tested students' control of written conventions derived from literature, universities, and the private school system. It paid attention to the development of formal, Latinate, standardized English, with heavy emphasis on accurate spelling and punctuation. There was little room for the "colloquial" or nonstandard varieties of English. The styles taught were largely literary and discursive, and the content reflected the White middle-class culture from which the course was derived. Thus students taking the exam in Africa, Asia, or the Caribbean had to respond to comprehension passages mentioning the London underground, British middle-class life, and obscure British idioms. The new GCSE examination is designed to be far more learner centered and flexible and to reflect language in use—oral and written. For the first time, the course is designed and marked by local teachers—and it can be assessed solely on course work. Where writing is concerned, the examination has several new features:

—The examination recognizes and places stress on the importance of writing that is appropriate for the context in which it is written.
—Teachers are encouraged to bear in mind, when setting tasks for the exams, "the linguistic and cultural diversity of society" (Secondary Examinations Council/Open University, SEC/OU, 1986).
—There is encouragement to students to include in their folders projects they research and write up themselves.

An official guide to the exam for teachers comments:

Emphasis [is] given throughout the national criteria to the appropriate and effective use of language for a wide range of purposes. . . . Students will be expected . . . to undertake different kinds of writing for differing goals and directed towards differing contexts. (SEC/OU, 1986, cited in Barham et al., 1988, p. 1)

The new syllabus suggests scope for the development of GCSE programs in schools that draw on community writing practices: Teachers can present subjects and materials that reflect the lives of their students, find scope for nonstandard varieties in written work, take a critical approach to the standard conventions, and produce tasks that reflect the writing practices of the "real world." They are encouraged to assess written materials on their effectiveness in communicating in real contexts. The examination is still very new, it was introduced for the first time in 1987, and this, and the fact that each individual school sets its own syllabus, makes it hard to generalize about how the exam is being put into practice across the country. However, we can consider two approaches that have been published:

(1)  Elizabeth A. Cripps (1988) *Longman Revise Guides: GCSE English*: This is "revision" textbook designed for students and written by a GCSE examiner. We will call this the "*Longman* example."

(2)  Northern Examining Association (NEA, 1989) *GCSE Examination 1990 English Syllabus B First Trial Marking 1989/90*: This is a manual circulated to GCSE teachers by the examining board so they can meet and compare their gradings of assignments. It includes a GCSE syllabus and sets of scripts from a London inner-city school. We will refer to this as the "NEA example" (although the publishers say explicitly that this manual is not a "model," in the sense of an "ideal" syllabus and set of answers, it does seem to be offered as an acceptable and realistic course for GCSE, and we know of several teachers who are treating it as such).

How far do these examples draw on community writing practices?

(1) Although the national criteria emphasize the importance of writing appropriately for different goals and contexts, the syllabi in both examples seem to overwhelmingly emphasize narrative/expressive "literary" styles and discursive writing.[4] In the *Longman* example, six out of eight chapters on writing styles deal with these two. Similarly, the NEA example has only two out of eighteen assignments that don't fall into one of these categories (or the category of "literature criticism").

The exam is still likely predominantly and uncritically to test and reward those written genres valued in academia. In practice, however, only a small percentage of students taking the examination will have the chance to study beyond school.

(2) This observation is confirmed by the fact that little weight seems to be given in either example to "the linguistic and cultural diversity of society." The *Longman* example offers one or two examples of nonstandard varieties in literature extracts but no opportunities for learners to write in a way that represents their spoken variety of English. In the NEA example, despite

having sample scripts from (we presume from content) Black students, there is only one text that reflects Black experience valuably, but almost tokenistically, in a story of slavery. There are a lot of examples of White working-class literature, which include use of nonstandard varieties, but again no explicit opportunities to write in these varieties.

We are not arguing here for teachers to abandon standardized written English—in fact, we believe strongly that all learners must have the opportunity to learn this variety and use it in their writing. However, we also believe the GCSE should specifically acknowledge and validate other varieties and promote discussion about their relative status.

It is important to note that the lack of Black literature in the NEA example may reflect the availability of texts in the school as much as teacher choice. For teachers to be able to recognize the "linguistic and cultural diversity of society" in their courses, they must have the means and support to acquire new resources and materials.

(3) Neither example seems to offer critical approaches to language study. The *Longman* example refers to the appropriate use of language, form, and style in writing as good "linguistic manners." This is very much a descriptive, noncritical approach to language awareness. There is no discussion of other grammars and other writing practices—though teachers could introduce these issues in class discussion. No links seem to be made in either example between language, status, and power.

(4) There is some evidence from the marking criteria in the NEA example that accuracy in spelling, punctuation, grammar, and syntax is still the main way of discriminating between passing and failing. It is one of two clear differences between a fail with grade D, where there should be enough accuracy to "make the writing easily understood" (NEA, 1989, p. 9), and a pass with grade C, where there should be "soundness in spelling, punctuation, grammar and syntax" (NEA, 1989, p. 10). The only other clear difference is the ability to select "style and vocabulary appropriate to the task"—far harder to assess clearly. One suspects that teachers will look to the difference between "enough accuracy to be understood" and "soundness" as the primary benchmark for passing. This seems confirmed by the advice of a training consortium to students in South East London taking the examination. They say, "Correctness in writing, accuracy in sentence construction, grammar and punctuation are *crucial*" (unpublished information sheet).

(5) Finally, the new GCSE offers the chance for students to explore kinds of writing more typical of practices in the community—letters, newspaper articles, advertisements, brochures, pamphlets, reports, and so on. In the community, however, the writing task is embedded in an institution/context

and in a complex range of activities. For these tasks to genuinely reflect community writing practices, tutors must enable their students to explore all these processes. Neither guide seems to encourage this. To illustrate this point, we are presenting a detailed critique of an activity from the NEA example.

Students are asked to complete a social work report following reading the play *A Taste of Honey* by Shelagh Delaney. This is a play about a young working-class woman in Liverpool in the 1960s who leaves home to have her baby and is helped by a young homosexual man. The exercise is to pretend you are a social worker visiting her and writing a report on her.

Students are asked to respond to questions on a form, such as:

- How does the client propose to support her child?
- Please give a long report on the suitability of this client for parenthood.
- Would you recommend that the child be taken into care or adopted? Please give reasons.

These guidelines for writing the report are notably at odds with current social work practice.[5] The guidelines, for example, imply that single parenthood would be grounds for considering a mother an inadequate parent in "real life." They encourage judgmental comments when, in practice, social workers must try and be as factual as possible. The task itself is inappropriate: Social workers would not be asked to recommend the child be taken into care or adopted after one visit. When writing the report, it would be important to know that social work reports are now open to clients to see and in many areas must be signed by the client. The style of the report would vary according to its purpose —for a case conference or for a court case. The social worker would be asked to discuss her report at a case conference or elsewhere.

This contrived example of writing for real purposes reflects a teacher's stereotyped view of what constitutes a social services report. It illustrates how writing in the community, even a particular style such as report writing, is embedded in a particular context and reflects that specific context in its form and content. As it stands, the activity is seriously misleading.

However, it could be adapted by a critical educator to bring important aspects of writing in the community onto the agenda. First, he or she would need to discuss the completion of this form as a literacy event in a real institution and in the context of the situation in which the writing is taking place. It would need an understanding of the role of social workers and the role of parents in our society, and the circumstances in which the state intervenes between parent and child. Second, the critical educator may use this example to broach issues of language status and power: she might begin by a discussion about the class, ethnicity, and status of most social workers; she might point to the importance of taking into account the author's identity and values, whose views have status at a case conference, and how written reports contribute to that status and so on. She might raise issues of ethics and discuss how to avoid author bias in such reports—and the implications of such bias. To be able to explore these exciting avenues, the course teacher would have to have resources and support from her school and the time to explore with her pupils. This would mean a change in commitment by the *system* as much as by the individual teacher herself.

It is possible, however, to incorporate community education practices and a critical perspective into the GCSE syllabus. An example can be seen in *Materials for GCSE Assignments with Language Awareness Focus*, by Harriet Barham and colleagues at Vauxhall College of Building and Further Education, published by the ILEA Afro Caribbean Language and Literacy Project in 1986.

These materials show how the new GCSE can take account of the writing practices, meanings, and values of learners and look at writing from a critical perspective.

Here we find (1) links being made between style, status, and power; for example, a discussion of the use of language in Alice Walker's *The Color Purple*; and an examination of two school reports to consider why they were difficult to read and what they were for; and (2) an active acknowledgment of one community's language culture and heritage—learners are encouraged to read and try writing in different varieties, including writing from community publishers and dub poetry.

This approach to GCSE seems to be moving closer to writing that acknowledges different cultural practices than that presented in the *Longman* example. At the same time, it does not lock students into those practices but asks them to examine them critically and develop from them. Although the situations are simulated, they are rooted in the Afro-Caribbean community, its culture, and its values. The GCSE structure has potential for this sort of interpretation, but it is doubtful how far in practice this will be explored by schools.

In practice, the GCSE examination, as mentioned earlier, is the primary means of maintaining dominant cultural values, and, as Bourdieu (1977) notes, the education system is designed to reward those already coming to school possessing the dominant cultural heritage. The GCSE is unlikely to change without structural changes within the education system itself. How-

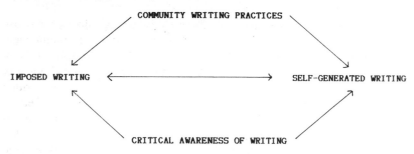

**Figure 9.2.** A Critical Approach to Learning to Write

ever, as we have seen, it is possible for GCSE teachers to effect some change within the new syllabus, even if this is only marginal in the system as a whole.

## THE ROLE OF COMMUNITY WRITING
## PRACTICES IN EDUCATION: SOME PRINCIPLES

In this section, we will draw on the examples above to suggest some answers to the questions posed in the introduction. Here we will outline some of the principles arising from these examples. Education with its roots in the community has to take account of the contradictions we mentioned in the first section of this chapter. It is not a question of teaching either imposed writing or self-generated writing. Educators need to find a way of synthesizing these two types of writing, which at first sight seem to be diametrically opposed. We suggest two ways of doing this. One is to recognize the writing practices in the communities from which learners come, so that whatever *type* of writing they are engaged in *ways of approaching it* are familiar. The second way of dealing with both imposed and self-generated writing is to include explicit discussion about the differential status of types of writing: what we call critical awareness of writing.

These elements are represented diagrammatically in Figure 9.2. The four outer arrows on this diagram suggest how attention to community writing practices and raising critical awareness can help to resolve the dilemma over whether to concentrate on functional (imposed) or expressive (self-generated) writing. The arrow in the center suggests that, within this framework, self-generated writing and imposed writing can support each other. The strengths developed through self-generated writing can empower learners in their efforts to deal with imposed writing. Critical awareness of the social context in which institutions impose writing tasks can, in turn, give writers the confidence to generate their own writing. What does this mean in practice? We'll elaborate on what we mean by each element in the diagram.

## Community Writing Practices

Educators need to draw community writing practices into the teaching of writing: the way writing relates to people's lives; people's strategies and processes; their perceptions, feelings, and attitudes. This means making sure that writing is discussed and seen as purposeful communication that is part of whole events inside and outside school (as advocated by Street, 1984 and ALBSU, 1987) and not an exercise for the teacher. They can do this by thinking through the uses of writing in complex and whole situations—relevant to the learners' own communities. Considering writing in community contexts shows us that meaningful writing is a part of a whole set of processes: deciding who to speak to, knowing what to ask for, making telephone calls, getting the right form, feeling confident that your demand is reasonable—all these together effect change. Educators could offer insight into how these processes interact, and support learners in carrying them through, rather than teaching how to write complaint letters in the English class and dealing with consumer law in social studies.

Another way of incorporating community writing practices in classroom activities is to encourage learners to share ways of "getting round the system" (for example, using a typist who has done "this kind of thing" before). Learners can draw on each other's skills when they write, write collaboratively, use word processors and spell checkers, ask others to read and comment on their work without it being considered "cheating." The discussion around writing needs to include how people perceive what they are doing, what they feel about it, and why. The new GCSE exam in Britain (case study 3) provides an opportunity for working in this way; further examples of how it might be done can be found in the publications of the National Writing Project.

The suggestions here apply to writing for school subjects too. Recognizing how writing is embedded in social context, collaborating, and recognizing how you feel are aspects of writing in the community that can make any type of writing easier.

## Imposed Writing

Education that validates community writing practices might be seen at its most straightforward as teaching adults and children the kinds of writing used by their families and in their jobs. This might run to some basic letter writing, filling out forms, list making, check writing, and so on. The Adult Literacy movement in the United Kingdom began with this kind of "functional" literacy, replacing "school literacy" with "everyday literacy." Street (1984), for example, strongly advocates the teaching of specific functional skills for specific purposes as "empowering" because it allows people to take control and use the system for their own purposes.

Certainly, control of these skills should be everyone's by right. But this is only one part of community writing. Case study 2 illustrates how functional writing means taking on, for the most part, imposed styles and limits writers because they cannot use language they identify with to express their own meanings and culture. If educators interpret "bringing community writing" into the classroom as no more than this, they are merely exchanging one imposed form for another: replacing "school writing" with "bureaucratic writing." Another disadvantage of concentrating on functional writing tasks, such as DHSS forms or letters of complaint, is that they demand the control of formal conventions remote from everyday speech. These conventions are derived from dominant groups' language practices and varieties and are less consonant with those of Black and White working-class communities—and certainly hard to acquire "on the spot" to deal with a sudden situation. To use literacy powerfully, the writer needs to be absorbed into formal conventions and have an understanding of complex institutional practice, which may be a lengthy, committed process. This writing is framed by the needs of the state and a ruling culture, and noncritical education that limits itself to everyday functional writing runs the risk of locking people into oppression.

## Self-Generated Writing

So imposed, functional writing alone is not enough. Simultaneously, education rooted in the community needs to offer ample opportunities for self-generated writing, especially in forms that may be closer to oral styles. It can provide opportunities for writers to share their writing with each other and publish it with varying degrees of professionalism (from photocopier to printed book) so that voices other than those of the dominant culture may be heard. Case study 1 (Marie) illustrates how, once writing becomes a self-generated activity in which one's own experience is allowable, it also becomes accessible. Community writing and publishing projects, and courses such as Fresh Start, can offer a space where "writing to get things said" and "writing to get things done" can develop, where writing that is an expression of value and culture can happen. Isaac Gordon's work on his publications (case study 2) is an example of this. This self-generated writing will teach many complex and transferable skills around writing. Individual student-centered learning that concentrates on self-generated writing takes "narrative and the oral tradition as primary modes," where the focus is on "meaning rather than form, as the form is socially constructed" (Bourne, Cameron & Rampton, 1988). This must be one aspect of an education grounded in community practice but not its whole. We cannot disregard the symbolic and communicative values of the statusful genres. Learning that fails to give students "the basics" in standard English and formal conventions disempowers them and deprives them of their rights to educational opportunity. (See *Whose Language? A Teaching Approach for Caribbean Heritage Students*, Craven & Jackson, 1985, for further discussion of these issues.)

## Critical Awareness of Writing

The process of learning to write needs to include both the use of self-generated writing and learning to take control when writing tasks are imposed. But these very different types of writing cannot be juxtaposed in a vacuum. We suggest that learners need to discuss these differences and develop a "critical awareness of writing." (See Fairclough, in press; Ivanič, 1988.) Critical educators can give those not of the dominant culture an overview of how certain conventions have acquired status. They can identify situations where the conventions are necessary and the times when they can be modified—or where it is even more powerful to flout them. They can locate the difficulties with "long words" not in the learners' deficiency in literacy but in sociohistorical factors such as preservation of "cultural capital" by dominant groups. Critical educators need to offer learners the opportunity to critically examine the "meaning" of literacy and, through critical language awareness, consider the links between decontextualized school prose and power and status.

Within the public domain, writing and literacy styles are determined by each institution, each with its own set of "discourse practices," each reflecting an institutional ideology. These are learned as people move into institutions. Preparation for this genre development, and critiquing it (Kress, 1982) needs to be part of critical education practice. The *Materials for GCSE with Language Awareness Focus* (case study 3) are an example of this.

We can offer learners experience of elite, decontextualized, expository conventions but, in addition, a critical understanding of how these conventions are linked to status and power. We can identify situations where these conventions are useful that are consonant with learners' own experiences in different communities. We can encourage learners to critique the conventions, and explore alternatives, and enable them to make choices on when and when not to use them. We can encourage learners to write in their own language varieties when they choose to, in full knowledge of the social act it may constitute. We can nurture self-generated writing as a firm foundation for meeting imposed writing demands with self-assurance.

## Summary

(1) The teaching of writing should include some or all of the following characteristics of writing in the community:

writing is part of a whole event and not an isolated event,

writing is purposeful,

writing is used not as a measure of intelligence and achievement but as communication,

there are different writing practices and conventions in different community and institutional settings, and

writing often involves collaboration and networking.

(2) It should give opportunities for learners to develop control over the "imposed," statusful types of writing:

discussing public domain writing and finding ways of being in control of it and

working on academic writing if it is part of their plans for themselves.

(3) It should also give learners opportunities for "self-generated" writing:

creating their own meanings and

giving expression to their own situations, experiences, values, culture.

(4) Items 2 and 3 need to be linked by explicit critical awareness of the differential status of writing varieties, including how

more powerful conventions are developed by powerful groups;

school sets up these expository, factual, and creative forms as "writing" per se;

these are not part of common culture but belong to powerful cultures; and

control of these is used as a measure of intelligence and achievement in testing and examination systems, which is apparently objective under the ethos of "equality of opportunity" but really gives dominant cultural groups easier access to statusful jobs and power.


## CONCLUSION


It is easier to work from learners' own meanings and words, desires, and perceptions at the less formal ends of education: in primary (elementary) and adult nonexamined classes. These are marginal, low-status sectors, but they are leading the way in developing learner-centered approaches to education.[6] They show what is possible in education generally if only the restraints of imposed curricula and criteria could be removed. We believe that the above principles are relevant to formal statutory education too: Classroom practice must have its roots in community writing practices so that no learner feels excluded.

School cannot hope to change dominant conventions, nor would it be fruitful to completely abandon them. Writing is a social practice: it has to conform to rules to communicate meaning. New rules or modifications must, therefore, emerge from cultural groupings and movements, not from individuals.[7] A critical approach to the teaching and learning of writing that is located in an understanding of class, race, and power may encourage people to control these conventions instead of being controlled by them.


## NOTES


1. One such description is from a report by ACACE in 1979, which describes people who have difficulty with literacy skills as "a hidden and largely defeated population, whom life has taught to keep their heads down and not expect much" (ACACE, 1979).

2. Gregory's term is *derived* meaning. We are using the term *self-generated* meaning here because we see a strong connection between Gregory's idea of "derived" meaning and Barton's

idea of "self-generated" purposes. Both writers are talking about the impetus coming from the writers themselves and not from some outside authority.

3. Courses termed *Fresh Start*, *New Horizons*, or *Return to Study* have recently grown in popularity in adult education in the United Kingdom. Typically, they are for adults with few or no formal qualifications and little experience of studying since leaving school. They are intended as a first step into education for women who want to try out formal learning and offer women a chance to explore their potential and consider new directions. The courses at the institute Marie attended are part-time women-only courses with child care. They are informal, are participative, and place emphasis on group discussion. Women are encouraged to share their experience and use this as a basis for learning; they also receive help with study skills.

4. The marking criteria for expressive writing rely on tutors assessing "convincingness and ability to interest and affect their responses" and control of "character, plot, dialogue, atmosphere and setting." It is likely that a teacher's view of "convincingness" will be drawn from dominant cultural values—largely stemming from traditional literature criticism. Similarly, discursive writing is assessed in terms of its ability to "use evidence to formulate and qualify generalizations and conclusions, and to consider a number of aspects of an issue in order to argue a case or present a balanced view" (NEA, n.d., pp. 11-12). These are undoubtedly worthy criteria but very much reflect the dominance of the statusful conventions of academic discourse; this and the minor role given to writing for other purposes and contexts suggests that, in practice, they may be only a token attempt to shift the emphasis away from traditional and elitist school writing practices.

5. This analysis is based on discussions with social workers in Greenwich Social Services Department in Southeast London. The overwhelming importance of writer identity is recognized in a report by the British Association of Social Workers, which attempts to set rules for the writing of social work reports. It comments on recording as follows: "A record system should reflect the fact that the perception, interpretation and recording of complex human interaction is always biased by the personal make-up of the recorder and the social context in which the record system is created and used, and therefore should be designed and maintained in a way which minimizes these effects" (BASW, 1983).

6. This issue is discussed in Keddie (1980).

7. On an optimistic note, greater ease of publishing may mean groups previously denied a voice may increasingly find an audience.


# REFERENCES

Adult Literacy and Basic Skills Unit (ALBSU). (1987) *Working together: An approach to functional literacy.* London: Author.

Advisory Council for Adult and Continuing Education (ACACE). (1979) *A strategy for the basic education of adults.* Leicester: Author.

Barham H. et al (1988). *Materials for GCSE assignments with language awareness focus.* London: Inner London Education Authority Afro-Caribbean Language and Literacy Project.

Bartholomae, D. (1985). Inventing the university. In M. Rose (Ed.), *When a writer can't write.* New York: Guilford.

Bloome, D. (Ed.). (1987a) *Literacy and schooling.* Norwood, NJ: Ablex

Bloome, D. (1987b). Introduction. In D. Bloome (Ed.), *Literacy and schooling*. Norwood, NJ: Ablex.

Bourdieu, P. (1977). Cultural reproduction and social reproduction. In Karebel et al (Eds.), *Power and ideology in education*. New York: Oxford University Press.

Bourne, J., Cameron, D., & Rampton, B. (1988). The Kingman inquiry: A briefing document. *Linguistics and Politics Newsletter, 5*. 3-21.

British Association of Social Workers (BASW). (1983). *Effective and ethical recording: Report of the BASW Case Recording Project Group*. London: Author.

Cook-Gumperz, J. (1986). Literacy and schooling: An unchanging equation? In J. Cook-Gumperz (Ed.), *The social construction of literacy*. Cambridge: Cambridge University Press.

Craven, J., & Jackson, F. (1985). *Whose language? A teaching approach for Caribbean heritage students*. Manchester: Manchester Education Committee.

Cripps, E. A. (1988). *Longman Revise Guides: GCSE English*. London: Longman.

Delpit, L. (1986). Skills and other dilemmas of a progressive Black educator *Harvard Educational Review, 56*(4), 379-385.

Edwards, J. (1986). *Working class adult education in Liverpool: A radical approach*. Manchester: Center for Adult and Higher Education, University of Manchester.

Fairclough, N. (1989). *Language and power*. London: Longman.

Fairclough, N. (ed.). (in press). *Critical language awareness*. London: Longman.

Gordon, I. (1979). *Going where the work is*. London: Hackney Reading Center.

Graff, H. J. (1979). *The literacy myth: Literacy and social structure in the nineteenth century city*. London: Academic Press.

Halliday, M. A. K. (1970). Language structure and language function. In J. Lyons (Ed.), *New horizons in linguistics*. Harmondsworth: Penguin.

Heath, S. (1983). *Ways with words*. Cambridge: Cambridge University Press.

Hymes, D. (1974). *Foundations in sociolinguistics: An ethnographic approach*. Philadelphia: University of Pennsylvania Press.

Ivanič, R. (1988). Critical language awareness in action. *Language Issues, 2*(2). Also available in Carter, R. (Ed.). (1990). *Knowledge about language and the curriculum*. London: Hodder and Stoughton.

Jolliffe, D. A. (Ed.). (1988). *Advances in writing research: Vol. 2. Writing in academic disciplines*. Norwood, NJ: Ablex.

Keddie, N. (1980). Adult education: An ideology of individualism. In J. L. Thompson (Ed.), *Adult education for a change*. London: Hutchinson.

Kress, G. (1982). *Learning to write*. London: Routledge & Kegan Paul.

Levine (1986). *The social context of literacy*. London: Routledge & Kegan Paul.

Martin, J. R. (1989). *Factual writing: Exploring and challenging social reality*. Oxford University Press. (Original work published 1985 by Deakin University Press.)

Moll, L,. & Diaz, R. (1987). Teaching writing as communication: The use of ethnographic findings in classroom practice. In D. Bloome (Ed.), *Literacy and schooling*. Norwood, NJ: Ablex.

Moss, W. (1987) *Breaking the barriers: Eight case studies of women returning to learning in North London*, London: ALFA/REPLAN.

National Writing Project. (1990). *Writing partnerships 1: Home, school and community*. Walton-on-Thames: Thomas Nelson.

Northern Examining Association (NEA). (1989). *GCSE Examination 1990 English Syllabus B First Trial Marking 1989/90*. Manchester: Author.

Odell, L. (1985). Beyond the text: Relations between writing and social context. In L. Odell & D. Goswami (Eds.), *Writing in non-academic settings*. New York: Guilford.

Richmond, J. (1982). *The resources of classroom language*. London: Edward Arnold.

Rose, M. (1988) Narrowing the mind and page: Remedial writers and cognitive reductionism. *College Composition and Communication, 39*(3).

Schwab, I., & Stone, J. (1987). *Language, writing and publishing: Work with Afro-Caribbean students*. London: Inner London Education Authority Learning Materials Service.

Secondary Examinations Council/Open University (SEC/OU). (1986). *English GCSE: A guide for teachers*. Milton Keynes: Open University Press.

Street, B. (1984). *Literacy in theory and practice*. Cambridge: Cambridge University Press.

# About the Authors

DAVID BARTON obtained his doctorate in Linguistics from the University of London in 1976 and was a Research Associate at Stanford University for five years. Since 1981, he has been a lecturer at Lancaster University. His current funded research focuses on community uses of literacy, and he has published articles on child language acquisition, the history of literacy, linguistic awareness, and adult literacy. He is a founding member of the Research and Practice in Adult Literacy group (Rapal) and an editor of its Bulletin.

ANDREA R. FISHMAN has been involved in public education for more than 20 years, teaching English in a variety of secondary and postsecondary settings. In 1982, she left the classroom to do research among the Amish as part of her doctoral studies at the University of Pennsylvania, from which she received her Ph.D. in writing in 1984. Returning to her high school classroom, Fishman wrote *Amish Literacy: What and How It Means* (Heinemann, 1988), detailing not only her research but its impact on her own teaching and its implications for public education. Her articles have appeared in *English Journal, Language Arts,* and *English Education.* She serves as a consultant for the Pennsylvania Department of Education and is a member of the NCTE/CEE Commission on English Education and English Studies. Currently, she is Assistant Professor of English at West Chester University in West Chester, Pennsylvania, and Associate Director of the Pennsylvania Writing Project.

SUE GARDENER is currently Vice-principal of Westminster Adult Education Institute, London. She has worked in adult education for over 20 years and as organizer, teacher, trainer, and writer about adult literacy since 1973. She was a founder worker at Hackney Reading Center, one of the centers pioneering the publication of students' writing, a founder member of *Write First Time,* and its Writing Development Worker from 1981 to 1984. Research interests usually succumb to work as organizer and teacher but include the social relations of written language, adult learners' perceptions of their learning, and the search for a history of adult education relevant to postimperial societies. Publications include *Conversations with Strangers:*

224

*Ideas About Writing for Adult Students* (ALBSU/Write First Time, 1985), *The Development of Written Language Within Adult Fresh Start and Return to Learning Programmes* (ILEA, 1985), and, as coauthor, *The Republic of Letters* (edited by Morley and Worpole, Comedia, 1982).

GERRY GREGORY taught for 12 years in secondary schools in London and Brazil before entering teacher education. He is currently Lecturer in Education at Brunel University in the United Kingdom, where he specializes in curriculum studies and language in education. His major research interest for a decade has been working-class writing and community publishing; Publications include "Community-Published Working-Class Writing in Context" in *Changing English: Essays for Harold Rosen* (edited by Meek and Miller, Heinemann, 1984). A second research interest is the role of language in craft, design, and technology education. Publications in this field include "Language in CDT Education" in *Studies in Design Education, Craft & Technology* (Summer 1989).

URSULA HOWARD is Vice-Principal of Kensington and Chelsea Adult Education College in inner London. She has worked in adult education since 1974, teaching and organizing adult literacy, Return to Learning programs, and women's studies. The publishing of student writing and community publishing have been active interests. She has been on the executive of the Federation of Worker Writers and Community Publishers as a member of QueenSpark Books in Brighton, and on the South East Arts Literature Panel. She is writing a Ph.D. thesis on the uses and meanings of writing in 19th-century English working-class life. She has published teaching materials and articles (often co-written) about literacy, adult education and unemployment, and local politics.

ROZ IVANIČ taught for 17 years in schools and colleges in Devon, London, and Stockton (California). At Kingsway-Princeton College in London, she was responsible for the Language Support Unit. Since 1986 she has been a lecturer in the Department of Linguistics and Modern English Language, Lancaster University, where she is an active member of the Center for Language in Social Life and the Literacy Research Group. She is a member of the editorial group of the *Rapal* (Research and Practice in Adult Literacy) *Bulletin* and has published teaching materials and articles, mainly on topics related to adult literacy, the teaching of writing, and critical language awareness.

CECIL KLASSEN has had training and experience over the last 10 years primarily in the field of ESL. This has included high school ESL, ESL in the workplace, community adult ESL programs, and academic ESL for adults. He branched off into the issue of literacy as part of his master's degree in Adult Education at OISE (University of Toronto) because of an interest in adult literacy programs for minority language groups that he brought back after teaching in South America. The chapter written for this book comes out of the research done for the master's degree. He is currently an ESL instructor in Vancouver at Douglas College in an academic ESL program. His research interests have expanded to the ESL/literacy combination in the workplace.

WENDY MOSS works in the Department of Continuing and Community Education, Goldsmith's College, South East London, and in the Adult Education Training Unit at the City Lit, London. She worked for 14 years with adult literacy groups, women's return to study courses, and as a community education worker at the Lee Community Education Center, Goldsmith's College. She has published materials on spelling (with Roz Ivanič) and letter writing, especially designed for adults, as well as *Breaking the Barriers: Eight Case Studies of Women Returning to Learning in North London* (ILEA/ALAA, 1986). She is a member of the editorial group of the *Rapal Bulletin.*

SARAH PADMORE has been a researcher in the Department of Linguistics at Lancaster University on the ESRC project "Literacy in the Community" since 1988. Prior to this, she was a teacher of Adult Basic Education for seven years.

BRIAN V. STREET is a Senior Lecturer in Social Anthropology at the University of Sussex. He has written extensively about literacy in both the Third World and in the United Kingdom and the United States. He is author of *Literacy in Theory and Practice* and edited *Literacy Research in the UK: Adult and School Perspectives* (with J. McCaffery). He organized (with A. Rogers) a Seminar for International Literacy Year at the Commonwealth Institute in London called "Literacy in Development: People, Language, Power." His next book, *Cross-Cultural Approaches to Literacy,* will be published in 1991.

JOANNA C. STREET obtained a first-class honors degree in social anthropology and then undertook some school research at the Institute of Education in London. She is now doing a Ph.D. in Art History and teaches cultural studies to art students at Goldsmith's College, London.